Hunts'

GETAWAYS

on the

UPPER MISSISSIPPI

Surprising worlds
close to home

MARY HOFFMANN HUNT

Midwestern Guides
Albion, Michigan

ISBN 0-9623499-3-3
Library of Congress Catalog Card Number 92-90870

A Midwestern Guides Book

**Printed by Malloy Lithographing
Ann Arbor, Michigan**

Mapmaker and editor: Don Hunt
Design consultant: Chris Golus

Midwestern Guides
504 1/2 Linden
Albion, Michigan 49224

CREDITS FOR ILLUSTRATIONS

Dickeyville Grotto: page 53. **Dubuque Chamber of Commerce:** pages 76-7 (Film Bureau), 85, 86, 101, 105. **Dubuque County Conservation Department:** p. 107 (painting by Gary Olsen). **Dubuque County Historical Society:** page 88. **Effigy Mounds National Monument:** page 139. **Galena/Jo Daviess Convention & Visitors Bureau:** pages 25, 26, 31, 35, 38. **Key Four, Fort Wayne, Indiana:** page 155. **Lyons Nature Center:** page 104 (drawing by Tom Roberts). **Roberts River Rides:** pages 79, 89. **Kuefler Photo:** page 132. **Merchants National Bank, Winona:** page 158. **Carson Ode:** page 181. **Southwestern Wisconsin Prairie Enthusiasts:** pages 13, 64, 180. Drawings by Gary Eldred. **Upper Mississippi Fish & Wildlife Refuge:** pages 6,7, 9, 15, 164, 165, 193, 194, 199, 200. **U. S. Army Corps of Engineers:** page 17. **Works Progress Administration (WPA)** Federal Writers' Project books: *Galena Guide* and *The Story of Mineral Point* were the source of linocut illustrations on 24, 28, 29, 33, 41, 49, 51, 56, 58. **Winona Convention and Visitors Bureau:** 4, 147, 150, 156, 160, 163, 166, 174, 175, 179. **Winona County Historical Society:** pages 152 and 172. **Wisconsin Division of Tourism:** pages 8, 61, 118, 122. **Wisconsin Department of Natural Resources:** pages 114 and 188 (drawings by Jim McEvey), p 128, 189, 191 (Dorothy Cassoday), 185 (Dean Tredt). **Wisconsin Historical Society:** pages 151, 197 (from the Wisconsin Historical Atlas, 1874). **Wisconsin Shakespeare Festival:** page 60.

Contents

Other Midwestern Guides publications
by Don and Mary Hunt

Michigan Fresh:
A guide to bakeries, farm markets,
cider mills, and herb farms.

Hunts' Highlights of Michigan

Hunts' Guide to West Michigan

Hunts' Guide to Southeast Michigan

Preface

The Upper Mississippi is an amazing place, completely unlike the big, muddy river that passes St. Louis, Memphis, Natchez, and New Orleans. The dramatic bluffs, picturesque river towns, and remarkable wildlife here are so alluring that it's already beginning to be discovered by German and Japanese tourists. Yet in a good many parts of the Middle West, you're more likely to hear about trekking in Nepal or terrific restaurants in Provence than about this beautiful upper stretch of the our continent's greatest river. That says a lot about how our unparalleled mobility has diminished our ability to appreciate places close to home.

This stretch of river looks like Germany's majestic Rhine, yet is clean enough to swim in. It's a protected natural area over 250 miles long, with many bald eagles and more kinds of birds and plants than anywhere else in the Middle West. The Upper Mississippi is over a mile wide at places and carries millions of tons of barge cargo a year, yet it's surprisingly accessible even for casual visitors. You can rent a canoe or houseboat and camp on its sandbars. The old river towns here are some of America's most distinctive and appealing, their steep streets loaded with ornate buildings from the past century. And you'll find the people who live along the river aren't caught up in today's rapid cycles of change.

Many thanks are in order. The following people were especially generous in reviewing material and supplying extra information and illustrations: Daryl Watson, Bill Butts, Ken Winge, and Kathleen Webster in Galena; Marilee Harmon, Jim Ryan, John Hail, Jan Oswald, and Jerry Ensler in Dubuque; Michael Douglas in Prairie du Chien; Al Thurley, Bruce Goebel, Greg Evans, and Mark Peterson in Winona; and Gary Eldred and Steve Huber of the Southwest Wisconsin Prairie Enthusiasts. Thanks also go to the managers of all the state parks included in this book. They are some of the most consistently helpful and broadly knowledgeable group of people in the United States.

The illustrations owe much to the photo resources of Bob Queen and the Wisconsin Department of Natural Resources; Janet Rother-Harris and the Wisconsin Division of Tourism; Hank Schneider and the U. S. Fish and Wildlife Service; and the State Historical Society of Wisconsin.

Now for a few other introductory comments:

◆ No one paid anything to be included in this guide.

◆ **Restaurants** were chosen primarily for the quality of their food. An effort was made to accommodate many kinds of budgets and eating requirements: families on a budget, vegetarians, people with restricted diets, as well as people who want to eat at the very best restaurant in town. I try to find good restaurants that cover all the bases. All the restaurants in our guides are independently owned (no chains), with local character and interesting settings whenever possible. Restaurant hours refer to hours food is served.

◆ **Lodgings** were similarly chosen for many kinds of budgets and tastes, from the top of the line to budget choices. All lodgings are places where I wouldn't hesitate to stay alone. Special emphasis is placed on lodgings with interesting settings and good views. Often they are the independents with older facilities that got the beautiful sites first. Another factor in selection is whether lodgings are in places where you can get out and take a walk, rather than having to use your car to get everywhere.

Quoted rates refer to two people in a room. Some lodgings have lower rates for one person, and most bed and breakfasts do. With motels and hotels, phones in rooms are assumed.

Bed and breakfasts do not have phones or TVs in rooms unless mentioned. Most restrict smoking. Relatively few have rooms with twin beds. Sometimes the bath, even a private bath, may be down the hall. If this really matters to you, inquire ahead. Half the point of staying at a bed and breakfast is unwinding and getting away from electronic interruptions. Many B&Bs do have a TV somewhere for guests.

Rates in the lodging industry are usually flexible. Sometimes they go up for special weekends; usually they go down in slow seasons. It always pays to ask about special deals and packages before making reservations. Many hotels and bed and breakfasts in vacation areas have attractive midweek rates part or all of the year. If you are combining business and pleasure, it's always worth asking about corporate rates. Many establishments are open to negotiation in the off-season, especially at the last minute, since lodgings lose earnings for each night a room stays empty. Good deals can be had if you can be comfortable asking, "What's your best rate?"

◆ Getaway destinations were chosen for their distinctive character and their variety of sights and activities for visitors. Reducing drive time and unpleasant local traffic was another factor. Some small, hard-to-reach places like Cassville, Wisconsin, and Guttenberg and Bellevue, Iowa, are merely mentioned because they lack a variety of nearby things to see and do. They'd be wonderful for lazy getaways, however.

◆ **Everything changes.** Places close. Hours are altered. Prices go up (and sometimes even down). Specific rates are stated to give an idea of relative prices, even though actual prices will be out of date before a year is up. *It's always best to call ahead and confirm hours.*

It's a pleasure to hear from readers, even critical ones. If you have any tips, complaints, additions, or comments, I'd like to hear from you. Write me at Midwestern Guides, 504 1/2 Linden Avenue, Albion, Michigan 49224.

Mary Hunt

Introduction:
The Upper Mississippi

With majestic bluffs, secluded backwaters, quaint river towns, and scenic trails, it's the Midwest's most surprising region.

THE BLUFFS AND VALLEY of the Upper Mississippi are surely one of America's most under-publicized national treasures. The great river curves languidly, making intricate channels and islands. Five hundred feet above it are the round tops of dramatic bluffs. The rosy light near dawn and sunset gives a gentle, timeless glow to the forested blufftops and the water below.

In most of the Upper Midwest, glaciers smoothed the landscape into gentle swells and rolls. But the glaciers missed this region. So the steep-sided hollows (known as coulees in parts of Wisconsin) remain. Many-branched tributaries with deeply carved valleys enter the great and ancient gorge of the Mississippi.

Nature, prehistory, and river traffic

Back in the 19th century, travelers compared this stretch of Mississippi scenery favorably with the legendary Rhine River Valley of Germany. While the Rhine is studded with castles, here there are fabulous natural areas that hardly exist in Europe: bluffs where eagles, hawks, and vultures soar, and winding channels and marshy sloughs full of birds and fish. Herons and egrets, sandpipers and ducks are common all summer long, and millions of migratory birds use the Mississippi Flyway as a giant superhighway to and from their southern winter homes.

The river's emotional power was recog-by many Native American cultures, going back over two thousand years. Surviving **Indian ceremonial mounds**, sometimes in the shapes of animals and birds, are clustered on many prominent river bluffs nearby, especially on the Iowa side, near Effigy

In geology and appearance, much of the Upper Mississippi is like the gorge of Germany's River Rhine (below). The gorge or trench of the Mississippi has the same high bluffs. It extends through the Driftless Region (untouched by glaciers) from Hastings, Minnesota, and the St. Croix River down past Dubuque and Galena. South of that, the Mississippi Valley becomes much wider, some 8 to 10 miles wide, and the bluffs are not so high or striking. ▼

Eagles are back on the Upper Mississippi

The bald eagle has made a big comeback since DDT was banned in 1972. In the Fish & Wildlife Refuge's McGregor District alone, over 600 eagles have been counted, and year-round resident eagles have established 19 nesting territories.

In winter, eagles are commonly seen around the open water, looking for fish, just below dams and at power plant outlets (at Nelson, Genoa, and Cassville, Wisconsin, and Lansing, Iowa). Most dams are good places to see eagles; those at Genoa, Wisconsin, and Harpers Ferry and Guttenberg, Iowa, are especially good. At **Sweeney's on the River** in Lansing, Iowa, you can even sit in the pleasant, window-lined tavern and see dozens of eagles.

The **best eagle-watching** is on **winter mornings**. During January, courting eagles soar and dive while doing maneuvers like side rolls, toe-touching, and talon-locking. Beginning in late January, they work on building nests in tall trees close to shallow waters with lots of fish. (They also eat waterfowl, turtles, small animals, and carrion.) Nests can be up to 8 feet in diameter and 2 tons in weight!

Seeing eagles in summer requires luck and the ability to identify immature birds. Mature birds are nesting and reclusive. To protect the birds, nest locations are not made public. Fledglings can be seen flying around nests in late June.

It takes five years for eagles to gain their adult plumage. They gradually change from mottled brown and white to have the familiar look of a mature eagle: white head and tail, with brown body. Eagles don't flock until winter. Then, concentrated around the few places with open water, they're seen in large numbers.

Mounds National Monument.

Every 15 to 30 miles, the Army Corps of Engineers' huge navigational **dams and locks** create their own slow-moving drama, as boatmen break up massive tows of barges and shuttle them through the locks. The boatmen's Louisiana accents are so thick that locals can't understand them.

Memorable 19th-century architecture & towns

There are a lot of splendid old buildings on the Upper Mississippi. **Galena**, Illinois, three miles away up a tributary, is preserved as it was a century ago by a sudden economic decline after 1857. It's by far the most remarkable of all the river towns. Although Galena was one of the region's preëminent commercial center through the 1850s, it's not actually on the Mississippi but near it. Today it has become a haven for urban refugees — artists, storekeepers, retirees, and others who have opted out of Chicago's intensity. Galena fills to overflowing with visitors in the summer and fall. Its food, shopping, and night life has more than a touch of urban sophistication, otherwise hard to find on the Upper Mississippi.

Nearly every river town of any wise has near it a blufftop park with a fabulous river view. **Guttenberg**, **Lansing**, and **Bellevue**, Iowa, and **Cassville**, Wisconsin, are pretty, remote small towns from the steamboat era. **McGregor**, Iowa (p. 114), tucked under bluffs opposite Prairie du Chien and the mouth of the Wisconsin River, is similarly sleepy, But it's easier to reach — via U.S. 18, a straight route to Madison.

Some river towns continued to prosper into the railroad era, then failed to develop much after 1900. As a result, they are unusually pleasant, settled small cities rich in Victorian architecture. Dubuque, Iowa (p. 72) has elabor-

▲ **In old river towns like Galena and Dubuque you can find many commercial buildings little altered from steamboating days.**

An excellent introduction to river life and history is Dubuque's Woodward Riverboat Museum building. Learn about the fur trade, the golden age of steamboats, steamboat cruise lines, the big pearl button industry based on river clams, boatbuilding, early small pleasure craft, and much more. ▼

Backwater canoeing on the Mississippi

Canoeing on backwaters and sloughs is a relaxing and quiet way to experience the reclusive world of wildlife. Shallow waters in many of these areas restrict most of the large, noisy motorized boats and let those people who are willing to paddle avoid crowded sandbars and heavy boat traffic in the main navigation channel.

Quiet canoeists may approach deer, great blue herons, egrets, perching bald eagles, waterfowl, beaver, muskrat, mink, raccoons, and, if lucky, river otters.

Detailed **river maps** and a **canoeing information sheet** are available from the Upper Mississippi National Wildlife and Fish Refuge office at McGregor, Iowa. Call (319) 873-3423 or stop by on weekdays or write the refuge, Box 460, McGregor, Iowa 52157.

Canoeists should use great caution near the strong currents at dam spillways. Poison ivy and stinging nettles cover most Wildlife Refuge lands, so finding a good campsite may be difficult.

Reaching the numerous openings to backwater areas means canoeists must often travel along the busy, open main channel. Sometimes canoeists even have to cross the main channel. Barge traffic, big pleasure boats, and high winds can make that a dangerous adventure. Barges, seen from afar, move so slowly they seem stationary. Up close, it's clear that they move right along, can't see vessels low in the water, and can't stop even if they wanted to. Ask refuge staff or boat liveries about good places to cross.

ate mansions and whole neighborhoods of 19th-century brick row houses. **Winona**, Minnesota (p. 146) has a beautiful turn-of-the-century downtown, handsome Victorian homes, and two distinguished Prairie Style banks. **Red Wing**, Minnesota, 60 miles up the river, is equally as attractive.

A magnificent place for birds, fish, and boating

Few outsiders realize that much of the Upper Mississippi consists of the enormous, 261-mile **Upper Mississippi River National Wildlife and Fish Refuge.** This superb natural environment, filled with islands and a maze of backwater channels, is a major migratory corridor for birds. It's also a fabulous public recreation area, more heavily used than Yellowstone, managed for wildlife and people by the U.S. Fish and Wildlife Service. Often two to four miles wide, it extends from Wabasha, Minnesota, just below Lake Pepin, all the way past Dubuque to Davenport, Iowa, and Rock Island, Illinois.

Nearly everywhere on the Upper Mississippi, the water is clean enough for swimming and waterskiing — a great surprise to many outsiders, who assume that all major waterways are necessarily contaminated with chemicals and agricultural runoff.

You can water-ski on the wide, deep pools just above dams, fish in numerous sloughs and marshes, watch birds, and canoe. Along the Great River Road on both sides of the river, public access sites and riverside turnoffs and parks are frequent. Hunting is permitted in most of the refuge. **Primitive camping on sand bars**, much enjoyed by canoeists and boaters, is allowed without permit for up to 14 days. (Poison ivy can be a problem.) Houseboaters like to anchor by sand bars and enjoy their own private beaches.

The Great River Road: enjoyable in small quantities

Seeing the Mississippi River by car isn't always that easy. In places the river is invisible because

▲ **The Mississippi Flyway is like a vast, heavily used superhighway during spring and fall migrations of birds. Bird-watchers enjoy finding unusual birds and seeing birds like eagles, tundra swans, and ducks and geese in great numbers at certain times of the year.**

Houseboating up a lazy river

A popular, inexpensive river vacation consists of renting a houseboat and taking it up to a sand bar, where you can fish, swim, and just laze around. Houseboats are shallow-draft, floating motor homes with a sundeck above the cabin. You don't need previous boating experience to rent one; rental includes an orientation lesson on how to pilot the boat and stay away from barges, how to read charts, and where to go to find good sandbars. The boats go about six miles an hour and stay in the main channel; for backwater fishing, you can take along a motor boat for an extra $30 a day.

From McGregor on a three-day weekend, boats can go from Dam No. 9 at Lynxville to Dam No. 10 at Guttenberg, a very pretty stretch of river with bluffs on both sides. Sample rates from Boatels in McGregor: for 8 passengers, $1,080/week; $640 for 3-day weekend or 4 midweek days. Off-season rates 25% off. 10-passenger boat: $685 for a summer weekend. 12 passengers $750.

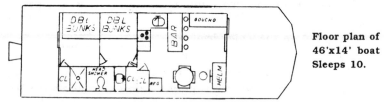

Floor plan of 46'x14' boat Sleeps 10.

Some businesses renting houseboats on the Upper Mississippi

Brochures have diagrams of interiors and details about what is furnished (quite a bit, including grill, ice chest, cookware and dishes), what to bring, fishing, and fishing boat rentals. Businesses are listed from south to north. Off-season discounts of 20-25% are typical. Inquire about cruising range on the river for weekend and full week rentals.

Dubuque: Family Marine, 3053 Lemon Street, Dubuque, Iowa 52001. (319) 583-8848. Based at Dubuque Marina.

Cassville, Wisconsin: Eagle's Roost House Boats, 1034 Jack Oak Road, Cassville, WI 53806. (608) 583-4454. Also rents canoes.

McGregor, Iowa: Boatels, Box 219, McGregor, IA 52157. (319) 873-3718.

Lansing, Iowa: S & S Rental, 990 S. Front, Lansing, IA 52151. (319) 538-4454.

Trempealeau, Wisconsin: Riverview Houseboat Rentals, RR 1, Box 1261-A, Trempealeau, WI 54661. (715) 985-3232. At Trempealeau Marina.

the road is on the opposite side of a broad flood plain, miles from the river. Or the road may be on the upland, past the bluffs and well away from the river. Or a town is wedged in the flats between bluff and river. If such a town becomes a city of 50,000 like La Crosse, the old river road may become a traffic-clogged commercial strip over 10 miles long.

On the Great River Road, the best river views anywhere along the Mississippi are between Red Wing, Winona, and La Crosse on the Minnesota side and from La Crosse to Prairie du Chien on the Wisconsin side.

Along the twisting, turning river valley, the typical road network of the late 20th century just doesn't apply. Maps can be deceiving, what with the hills and curves. It can take a half an hour or 45 minutes of tiring driving to get to a neighboring town that seems a short hop away on the map. Try going from Prairie du Chien to Dubuque, just down the river, and you'll understand. The upland, inland routes along ridgetops are usually much faster than the river.

The Great River Road concept was originated back in 1938 to focus visitor attention on the Mississippi River's scenic, historical, and recreational assets. Now the 3,000-mile river route along both sides of the river (that's over 6,000 highway miles) have been marked with the Great River Road's green pilot wheel sign. Having signs that mark the route overcomes one huge difficulty for visitors: how to find the changing way along the river, over various federal and state highways and county and local roads.

Camping and swimming on sandbars is a favorite activity of boaters on the Upper Mississippi. ▼

Down on the river:
a slow, sensuous world of its own

There's a world of difference between the Mississippi Valley and the upland farms not far away, up past the bluffs on the rolling plateaus and ridgetops of southern Wisconsin and neighboring Iowa and Minnesota. The Mississippi's special character is revealed in the memoirs of novelist and TV writer/producer Ben Logan. The son of Norwegian immigrants, he grew up on a diversified ridgetop farm near Gays Mills in the 1920s and 1930s. Here in his well-loved memoir, *The Land Remembers*, he describes the rare, unexpected summer holidays when his father decided work could wait, and fishing was the order of the day:

"Then we headed for the Mississippi, nine miles away. It was a different world in the broad river valley. The high bluffs towered above us on the Wisconsin side. Far across, in Iowa, were green, rolling hills. There was a strange quietness, no wind in the trees, the vast river moving slowly, silently. Even the trains, which roared into the quiet and then roared out again, didn't seem to change the silence. The sun boiled down, bringing new moisture up from the wet ground, turning the day hot and steamy. Even the people from along the river seemed different, quiet and lazy, moving slowly as if time didn't exist. Father used to say it took twice as long to get the car filled with gas in Lynxville as it did up on the ridge at Seneca.

"On fishing days, we became part of the lazy, timeless feel of the valley. If the fish were biting, that was fine. If they weren't, that was fine, too. We sat in unpainted, flat-bottomed rowboats, rocking gently, watching our corks floating on the smooth, dark water. . . . We fished in the main river and in the little lakes, called sloughs. Before the dam was built at Lynxville and the timber was cleared, there were hundreds of tree-covered islands with channels between them. Going out among the islands was like exploring an undiscovered world. The rowboat nosed silently through the dark water, great elms and willow and maple trees towering over us, birds singing far above in the sun. Father liked to row in the narrow channels, sending the boat skimming through the water with his long, sweeping pulls, the oars carefully feathered on the backstroke as though still cutting through the waves on the sea."

Ben Logan's **The Land Remembers** *is published by Heartland Press, an imprint of NorthWord Inc. The 281 pp.* **paperback** *is $11.95, the three-cassette* **audiotape** *$19.95. To order or to receive a catalog of NorthWord products call 1-800-336-5666.*

Like most aspects of automobile travel, driving the Great River Road has its advantages and drawbacks. If you attempt too long a stretch and get into hurry-up mode, your car will isolate you from the sounds, smells, and small sights of river life that make this area special. The bird, fish, plant, and animal life is amazingly diverse because of the river valley's varied habitats: wet prairies, upland prairies, sidehill "goat prairies," marshes, backwater sloughs and islands, sandbars, hardwood swamps, croplands, oak-forested bluffs, moist and dark ravines.

Even the people along the river are different and more relaxed. The river folks of Minnesota and Wisconsin tend to lead the more slow-paced life of Southerners. All that means you're missing the point of travel if you don't get out and walk, talk to people, or just sit and listen to the river sounds.

If you choose the right stretches of river, a leisurely riverside drive can put you in touch with places that really do seem to be in another world. Especially memorable are drives in the early morning, or at dusk, when the rosy, changing light is reflected in the river — a striking, silvery contrast to the dark, looming bluffs.

You can have a relaxing, even inspiring time on the Great River Road if you choose a scenic stretch or a loop of a reasonable distance — say, no more than 75 or 100 miles in a day — and get in the habit of stopping to investigate all kinds of things, from fresh fish shops and old riverside hotels to Indian mounds and blufftop vistas.

Where to find out more

Even though this book covers four states, almost everything in it is covered on the **Wisconsin road map**, free from the State of Wisconsin. It has roads on both sides of the river from Clinton, Iowa, to the Twin Cities. And it has a helpful mileage chart and information on state parks and historic sites. Get it from the Wisconsin Division of Tourism, Box 7606, Madison, WI 53707. Phone 1-800-372-2737 (from neighbor states, Mon-Fri 8-4:30) or 1-800-

The most picturesque small towns along the river include Guttenberg, McGregor, and Bellevue in Iowa and Cassville and Fountain City, Wisconsin. In Minnesota, Winona is an attractive small city with wonderful historic buildings; many people feel Red Wing, 56 miles up from it at the beginning of Lake Pepin, is even nicer.

A free introduction to the Great River Road is the 10-state fold-out map and highlights brochure. Get it from the Great River Road, Pioneer Bldg. #1513, 336 Robert St., St. Paul, MN 55101. (612) 224-9903.

Discover! America's Great River Road, a book by Pat Middleton, makes for interesting and helpful reading on a Great River Road drive, though it doesn't recommend what sections to choose. Get Vol. I, the Upper Mississippi, for $10 at area bookstores and museums, or from Heritage Press, Route 1, Stoddard, WI 54658.

What the land was like before it was plowed and cleared

"The valley bottoms and narrow ridges were originally covered with a deciduous forest. On the prairies of the broad upland levels, Pasque flowers, growing by the millions, spangled the wheat grass, beard grass, and buffalo grass. Later each spring came a profusion of rich blue bird's-foot violets, and white and pink shooting stars blossomed in mid-May. Though most of the prairie vegetation has been destroyed by cultivation and grazing animals, the steeper southern slopes and railway right-of-ways are still full. Among the remaining prairie plants, besides a wide variety of grasses, are the grass-like herbs called blue-eyed and yellow star grass and the herbs curiously named for fruit trees — ground plum, ground cherry, and prairie apple."

— from *Wisconsin: A Guide to the Badger State,*
in the WPA American Guide Series

The Prairie Mystique

Remnants of the great natural prairies that once extended from the eastern Dakotas to Wisconsin are treasured by prairie enthusiasts for their natural beauty and self-sustaining fertility. "The whole environment here favors grasses," explains Steve Huber, a wildlife biologist and member of Southwest Wisconsin Prairie Enthusiasts. "There's good rainfall, a moderate climate, a nice limestone bedrock. In the see-saw between forest and grass, the grass won here and grew for hundreds of thousands of years. Buffalo droppings and decomposing plant materials kept cycling back to form a rich organic soil."

All this was wrecked by the quick, easy cash crop of pioneers in Michigan, Wisconsin, and Minnesota — wheat. "They'd write back home, 'Wow! Come on out here!'" Huber says. "For 20 or 25 years they harvested thousands of years of nutrients."

When the soils gave out and the wheat belt moved west in the 1870s, it created an agricultural crisis that led to a less intensive use of the land, namely, Wisconsin's dairy industry.

But scraps of the old prairie are scattered throughout the region, often along railroad right-of-ways that escaped the plow. Small fires started by steam engines' burning cinders acted the same way as prairie wildfires and fires set by environmentally-aware Indians. They prevented woody plants from getting established.

A natural form of prairie still found today are the so-called "goat prairies" on bluffs that face south and southwest. These sidehill ➔

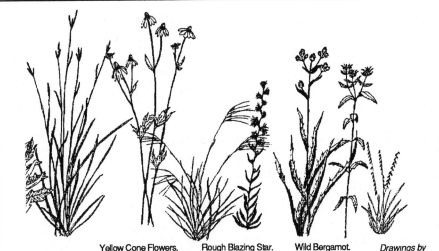

Yellow Cone Flowers.   Rough Blazing Star.   Wild Bergamot.   *Drawings by*
  Big Blue Stem.   Needlegrass.   Rattlesnake Master.   Side Oats.   *Gary Eldred.*

prairies, with slopes of 40 to 50 degrees, are natural solar collectors. They get so much direct sun that in winter the soil thaws each day. Continual freezing and thawing keeps any woody plants from becoming established. They're called goat prairies because the slopes are so steep only goats could graze here, though they never did.

Bike trails on abandoned railroad beds are a fine way to observe prairies without trampling them. The slightly elevated railroad beds are a help because prairie grasses have grown head-high by fall. From early summer into fall, each succeeding wave of prairie plants has to grow above the earlier ones to get enough sun to bloom. Wildflowers come first, followed by grasses like Indian grass and big bluestem.

Today prairies have attracted the attention of people interested in promoting sustainable agriculture that doesn't destroy the environment. Soils researchers are digging into native prairie remnants to study them and understand how these ecosystems renew themselves. Prairie promoters like those in southwest Wisconsin get together to collect seeds from prairie remnants, help landowners burn prairies to kill woody plant invaders, and help restore grown-over prairies. They are missionaries with a message. In Huber's words, "We have sprayed, over-grazed, plowed, and abused the soil so much, we don't even know what healthy soil is. This whole nation had better wake up to sustainable agriculture."

Any good guide to wildflowers of the Middle West will cover prairie flowers. Finding help in identifying grasses may be more difficult. For further information on enjoying and protecting Wisconsin prairies, contact Gary Eldred, Southwest Wisconsin Prairie Enthusiasts, 1492 Sleepy Hollow Rd., Boscobel, WI 53805.

432-TRIP (national, 24 hour recording). You can also get free, fat **guides on Wisconsin auto touring and outdoor recreation**.

To explore west away from the river, you would need Iowa and Minnesota maps. For a free **Iowa map** and *Discover Iowa* tourism book, call 1-800-345-4692 every day but Sunday. For the free *Minnesota Traveler* book and **Minnesota map**, call 1-800-657-3700.

Mark Twain's *Life on the Mississippi* remains the best introduction to the river in the golden age of steamboating, and it also includes some of Twain's best autobiographical writing. Read aloud, it's a wonderful companion on a lazy day canoeing or boating on the river. Twain learned the river in 1856 and 1857, when river traffic had not yet suffered from competition with railroads. He piloted steamboats until the Civil War disrupted river traffic in 1861. Two decades later, he looked back on the golden days of river transportation, revisited the river, and expanded upon his earlier reminiscences of his river career in the *Atlantic Monthly*. *Life on the Mississippi*, published in 1883, was the result. The Bantam Classic edition is just $2.50; there's also an Oxford edition at $4.95.

In *Nature's Metropolis: Chicago and the Great West*, William Cronon shows how Wisconsin's lakes and dairy farms, Iowa's grain and hogs all revolve around Chicago, as did the North Woods' lumbering era in its time. Cronon, an environmental historian and MacArthur Fellow, tells the story of how railroads and aggressive Chicago businessmen led to the Windy City's rise to dominate the nation's heartland over the old river city of St. Louis. This is ground-breaking scholarship, written so enjoyably that any thoughtful, curious student of our time and place can enjoy it. It's a W. W. Norton paperback, $15.95.

Each state prepares its own publication about places of interest to visitors along its portion of the **Great River Road**. These are not always as widely distributed as many brochures, so you may want to request them specifically from these offices:

"The tonic of wilderness" was the highly touted attraction on fashionable tours of the Mississippi frontier in the 1850s. Steamboats left from steamy St. Louis or bustling Galena and passed by the forested bluffs, Indian villages, and occasional prehistoric pictographs, clear up to St. Anthony's Falls at Minneapolis.

♦ Minnesota Dept. of Transportation, Environmental Services Section, Room 124, Transportation Bldg., John Ireland Blvd., St. Paul, MN 55155. (612) 296-5770.

♦ **Wisconsin** Division of Tourism, 123 W. Washington, Box 7606, Madison, WI 53707. Neighbor states, Mon-Fri: 1-800-372-2737. National: 1-800-432-TRIP.

♦ **Iowa** Dept. of Economic Development, Bureau of Tourism & Visitors, 200 E. Grand Ave., Des Moines, IA 50309.

♦ **Illinois** Dept. of Commerce, Bureau of Tourism. 1-800-ABE-0121.

Establishing the Upper Miss Refuge in 1924 was the first major conservation victory of the Izaak Walton League, founded to encourage fishing. It was among the conservation lobbies formed after 1900. Outdoor lovers saw that so many natural areas had turned into farms and cities that common kinds of wildlife could soon vanish like the passenger pigeon unless government became a steward of the land.

The **U.S. Fish & Wildlife Service** is an excellent source of information about wildlife and recreation in the Upper Mississippi National Fish & Wildlife Refuge. Write: 51 E. Fourth, Winona, MN 55987, or phone (507) 452-4232. Here's what is offered upon request:

♦ A **general brochure** describes the refuge and recreation opportunities, with a small-scale map.

♦ **Detailed river maps** of areas between each lock and dam (from #4 through #14) show the main channel and channel markers, along with backwater sloughs and lakes. The river is always changing, so maps are inevitably approximations. The wide maze of sloughs and lakes upstream from Dam 9 above Lansing, Iowa, offers the best canoeing. Ask for the informational sheet on canoeing in the area.

♦ Interesting, informative sheets include, among others, **"Wildlife Viewing Opportunities in the McGregor District"** and separate sheets on bald eagles, great blue herons, raccoons, and river otters. **"Canoeing"** and **"Camping"** sheets have many helpful hints.

♦ **Checklists of birds**, mammals, fish, reptiles, and amphibians observed in the refuge.

Chambers of commerce can provide information on local boat rentals.

The Driftless Region — hollows and bluffs in the heart of the Midwest

The continental glaciers of the last ice ages drastically altered the surface of most of the Middle West. They created belts of lakes and bulldozed away hilltops. They carried rock from the Canadian Shield and filled the older, deep valleys with the accumulated local sand and gravel and rounded rocks and pebbles from far away.

Of all the northern two-thirds of the Midwest, only in the surprising Driftless Region do the older, preglacial landforms survive. The lobes of the most recent glaciers entirely missed the driftless (that is, unglaciated) area of southwestern Wisconsin and the neighboring parts of Iowa, Minnesota, and Jo Daviess County, Illinois. There the ancient limestone plateau has been eroded and shaped for almost 400 million years, creating a drainage system of rivers with many tree-like branches.

It's a landscape of great contrasts: deep-cut valleys, often with dramatic limestone and sandstone outcrops, and on the high ridgetops, gently rolling plateaus and long vistas. Driving along the ridge, you'd never suspect the valleys were there. Coming down into the hidden valleys is a whole different world, where roads and rivers twist and turn.

The Mississippi is its most beautiful where it cuts through the Driftless Region. The bluffs are most spectacular, the interior valleys the most charming. This sizable part of the Midwest has hills and hollows that look like Appalachia. Delight-

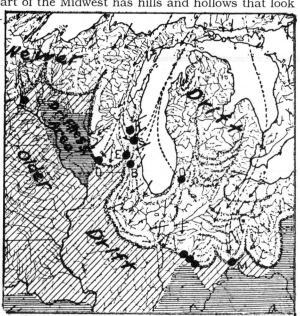

ful valley bike trails in beautiful bluff country are Iowa's Heritage Trail west of Dubuque (p. 106), Minnesota's Root River Trail through Lanesboro (p. 181), and Wisconsin's Elroy-Sparta, Pecatonica, and Cheese Country trails.

Generalized map showing depositis of glacial "drift"(deposited matter) in the Middle West.

The story behind the Upper Mississippi's dams

Building the system of locks and dams on the Upper Mississippi is one of those monumental projects of engineering that captivated the imaginations of a generation of Americans in the Depression years of the 1930s.

Before any dams were built, the Upper Mississippi had formed a series of pools caused by naturally occurring constrictions — built-up snags, narrow bluffs, and such. Between Minneapolis and St. Louis, the river level drops 420 feet, with many bends. Below the confluence of the Missouri River at St. Louis, the channel is deeper and straighter.

During the golden age of steamboats, the navigability of the entire river was a constant worry. To pilot shallow-draft boats on the constantly shifting channel was an art and skill of the highest magnitude, as Mark Twain made clear in *Life on the Mississippi*. In dry summers, river traffic on the Upper Mississippi sometimes stopped altogether. The river could cut a new channel, leaving ports and river towns high and dry. In 1857, Winona's early settlers had to dump tons of limestone above Latsch Island to force the main channel back into its old place by their thriving frontier port.

Beginning in 1878, the Army Corps of Engineers undertook various navigational improvements on the Upper Mississippi. First they dredged the river and narrowed channels to insure a 4 1/2-foot channel. But by the 1880s, riverboats had become obsolete in of hauling freight. Railroads won out

Barge-watching on the Upper Mississippi
Each barge holds the equivalent of 14 to 18 rail cars or 58 to 62 semi loads. Downbound barges carry mainly corn, soybeans, wheat, and other agricultural products. Common upstream cargoes consist of fertilizer, cement, coal, and pipe from Pennsylvania.

once a network of rails crossed the country.

A 6-foot channel was authorized in 1907, but it couldn't keep up with the big new barges used on the Lower Mississippi, with drafts of 8 1/2 feet. Long tows of the big barges could hold two to four times as much cargo as a railroad train. Shifting bulk cargo from one sizebarge to another, called "breaking of bulk," involved costly handling. That put the Upper Midwest at a great disadvantage in shipping its grain and receiving coal, oil, and other bulk products.

Widespread fear of permanent decline for the Upper Midwest

In the 1920s, the entire nation suffered from an agricultural depression. Business leaders and farmers of the Upper Midwest, and politicians representing them, feared their region would slip into permanent decline. After steamboat traffic fell off, for awhile the lumber boom had sustained Upper Mississippi river towns. But by the 1920s these boom times were long over. The Panama Canal made it cheaper to ship goods from coast to coast than from the Upper Midwest to either coast. Railroads serving the Upper Midwest had little competition from shipping on inland waterways, so they could often charge monopoly rates. The difference in shipping costs caused some Minneapolis businessmen to move away.

As secretary of commerce from 1921-1928, Herbert Hoover (an engineer himself) became the leading advocate for constructing a 9-foot channel on the Upper Mississippi. It would help integrate the nation's economy and solve the agricultural crisis, he argued. As President, however, he withdrew support during the Depression because he opposed any kind of deficit spending. But under Roosevelt, the National Recovery Act funded the 9-foot channel project.

Engineering challenges to preserve wetlands and prevent ice buildup

Designing the 9-foot channel required some engineering innovations. A series of fewer, higher dams would have been cheaper to build and able to

Barge tows *average 3 to 8 miles an hour; the speed depends on wind and weight. They operate 24 hours a day in shipping season. Tows on the Upper Mississippi are limited to 17 individual barges northbound, 15 southbound. Below St. Louis, there aren't as many turns on the river, and barge tows can be from 30 to 100 barges long.*

generate electricity, too. But high-crest dams would have flooded too much of the area immediately above them. The Upper Mississippi has a wide flood plain, from half a mile to two miles wide at the logical lock and dam sites. Many towns, railroad tracks, and farms had been built on or near the flood plain. Moreover, the Upper Mississippi Wildlife Refuge had already been established. Too many of the the wetland habitats it protected would have been turned into lakes by high dams.

So the decision was made to build a series of more low-crest dams — 27 in all. These would also be safer to operate and make it easier to maintain a channel.

Winter accumulations of ice and debris were another challenge. The most economical way to let water go over the dam and adjust water levels were Tainter gates, swinging from an upper pivot. But Tainter gates could be no wider than 35 feet — too narrow for masses of ice and debris to pass through. And ice formed on them in winter, making them hard to move.

A Swedish engineer invented the roller gate, which could be 80 feetwide or more. These large cylinders with toothed ends move up and down an inclined track in the concrete piers flanking each gate. They operate much more reliably in freezing weather. The Upper Mississippi dams used a combination of gates for the first time: mostly Tainter gates, with enough roller gates to allow ice to pass through.

Locks were 110 feet wide by 600 feet long, which allows two rows of three barges abreast, or one row plus a tug, be locked through at once.

With a new way of shipping bulk commodities cheaply, commerce on the Mississippi did indeed revive, as intended. Shipping coal and oil led the way; grain didn't become significant until the mid-1950s. Today almost half of all shipping on the Upper Mississippi consists of grain and other agricultural products.

A typical Upper Mississippi lock and dam locks through about 5,000 boats a year. For a typical barge tow, it takes about an hour and a half from the time the slow-moving tow pulls alongside the lock and is uncoupled, until each section has been locked through and the tow reassembled.

Galena, Illinois

Once a wealthy center of river commerce, Galena was frozen in time by economic stagnation. Now this charming town has been reborn as a popular weekend getaway spot.

GALENA is the Upper Mississippi's most striking and best-preserved old river town. Not surprisingly it has become a picturesque getaway and shopping destination, and also a golf and ski area geared to Chicagoans.

Back in the 1840s, when Chicago was still a raw frontier outpost, Galena had developed into the elegant business, social, and political center of the upper Mississippi. Just a decade earlier, Galena was still a remote frontier town swarming with young adventurers hoping to strike it rich in the lead diggings that had been opened 10 years before. In the 1830s and 1840s, the rush to mine lead resulted in booms in wholesale and retail merchandising, steamboating, and banking as well as in selling land and mineral rights.

Many of Galena's settlers were Southerners who had come up the Mississippi from Missouri, which had its own lead-mining region southwest of St. Louis. The elaborate mansions they built on Galena's steep hillsides will satisfy the most romantic of tastes. Most of Galena was built in Greek and Italian revival styles of the 1840s and 1850s.

Distances from Galena
180 miles to Chicago
300 miles to Minneapolis
90 miles to Madison
167 miles to Milwaukee
77 miles to Rockford
15 miles to Dubuque

With its crooked streets and striking hillside views, Galena looks more like an old European city than typical Midwestern towns with their regular grid street patterns. Some streets become stairways, just like in Rome. ▼

▲ **Galena's riverfront, though still busy with steamboats in this 1856 lithograph, was being threatened by the new railroad (left) and by silt from eroded hillsides that miners had stripped of trees.**

In 1857, Galena was entering its third decade as the reigning commercial center on the Upper Mississippi and one of the wealthiest cities in Illinois. No one could then imagine that the city had already reached its greatest size, and that the Civil War would soon completely change the patterns of the region's commerce.

To be closer to the lead mines, Galena itself actually developed three miles *east* of the Mississippi at the head of navigation on the Fever River. (The river's name probably didn't refer to sickness. It was possibly a corruption of *fevré*, the French word for bean. Image-conscious city leaders changed its name to the Galena River in 1854.)

A museum of mid-19th-century architecture

Economic stagnation after 1857 preserved Galena's mid-19th century cityscape virtually intact. Its stock of historic buildings includes modest workaday storefronts and cottages, dignified churches, early Federal and French vernacular houses, a sprinkling of elaborate Queen Anne Victorian houses, and some palatial mansions with massive columns that seem straight off the set of "Gone with the Wind."

Today Galena has been restored and shined up as an architectural treasure. What makes it so unusual is that virtually the entire built environment of the 19th century remains intact, down to stone

A colorful, more detailed view of the lead rush can be found in the chapter on Southwestern Wisconsin, pp. 47-71.

A superb look at lead mining, its geology and history, is at the interesting Mining Museum in Platteville, 30 minutes north of Galena (p. 61). It includes a good lead mine tour.

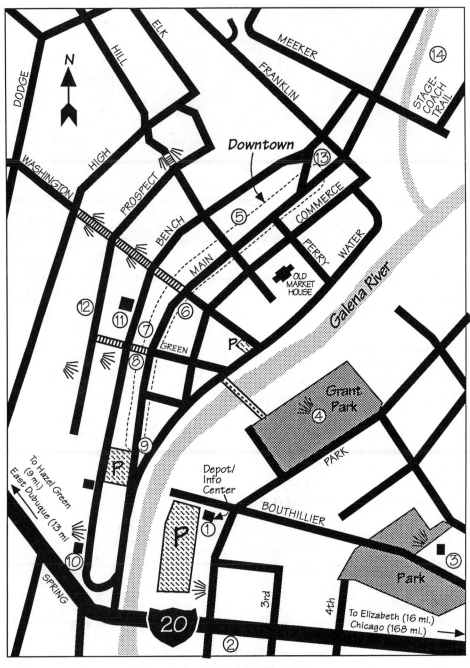

• GALENA •

GALENA MAP NOTES

① **Depot/Visitor Info Center.** Stash your car, get The Galenian inside, and prepare to explore Galena on foot. P. 28.

② **Park Avenue & Third St.** Many impressive houses here.

③ **U.S. Grant Home.** Furnished much as it was when local admirers gave it to the returning hero in 1865. P. 38.

④ **Grant Park.** Fabulous view from hillcrest plaza, picnic tables. Playground on Park Ave. P. 41.

⑤ **Main Street.** Block after block of commercial buildings from the 1850s—unparalleled in the Middle West. Shops with collectibles, antiques, fudge, good books. P. 29.

⑥ **Jakel's Galena Bäckerei.** Terrific German-style breads & tortes, cookies & Brötchen. Amazing decorated cakes. P. 35.

⑦ **Old General Store Museum.** One woman's affectionate tribute to a beloved American institution. P. 34.

⑧ **Main St. Fine Books and Manuscripts.** Civil War material is the specialty of this friendly, classy used & rare bookshop. Historian/bookseller Bill Butts knows a lot about Lincoln. P. 32.

⑨ **Galena River Wine & Cheese.** Another friendly, knowledgeable merchant with a choice array of local & imported cheese, reasonably priced. Stop here for a great picnic! P. 36.

⑩ **Public Library.** Beautiful interior, tiled fireplace with wisteria motif, nice view from steps. Good rest stop on a walk. Open Mon 1-8, Tues 1-6, Wed 1-8, Th 9-6, F 1-6, Sat 10-5.

⑪ **Galena/Jo Daviess Historical Museum.** Slide show here is an excellent overall introduction to Galena history. Interesting artifacts intelligently presented. Thomas Nast painting of the surrender at Appomatox is a knockout. P. 36.

⑫ **Bench and Prospect streets.** "Quality Hill," Galena's elite neighborhood. Many ornate homes are now B&Bs with fabulous views. P. 30.

⑬ **Kingston Inn.** Laid-back theatricality with singing wait staff, pianist, excellent food. Reservations advised. P. 43.

⑭ **Stagecoach Trail.** Scenic historic backroads route to Warren (good cheese factory tour) and remote Shullsburg, Wisconsin (summer lead mine tour, interesting architecture, inexpensive new restaurant in restored hotel/cheese shop). P. 42.

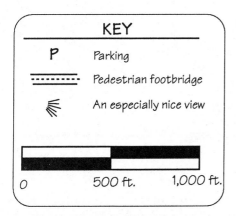

KEY

P   Parking

---------- Pedestrian footbridge

≪   An especially nice view

0   500 ft.   1,000 ft.

retaining walls, barns, carriage houses, and iron
fences. The population has shrunk considerably
from its peak of over 14,000 in 1857 to 3,900.

For a hundred years Galena residents had just
enough money to maintain their homes, but not
enough money or development pressure to demol-
ish the old central city and build bigger. Lead and
zinc smelting continued into the 20th century, and
two 19th-century foundries still operate today —
one right in the heart of the historic downtown,
next to the Old Market House. Jo Daviess County's
strength in dairying and raising beef bolstered the
area's economy.

Some new buildings were built, up through the
1890s. But in the mile-long elliptical bowl that visually defines the city, hardly a building from the
20th century exists except for the old high school
and the impressive Carnegie library, both erected
in the first decade after 1900. Streets were never
widened to accommodate streetcar lines or rush-
hour traffic. No areas were razed for big office
buildings or civic centers. No suburbs were built.

Stay at a log cabin or a magnificent mansion

Thanks to the timely intervention of preserva-
tionists and a preservation-minded mayor in the
early 1960s, Galena has been revived by history-
conscious tourism. Galena's picturesque look and
low real estate prices made it natural for week-
enders from Chicago to pick up quickly on the
country inn idea first popularized in New England.
History-minded visitors today can stay at palatial
hillside mansions, country log cabins with every
modern convenience, farmers' hotels, Queen Anne
houses full of nooks and crannies, simple row
houses and frame cottages, a nearby stagecoach
stop, or Galena's leading hotel, where Ulysses S.
Grant was triumphantly welcomed home as the
leader of the victorious Union army. Historic
accommodations may be homestay bed and breakfasts, self-contained suites with kitchenettes,
professionally managed inns, or motels. Conven-

*Seeing the Mississippi
from Galena*
*The great river is off the
beaten path, away from
tourist crowds, accessible
only by gravel roads.*
2 miles from town: *take
West St. off U.S. 20 on
Galena's west side. It
becomes Ferry Landing Rd.
Boat rental at Schubert's
Landing (815-777-0622).*
**Striking views from
sheer limestone bluffs:**
*take 4th St. off U.S. 20 on
the east side. It becomes
Blackjack Rd. Follow signs
to Chestnut Mt. ski area.
Warning: gravel may
damage perfect paint jobs.*
Fishing boat rental *from
Moon's Little Acres, (815)
591-3383.*

*A handy aid to back-
roads adventures
and activities from
downhill skiing to riding
and golf is the free Jo
Daviess Co. Recreation
Guide and Map. Get it at
the Visitors Bureau in the
depot (p. 28) or call (800)
747-9377.*

tional motels range from a new luxury motel with indoor/outdoor pool to clean, simple 1950s-era ma-and-pa motels.

Hilly terrain ideal for golf and skiing

In recent years the Galena area, now only two hours from Chicago's ever-expanding northwestern suburbs, has also become something of a resort, despite its harsh continental climate. (Summers are hot and muggy; winters are very cold.) All of Jo Daviess County is in the Driftless Region, untouched by glaciers. Its high ridges and steep-sided hollows are unlike anything else in Illinois. The resort developments of Galena Territory, Chestnut Mountain, and Eagle Ridge make use of the landscape's natural affinity for downhill and cross-country skiing, golf courses with river vistas, and recreational lakes created in narrow valleys.

Artists, academics, and various creative professionals from Chicago have found they could get a weekend cottage for very little money, compared with prices in Chicago and waterfront vacation areas. A good number of people who have been transferred to nearby Dubuque decide to settle in Galena and commute. Today, despite the growth in tourism and second homes, real estate remains remarkably inexpensive by standards of large metropolitan areas. Real estate circulars list handymen's specials on large lots for $15,000 and under, and renovated small houses for $40,000

▲ A two-day river cruise from LeClaire, Iowa (just north of Davenport) to Galena comes highly recommended for its scenery and the 19th-century atmosphere of its boats. One boat, the Julia Belle Swain, really is an old steamboat (with a steam calliope, too).

Entertainment is provided by banjo players, storytellers, dance hall singer-dancers, and the captain, who points out passing sights. Fares ($195/ person) include all meals, overnight at Chestnut Mountain Resort with a pool and a morning tour of Galena. In Illinois call (800) 237-1660. Otherwise: (800) 331-1467.

Cross-country skiing at beautiful Eagle Ridge Resort
61 K groomed trails through woods. Lessons, sledding, ice skating. Nov.-March. $6 trail fee.

and under, while fully renovated mansions used as inns may sell for $200,000 and up.

Since 1991, riverboat gambling (p. 88) has shifted many visitors' focus from Galena to Dubuque, which pioneered it. Galena used to be the area's major destination. Side trips took in Dubuque and its quaint funicular railway, and its opulent mansions. Today tour busses are more likely to head for the greyhound track and Casino Belle in Dubuque. Now several cities in Illinois, Iowa, and possibly Wisconsin are joining the riverboat gambling bandwagon, including East Dubuque in Jo Daviess County.

High-caliber local entertainment an extra plus

Still and all, there's nothing remotely like Galena. The charm of its architecture and hilly site can't be matched. The variety and quality of its historic accommodations are outstanding. With over 50 specialty shops and antique shops, the recreational shopping is the best in the tri-state area — though hardly as interesting as what's to be found in Chicago, Madison, or Minneapolis. Galena also offers quite a variety of high-caliber resident entertainment — from folk singers at the Spring Street Tavern and singing waiters at the Kingston Inn to the Main Street Players and the Galena Chamber Ensemble, composed of musicians from

Golf in Galena
*Two 18-hole championship courses and a 9-hole course at **Eagle Ridge**, in beautiful wooded hill country east of Galena. Indoor golf driving and video analysis in winter. 18 holes $68, or $38 after 3 p.m. Res. required. (815) 777-2500. 9-hole Galena Golf Club on rolling hills: $8 weekdays, $9 weekends. (815) 777-3599.*

Downhill skiing overlooking the Mississippi
at Chestnut Mt. Resort. 16 runs, 1 quad & 2 triple chair lifts. 475-foot vertical drop, 3,500 feet longest run. Night skiing. Thanksgiving to St. Pat's. (800) 397-1320.

Jim Post, nationally known folksinger-songwriter and a Galena resident, has recorded "Galena Rose," his fascinating and popular portrait of Galena's lead rush days. Each song depicts the hopes and dreams of real people who came to Galena, from the members of the founding Meeker colony of entrepreneur-pioneers to an Indian mourning the loss of his ancestral land. Tapes are for sale for $10 at Cover to Cover and Main Street Fine Books.

the Chicago Symphony, Northwestern, and Dubuque.

You're not really getting *away* from Chicago when you go to Galena, especially in the busy seasons. If you're looking for that getaway feeling, come in early May, when the daffodils and redbud are out in profusion, or at lilac time around Memorial Day. That's the perfect time for long walks that show off Galena in all its glory, before the summer crowds and fall fill up its winding streets.

Midweek is nicer
Galena can be uncomfortably crowded on weekends in summer and fall, with so many people that it doesn't seem like any kind of a getaway at all. Midweek (Mon.-Thurs. nights) it's much less crowded and often cheaper, too. Off-season rates apply Nov.-April.

WHEN TO VISIT

Spring: The best time by far to visit Galena. Through mid-June, even weekends aren't crowded. Lots of lilacs. beautiful pointillist effect of long views at leaf-out time. Great weather for walks. Spring homes tour least crowded.

Summer: Weather is often hot and muggy. Weekends are crowded. See town in the uncrowded morning, plan outdoor recreation, cool lead mine tours for later.

Fall: The weather's nice in Sept. & Oct. But town is often crowded beyond its carrying capacity — always at color time in early and mid Oct. The color isn't that great, either. But it's good for golf, outdoor recreation.

Winter: No crowds. Relaxed atmosphere reigns in town, when interesting retailers have plenty of time. Most shops stay open. Excellent downhill and cross-country skiing.

ANNUAL EVENTS

Spring homes tour: 2nd weekend June. $10. **Galena Arts Festival:** 3rd weekend June. **Willow Folk Festival:** 2nd weekend Aug. in Stockton. **Fall homes tour:** 4th weekend Sept. **Galena Country Fair** and **Civil War Encampment**: 2nd weekend Oct. **Country Christmas**: strolling street carolers, lamplight tours, homes tour, Santa parade, including fancy dress **Mistletoe Ball** (1st Sat. in Dec.). From Thanksgiving to Christmas.
For a calendar of all events, call 1 (800) 747-9377.

ENTERTAINMENT

Galena Chamber Ensemble: 4-concert season (Sept., Dec., March, May). $8. **Main Street Players:** high-caliber local theater in excellent, air-conditioned space at beautiful Sinsinawa Mound (p. 56). Every weekend, June-Oct. $8. (815) 777-0410. **Remembering Old Galena:** worthwhile musical look at Galena's colorful history, from the Main St. Players. At DeSoto House, 203 S. Main. Mid-June thru Oct. $7. **Bingo:** Every Thurs. at Turner Hall, S. Bench St., 7 p.m. Proceeds to save hall. **Live music nightly:** spirited singing waiters, very good food at **Kingston Inn**. Reservations suggested. (815) 777-0451. Folk music at **Spring Street Tavern** in Farmers' Home, 334 Spring, 8:30-11 except Sat. **Live weekend music at nightspots:** Folk, blues, jazz at **Benjamin's**, 103 N. Main. (815) 777-0467. Bluegrass, country, folk at **Green St. Tavern** in DeSoto House (815) 777-0090. Cabaret at **Silver Annie's**, (815) 777-3131.
For a complete nightlife listing, call 1 (800) 747-9377.

The Illinois Central depot

was built in 1857, shortly after the railroad arrived. Galenians had always perceived the railroad as a threat to their city's prosperity, based on river transportation and linked with St. Louis. When the Illinois Central located its roundhouse and shops in Dubuque, Dubuque gained the advantage for later industrial development.

Stop at the depot first!
Good information and lots of parking

In the busy season, parking on downtown streets fills up by noon, but the **Galena/ Jo Daviess Visitor Information Center** at the old **Illinois Central Depot** usually has **plenty of free parking**.

Where: The old depot is visible from U.S. 20 across the Galena River bridge from downtown. Turn north onto Park Ave. and go one block. The depot is on Park at Bouthilllier. Plenty of parking is behind it.

Open: Monday through Saturday 9-5, Sunday 10-4.

Phone: (800) 747-9377 (recorded info & events). (815) 777-3557 (questions).

Inside, there's loads of visitor information, not only about Galena and Jo Daviess County but about neighboring places in Iowa and Wisconsin. There are **menu notebooks** of local restaurants and **photo-notebooks of inns** and bed and breakfast establishments, with color photos of exteriors and typical rooms. Also on hand: **public restrooms** and **phones**.

The brochures can be overwhelming if you don't have a specific interest in mind. Here's what's most generally useful:

◆ Coordinated **Jo Daviess County guides** to lodging & dining, events, antiquing, historic attractions, outdoor recreation, art galleries & studios. All are well organized, comprehensive, and easy to use. The **county recreation guide** has a detailed county road map for backroads adventures.

◆ *The Galenian.* The chamber of commerce's free magazine/guide includes the best overall maps, a seasonal events listing, an outstanding 2-page timeline to fill you in quickly on relevant local history, and numerous interesting articles on local history, written by top local authorities. Worthwhile ads, too, and restaurant menus.

◆ **"Walking Tour of Historic Galena."** Two-part architectural/historical tour of Main Street and Beach Street, totaling about 1 1/2 hours plus stops.

POINTS OF INTEREST

Downtown Galena and Quality Hill: shops and points of interest

Along Main on the 5 blocks between Water and Franklin. Free parking is on the street (fills up early in season; 2 or 3-hour limit rigorously enforced), in a lot opposite the V-intersection of Water, and at the foot of Washington. Ample all-day parking is across the river by the depot/visitor info center.

This is pretty much what prosperous centers of commerce looked like at the time of the Civil War: rows of brick storefronts, mostly three or four stories high and three windows wide across the upper stories. Occasionally a larger business block was as wide as several storefronts. Upper stories were used as offices, as residences for merchants, and as boarding houses. It's a tight, dense environment, meant for walking and certainly not for cars.

After several fires in the 1840s, new buildings were required to be brick. That creates the unifying wall effect of Main Street, together with the fact that most stores were built within a 10-year period of compatible styles. One noteworthy difference from Galena's heyday in the 1850s is the number of big plate-glass windows. That technological innovation by 1880 or so replaced smaller, multiple-paned storefront windows.

For most of the 20th century, Galena's streets have fascinated artists and visitors. Lorado Taft, Chicago's leading public sculptor around the turn of the century, was part of a group of artists who visited the area frequently. He declared that "every stick and stone of Galena was precious to the artist and student," and he "urged that the city's architectural relics be kept as close to their original state as possible," according to the WPA *Galena Guide* published in 1937.

The *Guide* continues, "Modern business thrives within walls which witnessed the barter of lead

A Walking Tour of Historic Galena *is an informative annotated map emphasizing architectural styles, dates, and builders. It tells a lot about 63 buildings on Main and Bench streets. It's free at the Galena Historical Museum (p. 36) and the Depot/Visitor Info. Center (p. 28).*

miner and Indian. . . . There has been little need for new buildings in a town which was sturdily built to accommodate [a far greater population] in the 1850s."

Today's downtown conveys the look of old Galena even better than that of 50 years ago, when Art Deco fronts covered street-level façades. The current **sign ordinance** allows only signs of a size and style reflected in 19th-century photographs of Galena. New street lamps with the height and style of old gaslights enhance the 19th-century look. On Main Street, façades built to house several narrow shops disguise fairly large-scale uses such as a big drugstore, the VFW social hall, even a large parking garage next to the De Soto House Hotel.

Of the four main streets that parallel the Galena River and climb the steep hill, each has a distinctive character worth exploring. **Commerce Street**, closest to the river, was once lined with blacksmiths, livery stables, warehouses, and workshops. Also on Commerce are the splendid **post office** (p. 32) and the **Market House**, now a state historic site where visitors can see an slide-tape show on Galena architecture (p. 35). Floods were a problem here until dikes were built after World War II. Today it's interesting to see how the look of old Galena along Commerce Street accommodates two sizable supermarkets, a Kraft cheese plant, a foundry, a drive-in bank, and a lumberyard without looking either out of place or cutely historic.

Main Street was, and is, Galena's only retail district. It's a level street, fitted into the curve of a bowl that rises so steeply behind it that what's the ground floor on the front of some buildings is two stories below grade at the rear. Odd little walled patios, backyard terraces and retaining walls can be seen from Bench Street, Galena's earliest show street. Two public stairways lead up to Bench Street at Green and at Washington streets; court–yards and balconies overlook them, too.

Bench Street is the home of many fine Greek Revival and Italianate homes, five beautiful churches, Turner Hall, and a grand library.

A recommended plan for touring Galena

◆ *By foot is best. The wonderful details of architecture and scenery stand out.*

◆ *Save the morning for a walk. The morning light illuminates the lovely details of downtown Galena's east-facing historic streets and gardens. By mid-afternoon, downtown streets are in the shade. By that time, if it's hot and muggy (as it often is in summer), air-conditioned shops will be a welcome change.*

◆ *Park your car at the Depot (p. 28) and forget about it.*

◆ *Get an overview of Galena at the historical museum (p. 36); you'll have a better understanding of what you see.*

◆ *Have a picnic lunch with a fine view (p. 35). Use restaurants as air-conditioned snack and rest stops in the afternoon. Save your time and money for a relaxed dinner.*

Galena
is also the name for lead sulfide, the brilliant blue-black mineral which when smelted yields lead.

Dramatic architectural
details and widespread
use of stone reward visi-
tors who explore Galena
by foot. The beautiful
First Presbyterian
Church on Bench Street
represents the hard
work of frontier mis-
sionary and abolitionist
Eratus Kent, who asked
the American Missionary
Society to send him "to
a place that is so hard
that no one else will
take it." He helped
found Beloit and Rock-
ford colleges.

Prospect Street is, like Bench Street, a hillside
street with fine homes and a splendid view of the
Galena River valley. Together they are the main
streets of "Quality Hill," Galena's elite residential
district of the 1850s. Built up after Bench Street
had filled in, it has a later mix of styles: Italianate,
Queen Anne, French Second Empire, Romanesque
Revival. The old high school (now condominiums)
dominates the skyline with its mass and prominent clock tower. The picturesque roofs, steeples,
and towers of Bench and Prospect streets lend
great charm to the view of town from the pedestrian bridge and Grant Park (p. 41).

Galena's over 50 **specialty shops** are concentrated in a half mile of Main Street. Most close at
5. The stores feature mainly home accessories,
country and Victorian things, mostly ordinary antiques, candy, and sportswear. Few are so distinctive that they couldn't be found in dozens of other
visitor destinations a few hours north of Chicago.

Here's a **short, select list of downtown sights**

*If you can't get around
easily,*

*plan on having someone
drop you off by the down-
town destinations that
seem most interesting. The
Chamber of Commerce is
planning to start a shuttle
bus. There are bus tours,
but their narrated history
is said to be overly romantic. You can see a lot of
interesting houses from
your car.*

that stand out. They could be seen in an afternoon, if you want to limit shopping to an hour or two. Commercial tourist attractions of lesser interest have been omitted. *(This tour starts at the Green Street foot bridge. The bridge takes you from Grant Park and convenient all-day parking at the depot over the Galena River to downtown.)*

◆ **U.S. Custom House/Post Office.** *Green at Commerce.* Built in 1857 in an especially elaborate version of the Renaissance Revival style, this is a monument to Galena's political influence during its heyday. The ornate interior is little altered. Congressman Elihu Washburne got the federal government to build the post office. A few years later he would successfully recommend that U.S. Grant, then the colonel of a volunteer unit, be appointed brigadier general before he had even seen action. The construction supervisor of the post office job was a Seneca Indian, Ely Parker. When Grant became a general, he made Parker chief of his staff, and as President, named him commissioner of Indian affairs.

◆ **The Toy Shops in Galena.** *310 S. Main. (815) 777-0383. Open daily 10-5.* General Grant, in the person of impersonator Paul LeGreco, can often be found here, along with a very large selection of toy soldiers and vividly detailed military miniatures, 2 1/4" high and made of pewter. Upstairs are all sorts of other toys: windups, wood toys, educational toys, Playmobil, and more.

◆ **The Friedl Collection Ltd.** *304 S. Main. (815) 777-0599. From mid-April-Dec. open Mon-Sat 10-5, Sun 11-4. Otherwise: Open Fri-Sun only.* Thomas Friedl shows his own well-regarded photographs of Galena, along with hand-crafted stoneware and raku, jewelry and decoys.

◆ **Main Street Fine Books and Manuscripts.** *301 S. Main at Green St. stairs. (815) 777-3749. Open 9-5 every day but Tues & Wed.* The front display counters showcase local memorabilia, political portraits and letters, autographs, and railroad maps, and do it so appealingly and professionally

Why Jo Daviess County?
The name honors Col. Joseph Hamilton Davis, Kentucky lawyer and Indian fighter who died in the Battle of Tippecanoe (1811). In 1827, when the county was formed, Southerners dominated the Illinois legislature and left their stamp on state place names. "Jo" was added to the county name to distinguish it from another Illinois legislators also named Daviess. It is generally pronounced the same as "Davis."

Grant lives on in Galena
at The Toy Shops, 302 S. Main. Portrayed by military history enthusiast and toy store owner Paul LeGreco, Grant is on hand from May through December to answer any questions visitors may have. The general dines with visitors Saturdays and Sundays at 6 and 8 at the DeSoto Hotel (815-777-0090). Other appearances may be arranged by calling (815) 777-0383.

Streets turn into public stairways on Washington and Green streets. They offer good views across the valley and into the odd little patios and balconies permitted by the dramatic change in grade.

that some people think they've wandered into another museum. Specialties include Americana, American literature, Civil War, and Lincolniana. Co-owner Bill Butts, a historian by training, worked for a Lincoln expert before chucking city life and setting up shop in Galena. Not all books here are rare or expensive, but everything, from first editions to inexpensive paperbacks, is carefully chosen, clean, and exceptionally well organized. Good browsing for casual readers.

◆ **Cover to Cover.** *221 S. Main between Green and Washington. Open daily 10-5. (815) 777-3931.* This rambling bookstore has lots of interesting browsing, new and used: a good selection of regional material, vacation reading, a good children's section, lots on history and crafts. Romances, printed ephemera, old magazines, and a good number of sets are in back, along with a roomful of used books.

◆ **DeSoto House Hotel**, *230 S. Main at Green.* Galena merchants built the biggest hotel in town, opened when the Illinois Central Railroad arrived in 1854. Lincoln spoke and stayed here when he helped organize the Republican party in Illinois in

Spring is best of all in Galena
The prettiest months with the best weather are May and June.

1856; Grant's triumphal welcome to his adopted home town was held here in 1865. Upper floors were later removed, and the remodeled interior, though vaguely historic in feeling, is too slick and standard to seem authentically old.

◆ **Old General Store Museum**, *223 S. Main across from DeSoto House. June-Oct. open daily 10-4 more or less; in May, Nov & Dec open Sat & Sun 10-4. $1 admission. (815) 777-9129.* Many visitors think they've stumbled upon an unusual antique shop when they come upon this quaint store crowded with merchandise from the last decades of the 19th century. Actually it's a very personal museum — not the product of professionals trained in museum techniques, but the heartfelt life work of a lifelong saver and innate preservationist, the late Marie Duerrstein.

Posed figures with delightful handmade papier-mache heads evoke characters from Duerrstein's own past and give the museum more the feel of a folk art environment than a meticulously research-ed recreation. Still, the atmosphere is authentic in spirit — authentic enough to have been used as the store where actress Liv Ullman shopped in "The New Land," the film based on Ole Rolvaag's *Giants in the Earth.* The museum's founder was a seam-stress by trade. She wanted to pass on to younger generations the atmosphere of her aunt's general store at nearby Guilford, where she played as a girl before World War I. In 1957, when Duerrstein was 52, she decided to rent this onetime hardware store as a community museum, and went about collecting donations from the attics of friends and merchants. Ancient, unsold merchandise was cleared out of many a loft stockroom to supply the bolts of cloth, button samples, ribbons and sewing notions, hatpins, stockings, new shoes, oil lamps, and the like that fill the old counters and shelves. Duerrstein made many costumes for Galena home tours and parades, and she paid special attention to costumes

Sinsinawa Mound is a beautiful and historic convent complex a few minutes north of Galena in Wisconsin. It's the mother house of the Sinsinawa Dominican Sisters, and visitors are welcome to come and learn about their diverse activities, from sustainable agriculture to art and entrepreneurship. For details, see p. 56.

Shakespeare, the Chicago Bears, a top sausage shop
There's a lot to see and do just north of Galena in Wisconsin. See Southwestern Wisconsin chapter, pp. 47-71.

on museum mannequins. Museum staff are likely to be her friends.

◆ **Carl Johnson Gallery.** *202 S. Main. Open daily 11-5. (815) 777-1222.* Attractive watercolors and etchings of scenes in Galena and other places, here and abroad, the artist has visited.

◆ **Jakel's Galena Bäckerei.** *200 S. Main. Open daily 7-6, Fri & Sat 7-7. Closes 1 hour earlier Nov-April. (815) 777-0400.* This Old World bakery turns out quality European specialties like German black bread and Brötchen and Linzer tortes, at very reasonable prices. Sauerkraut rye at $1.39 for a 1-lb. loaf is the most expensive of 23 kinds of bread, while tortes run from $1 to $2.10 a slice. Poppy-seed amaretto torte is a specialty; pretty decorated cookies are nice treats to take home. Cake decorating here is unusually elaborate, and creative, too — often more like cake landscaping, with tiny scenes.

◆ **Nelson's Bakery,** *118 S. Main. Mon-Fri 6-6, Sat to 5. (815) 777-1373.* At this folksy, old-fashioned bakery, you can sit at a Formica counter and have coffee and tasty 35¢ muffins. The prices on breads and cookies are old-fashioned, too.

◆ **Old Market House.** *On Commerce between Hill and Perry. Free admission. Open daily 9-5 except Thanksgiving, Xmas, New Year's. (815) 777-2570.* When it was built in 1845, this Greek Revival market hall was hailed as a convenient equivalent of a contemporary supermarket The second floor accommodated city council chambers and offices. Now it is an Illinois State Historic Site. The plain interior is much as it was when built. A **slide show on Galena architecture**, shown on the hour and half hour, is a walk through 19th-century styles, illustrated by local examples within the context of

A lunchtime picnic is the way to enjoy Galena's beauty while avoiding tourist crowds and overpriced food. Stop at Jakel's Bäckerei and the Galena River Cheese Co. (p. 36) for great bread and cheese. Then go across the Green St. footbridge to Grant's Park, with its fabulous view of downtown and Quality Hill. Across from the Grant Home is another pleasant picnic spot without the view.

Galena's peculiar history. It's worthwhile but rather dry. Changing **special exhibits** are on the second-floor and in the basement.

Galena River Wine and Cheese

At the Saturday-morning farmers' market,

held from 7 to 10 a.m. from May through October, the market house regains its bygone bustle. Fresh seasonal produce (often organically grown), perennials, and fresh flowers, ornamental corn and dried native grasses, honey, jams and jellies—it's quite a satisfying array of specialties.

Open daily 10-5 year-round.
420 S. Main just inside the flood gates. Parking next to Galena Cellars Winery across the street. (815) 777-9430.

If you're put off by fancy gourmet shops that sell attitude as much as food, you'll love the friendly, knowledgeable, down-to-earth service here. Co-founder Ken Winge has gladly traded the pressures of the Chicago investment world for working long hours in this relaxed and beautiful setting. (The big space goes back to 1845, when it was a warehouse for provisioning steamboats. Today it is oak-paneled and accented with antiques.)

This is where to go for a one-stop sampling of select Wisconsin and Illinois cheeses, including Belmont Brie and a four-year-old, super-sharp Wisconsin Cheddar. Imports aren't neglected — there's English Stilton, Swiss Emmenthaler and Gruyere, and many specialty cookies, pastas, preserves, etc., both imported and domestic. But the attention paid to quality regional products makes this store stand out. Ask for a taste of delicious Galena's Favorite summer sausage, made from an 1879 family recipe. Patés, Usinger's sausage from Milwaukee, cold cuts, crackers and good rye bread, and juices make this the perfect stop for putting together a memorable picnic lunch. Don't miss Sioux City cream soda, sarsaparilla, and root beer, old-timey novelties at just 60¢ a bottle.

Galena/Jo Daviess County History Museum

Galena Cellars
at 515 S. Main just inside the floodgates makes fruit wines (raspberry, strawberry, blueberry, even rhubarb) and some dry grape wines and seasonal specialties like May wine. Mostly $6-$7/bottle. Tastings, free tours. Open daily at 9 a.m. year-round.

Open daily except Thanksgiving, Christmas, New Year's 9 a.m.-4:30 p.m. $3 adults, ages 10-18 $2, under 10 free.
211 S. Bench, one street up from Main, between Washington and Green. (815) 777-9129. Mostly air-

conditioned.

Housed in a grand mansion, this museum has a lot of really wonderful stuff, and a memorable setting, too. It's located in the center of Bench Street's stately parade of fine houses and churches. The 1858 Italianate mansion still has much of its original architectural detailing. What's most impressive is its steady focus on using artifacts to convey an understanding of this unusual town and county and the forces and people who shaped it.

Start your trip to Galena by seeing the fine **audiovisual presentation**, shown on the hour. Nowhere else in town can you get such an intelligent overview of how Galena came to be — and to be preserved. In the main exhibit hall is **"Peace in Union,"** a compelling, life-size painting by Thomas Nast, the preeminent illustrator of the Civil War era — and the inventor of the popular American image of Santa Claus. His 1895 painting depicts Lee's surrender to Grant at Appomatox. "There is deep understanding by the artist of this great hour in American history," writes museum director Daryl Watson. "Every detail in it is complete. . . Lee in perfectly groomed boots and uniform, Grant with mud-caked boots and careless coat and tie." Other displays are on Nast himself and Galena's nine generals — townspeople who volunteered with Grant, joined his staff, and rose with him.

This is not a slick museum. Some display techniques are informal, even amateurish. What's much more important is that the writing and ideas conveyed are consistently intelligent, whether the subject is dolls and toys of the rich and the poor, or Galena's distinctive lead-glazed pottery, or the Black Hawk War (actually a series of skirmishes) and its causes.

"Diggers, Smelters, Steamers" tells the story of the pioneers drawn by the lead boom and steamboat traffic it created. Newly upgraded for 1992 is a new exhibit on **geology and landforms**. It's no coincidence that lead deposits were in the southern part of the Driftless Region, where the glaciers never came, or that lead deposits are in

What led to Galena's sudden decline after 1857

♦ *Silt from erosion made the shallow Galena River less reliably navigable.*

♦ *The coming of the Illinois Central Railroad in 1854 competed with Galena's river trade as the Wisconsin lead region's main port.*

♦ *Lead production dropped as the easiest deposits gave out.*

♦ *The nationwide Panic of 1857 hit overextended areas like Galena especially hard.*

♦ *The Civil War disrupted the Mississippi's north-south trade routes that tied Galena to St. Louis and New Orleans. It strengthened east-west routes and Chicago's key position on them.*

♦ *Local complacency and polarization between Republicans and Democrats deprived Galena of strong local leadership.*
—Adapted from article by Daryl Watson in *The Galenian* (p. 28)

the highest part of Illinois. Understanding the varying sentiments of Jo Daviess County residents toward the Union cause is illuminating for people who have the mistaken notion there were neat divisions between Yankees and Southerners.

It's fascinating to see photographs of Galena's riverfront back when it bustled with steamboat traffic, and again when floodwaters rose high. The upstairs **river gallery** uses rare photos and drawings to tell the story of the Galena River, from early explorations to the 1951 dike and floodgate project of the Corps of Engineers.

The small **gift shop** has a fine collection of regional books, cards, and historic documents, and replicas of Victorian graphics.

Ulysses S. Grant Home

Open 9-5 daily except New Year's, Thanksgiving, Christmas. No admission charge.

Across the river from downtown. On Bouthillier St. midway up the hill. From U.S. 20 on the east edge of the old part of Galena, turn north onto Bouthillier. From the Illinois Central Depot on Park north of U.S. 20, go east up the Bouthillier hill. (815) 777-0248.

"I guess I was expecting it to be a little more palatial," sniffed a woman in an expensive sweater as she left the restored home of the Union's greatest general. She apparently expected more than this ample, solid, moderately stylish Italianate brick house, built in 1860 and given to the Grants at the war's end in 1865.

The year before the Civil War began, Grant had come to Galena to work in his father's big leather firm. He was at a low point, having resigned from the army because he refused a second assignment that would have kept him from his beloved wife and family. Grant's judgment and perspective on politics and military matters made a good impression on influential local citizens, who encouraged the revival of his military career.

After the war, 13 local Republican admirers purchased this house for their hero. If you come here

Use the museum as a cool rest stop
If you are planning a long walk up Bench and Prospect streets and beyond, you are welcome to return to cool off, see more in the museum, and sit down in the video room seats when not in use, or see the show again.

A quick, chatty read about Grant in Galena
Stephen Repp's self-published Ulysses S. Grant: The Galena Years ($6 or so at both local bookstores) is an engaging little book full of interesting vignettes about Grant at work and at home, drawn largely from letters and writings of Grant and others.

expecting to be impressed with Victorian splendor, you're in for a disappointment. The Grants only lived here a few months, all told, and they didn't choose the furnishings. The gift house came fully furnished — in the latest upper-middle-class style, but not really ostentatious in any way.

It has just enough gilding and impressive dignity to be suitable for entertaining important guests, while still being a comfortable and livable home. That's just the way the Grants would have wanted it. Though the opulent, mansard-roofed Second Empire style of public buildings during his administration is sometimes called "the General Grant style," Grant was a quiet, unassuming person with simple tastes and a great fondness for family life. His wife, something of a Southern belle, had more of a taste for elegance.

The house has been restored to its 1868 appearance, and most of the original furnishings remain. So if you enjoy seeing a sort of ideal upper-middle-class house from just after the Civil War, without family heirlooms, you will find a lot to enjoy about this well-done restoration. The **kitchen** is quite modern for its time. The **garden** and yard plantings are characteristic of the period: the kitchen garden is interesting, and the redbud and lilac are beautiful in May and June — the best time to visit Galena. The site is splendid; a knoll just west of the house has a **fine view** of Grant Park and the buildings of downtown Galena beyond it.

A guide tells a bit about the house while taking visitors around. In the **log cabin** in the **park** across the street, there's an exhibit on Grant's life, but the person is lost in the details. That's a shame, because you don't have to be a military history fan to enjoy learning about this admirable, level-headed, courageous man who went from being a business failure to a military hero in two years. **Picnic tables** are in the shady park; it's a nice place to stop.

More on Grant

The Personal Memoirs of Ulysses S. Grant is considered one of the best autobiographies of the 19th century. Grant, a great smoker of pipes and cigars, was dying — with much pain — from throat cancer as he heroically completed it. The book's tremendous success saved his family from poverty after an investment partner turned out to be a swindler. It's rentable on tape, complete, from Books on Tape, Box 7900, Newport Beach, CA 92658, or at many libraries.

A much shorter contemporary biography is William McFeely's Pulitzer Prize-winning Grant: A Biography, available in paperback.

Grant and Galena

◆ **Jesse Grant's leather store: an important part of Galena.** U. S. Grant's father's Galena leather store was just part of a far-flung family business. It was typical of the kind established by smart, enterprising men who took advantage of new markets on the booming frontier. Jesse Grant's tannery was on the Ohio River, not far from the family home where his children grew up. His stores in La Crosse, Wisconsin; Galena; and Cedar Falls, Iowa, took in hides, shipped them to Ohio to be tanned, and received finished leather and leather goods. The store where U. S. Grant clerked was at 124 South Main.

◆ **The vicissitudes of Grant's career.** Grant was a West Point graduate and career army officer, but his love of family life caused him to quit the army in 1854, after a promotion would have brought a second long separation. He tried to establish himself near his wife's parents' home outside of St. Louis. First he tried farming. (Grant's Farm, which he called Hardscrabble, is now a visitor attraction owned by the Busch brewing family.) Then he lost money in real estate investments. In 1860, he took up his father's offer to work at the Galena business run by his brothers. People he met on business in the area loved to hear this well-spoken, perceptive officer talk about the Mexican War. (Grant did not support the blatantly imperialistic war but served in it.)

◆ **Apolitical but committed to the Union.** Grant was never a very political person. First a Whig, later a Democrat until well into the Civil War, he had voted only once before becoming President. Though many Democrats in Galena and elsewhere had Southern sympathies, and though Grant's own father-in-law owned slaves, Grant was deeply committed to preserving the Union. When war broke out, he immediately recruited a volunteer unit and drilled it.

◆ **Grant's springboard to prominence.** As one of the few professionally trained officers of Galena's volunteer unit, Grant stood out. That paved the way for his rapid ascent, along with help from Elihu Washburne, the congressman from Galena. Washburne soon had Grant appointed brigadier general. In Galena, Washburne and other local Republicans had come to admire Grant for his unusual combination of tact, honesty, forthrightness, and independence. Grant was a quiet man, an interested listener who didn't hesitate to offer opinions when asked. Those qualities, together with his decisiveness in battle and his ability to manage men and supplies, accounted for his military success.

Grant Park

*Between Park Ave. and the Galena River, 2 blocks
north of Hwy. 20/Decatur St. A footbridge across the
Galena River connects the park with Green St.
downtown.*

This extremely pleasant little park has two
fronts and two personalities. The west-facing side
and hilltop is a formal plaza with benches, centered around a bronze state of U. S. Grant. The
view across to downtown is splendid, especially in
the morning light. **Picnic tables** are under a
pavilion and scattered around the hill crest, to
take advantage of the fine view would be a nice
place to enjoy a sack lunch. Along the park's
Park Avenue frontage, the park functions more as a
neighborhood recreation center, with a **playground** and **basketball court**.

H. H. Kohlsaat acquired the park for his home-
town in 1890 as a site for a memorial to its most
famous citizen. Born here, he left Galena as a boy
with his parents. Like many Galenians after the
Civil War, they decided to invest their money and
energies in Chicago. There he
made good as a publisher.

The statue, by Danish sculptor
Johannes Gelert, shows Grant at
44, just after he returned from
the Civil War. When Mrs. Grant
saw the model for it, she said
she didn't like the hand in the
pocket. Kohlsaat offered to change
it, but the widow answered, "Oh,
no! Leave it as it is, but dear me,
I've told that man twenty times
a day to take his hand out of his
pocket."

*A Civil War
encampment
is held in the park across
from Grant's house each
Columbus Day weekend.*

*Lamplight tours
of Grant's home
are held for spring and fall
homes tours, and on three
Country Christmas
weekends beginning
Thanksgiving weekend.*

A walk through
the east side

*Begin at the Old Depot/Chamber of Commerce, on
U.S. 20 just east of the Galena River.*

Galena's attractive east side has an interesting

mix of impressive mansions and middle-class homes. The yards are large, with room for gardens. This a fine place to walk and make your own discoveries, what with redbuds and lilacs in spring and a wealth of decorative detail on porches and bay windows. Some high spots offer outstanding views of downtown Galena across the river. Use the overall map in *The Galenian* (p. 28) to plan your own walking tour.

Galena Rock Shop

Hours vary. Open most weekends.
713 South Bench, 1 block south of U.S. 20. (815) 777-1611.

It's easy to overlook the interesting old parts of Galena that are off and away from major attractions. On a visit here, you'll see minerals and fossils from all over the world, collected by mineralogist Mike Bergmann in his role as partner of MinSpec Mining Corporation, *and* you'll see an unusual French house from 1836, reminiscent of early homes in old French-style river settlements like St. Louis and Ste. Genevieve, Missouri.

Warren Cheese Plant

Open weekdays for cheese sales and free tours some mornings. For tours, call ahead to make sure cheese is being made. (815) 745-2627.
415 Jefferson at Belleview in Warren. Where Stagecoach Trail turns to the left, at Belleview, turn right. Plant is in 2 blocks.

Though pizza parlors are this cheese factory's major customers, it makes two specialty mozzarella-type cheeses of note. Its string cheese placed first in a 1984 world competition. And cheesemaker-owner John Bussman (who may be your tour guide) invented Apple Jack cheese, named in honor of the nearby Apple River. It uses cultures from Swiss, Cheddar, and Monterey Jack cheeses for a semi-soft, creamy white cheese that can be melted, frozen, and aged up to three months, much longer than mozzarella.

*A beautiful, scenic drive is due east out of Galena along **Stagecoach Trail**. A major route through the old lead region, it follows a beautiful wooded valley and passes many buildings from the 1830s and 1840s. Two destinations are each about a half hour away. At Scales Mound, go north on County Rd. 4 to the interesting old mining town of **Shullsburg** (p. 58). Highlights are Shullsburg's lead mine tour and new restaurant. Or continue on Stagecoach Trail to **Warren** with its cheese factory.*

A major beef and dairy region
In Illinois, Jo Daviess County is #1 in beef cattle and oats, #2 in dairy cattle and hay. Its rich limestone soil s are excellent for alfalfa, grazing, and oats. Kraft makes Swiss cheese in Galena and nearby Stockton.

Just 20 minutes away in Dubuque
An old funicular railway, an excellent museum on riverboats and river history, palatial 19th century homes, and Iowa's pioneer of riverboat gambling enterprise. See p. 72.

RESTAURANTS & LODGINGS

Illinois sales tax is 6%. In addition, lodgings in Jo Daviess County charge a 3% room tax.

GALENA (population 3,910)

Chestnut Mountain Resort. *From U.S. 20 on the east side of Galena, take 4th St. south. It becomes Blackjack Rd. Follow signs to Chestnut Mt. ski area. (815) 777-1320. Open daily for 3 meals, year-round. Breakfast: 8-11. Lunch: 12-3. Dinner: 5-10. Major credit cards. Full bar. Separate bar area.*

Better-than-average hotel food in the Galena area's only restaurant overlooking the Mississippi. Blufftop setting has a terrific view. Chestnut Mountain is a ski resort; summer amusements available to diners include hiking trails, a miniature golf course, and Alpine Slide. (Like a water slide with no water. Sliders go back uphill on a chair lift.) Casual setting. Seasonal menu. Sample dishes: French toast for breakfast, $3.50 with choice of meat. For lunch, big burgers, $3.50, meal-size salads (taco, dilled chicken salad, chef) around $5. Dinners include relish tray, salad, rolls, starch. Catfish $11.50, prime rib $16. Also: ribs, pork chops, chicken. Not a lot for vegetarians except for summer salad bar (about $5). Kids' menu.

Grant's Place. *515 South Main over Galena Cellars Winery, just inside the floodgates. City parking lot next door; may be full. (815) 777-3331. Open daily year-round, 11-10, except closed Tues in winter. Visa, MC, AmEx. Full bar.*

Pub with 6 TVs for sports. Known for good basic sandwiches and fast service. Popular picks: bowl of soup and sandwich ($4.25), 1/3 lb. burger with pickle, slaw, fries or housemade potato salad ($4.50), Philly sandwich. Dinners in evening include baked potato or french fries, dinner salad, rolls. From $7 (beer-battered smelts) to $12 (shrimp, steak). Broiled fish available.

Jakel's Galena Bäckerei & Cafe. *200 South Main at Washington. (815) 777-0400. Open daily year-round. Sun-Thurs 7 a.m.-5 p.m., Fri & Sat to 6 p.m. No credit cards. Out-of-town checks OK. No alcohol, no smoking.*

Excellent European-style bakery (p. 35) has 40-seat, fast-serve cafe featuring 100% Colombian coffee, brewed the German way; a dozen juices; and its own baked goods, including several hearty stuffed croissants ($2.25-$3.10) for breakfast and lunch: ham and egg, chicken breast, broccoli & cheese, etc. Also, beef stew in a bread container ($3.10).

Kingston Inn. *300 North Main at Franklin, on the north end of downtown. (You might find parking on side streets.) (815) 777-0451. Open daily year-round except for being closed for one day a week in winter (day changes; call ahead). Seatings on the half-hour from 5:30 to 9:30. May be open for lunch at 11:30 in summer and fall. Opens at 4:30 Sundays, May-Oct. Reservations advised, not always necessary. Visa, MC, Diners. Full bar. Separate pub area.*

A singing wait staff serves what's widely considered the best food in town. Pop standards of the past century are the typical musical fare, performed competently with casual gusto and piano accompaniment. The European/American menu reflects the owners' eclectic national backgrounds (one is from Spain) and makes vegetarians and dieters happy. Imaginatively improvised atmosphere is comfortable, not fancy. Feels like a warm family party. Dinners run from $10 to $20. Favorite dishes include delicious roast duck, New Orleans jambalaya with the requisite crawfish, shrimp, ham, chicken ($14), besubo (an Atlantic whitefish) in a Spanish tomato-green pepper sauce, and Iowa pork chops ($14). Dinners include interesting salad bar, starch, homemade bread. Lunch, when offered, is sandwiches and other pub food, served without singing wait staff. Ask about special December **holiday shows** with flamenco guitar.

Log Cabin. *201 North Main at Perry on the north side of downtown. (Try parking on Commerce in evening.) (815) 777-0393. Open Tues-Sat 11-11, Sun 11-10. Cash only. Full bar.*
Family restaurant is a longtime favorite with discriminating locals. Recommended lunches include croissant sandwich, soup ($4), Greek salad (about $5). Good Greek chicken (baked with lemon, oregano, olive oil) is $7.50 at lunch and dinner. 1-lb. ribeye steak a dinner favorite at $13. Entrees include salad, starch, relish tray, roll, coffee. Piano player Fri & Sat evenings. Reservations advised for 6 or more. Ice cream drinks a specialty.

Market House Tavern. *204 Perry between Main and Bench at north end of downtown. Upstairs (no elevator). (815) 777-0690. Open daily year-round. 11:30-2 (to 2:30 in season) and 4-9 (to 9:30 Fri & Sat, to 8 Sun). Visa, MC, Disc. Full bar. Pleasant bar area.*
Dependable, slightly upscale pub food. Good view of Main Street bustle from upstairs windows. Highly recommended: 1/2 lb. Tavernburger ($5 plus extras), $7 steak sandwich, Crab Louis salad ($8.50 full order, $5.25 half order). Meal-size garden salad $3.75, chef salad $4.25, veggie pita $5. Fish, steak, chicken entrees come with appetizer basket, starch, salad. Pasta Alfredo a specialty ($12 with chicken or shrimp).

Silver Annie's. *124 North Commerce at Perry, on the north end of downtown. (Parking often available in bank lot across Commerce. (815) 777-3131. Food served 5-9:30 (from 4:30, June-Oct). Reservations usually necessary, at least a few weeks ahead on busy weekends. Major credit cards. Full bar.*
Tiny, 34-seat spot features Gibson Girl decor, good Italian and American food, after-dinner cabaret "A Detour in Time." Piano, vocals, and guitar by the owners, Percy and Peaches, and Dan the Music Man. Music spans the last century and the spectrum from folk to Phantom of the Opera, with special emphasis on the 1930s. Patrons often sing along. Dinner favorites: fettucine Alfredo, cooked to order ($10.25), grilled halibut, smothered pork chops in wine-veloute sauce. Lasagna a vegetarian hit. Prices from $8 (spaghetti) to $15 (steak and scampi). Entrees include starch, soup or salad, garlic bread. All desserts homemade.
See also: **Hazel Green**, p. 69 **Shullsburg**, p. 59.

Best Western Quiet House. *(815) 777-2577. 9923 Route 20, at the crest of the hill on the east edge of town.* 42 rooms on 2 floors. Standard rooms $87, fantasy suites (Lincoln Log Cabin, Roman Huntsman, Grand Presidential, etc.) to $187. Very large, attractively decorated rooms with restrained country theme. All have balconies, half have nice views of country, half face cemetery and strip. Next to Happy Joe's restaurant. A hike to downtown, not far from Grant's home. Good-sized indoor-outdoor pool, whirlpool. Pleasant lobby with sofas, game tables, fireplace. Coffee in lobby.
Luxury motel with beautiful indoor-outdoor pool.

Craig Cottage. *(815) 777-1461 or (815) 777-0482. 505 Dewey (the northern extension of Main) in a quiet residential neighborhood.* $90/couple, $105/family, $120/ 2 couples. 20-25% midweek discount, plus discounts for multiple nights. 650-square-foot brick house on 2 levels. Owners live across street. Two-story rear porch & deck overlook wooded river valley. Built in 1827, rebuilt in 1960s for rustic country look. Once featured in *Country Living*. Operable stone fireplace in downstairs family room. Double bed upstairs, sofa bed downstairs. Complete kitchen with staples, microwave, washer-dryer, 3-season back porch, grill on rear deck. Two blocks from north end of downtown.

Choice example of short-term rentals: picturesque, private, and reasonable

DeSoto House Hotel. *(800) 343-6562. (815) 777-0090. 230 South Main at Green. Parking ramp adjoining.* 55 rooms on 2nd and 3rd floor. 55 rooms with baths. In-season rates: $89-$109. Off-season $10 less. 4 suites: $129-$149. 1855 hotel in the center of downtown is a favorite choice for tour groups. Good location for people who want to be in the center of things or who can't walk too far. Especially good views from rooms facing either Main or Commerce. Cable TV. Courtyard dining room in 4-story atrium, Green St. Tavern. Antique reproduction furniture, pleasant but bland decorating, renovations without old trim make most of the interior seem new, not old.

Historic hotel in the center of downtown Galena.

De Zoya House. *(815) 777-1203. 1203 Third, south of U.S. 20 at the end of a dead-end residential street.* Bed and breakfast in family home. 4 rooms with baths. $75 weekends, $65 midweek. Air-conditioned. Full breakfast. No smoking in rooms. Guests may use balcony, screened porch, library/TV room. Dignified, large 1830s stone house beautifully furnished with Federal antiques (1780-1820). Walking distance to downtown. In quiet neighborhood of interesting historic homes, good for walks.

Antique collectors' treasure from the 1830s

Eagle Ridge Inn & Resort. *(800) 892-2269. (815) 777-2444. East off U.S. 20, 6 miles southeast of Galena.* 20 rooms in main lodge, 60 in 3-story detached units. Weekend in-season rates $165 to $225 (with Jacuzzi and fireplace). Extra day half off. Midweek rates in off-season are much less. Many packages (romance, golf, casino, family, ski, Christmas, riding) include meals at inn. Inn overlooks 220-acre lake at center of 6,800-acre golf resort. An unusually beautiful setting in a hilly valley characteristic of Driftless Region topography close to its most dramatic. Many areas of mature woods contrast with rock outcrops and open space. Rustic architecture of inn and privately owned Galena Territory resort homes is handsome, not cute. Wonderful for wildlife. Over 60 K cross-country ski trails. 45 holes of golf. Rated by Golf Magazine as one of best golf resorts in the world. Riding center. Rent sailboats, canoes, cats, paddleboats on lake. Large indoor pool. NOTE: Rental homes and condos in Galena Territory can be better values than the inn. Inquire at Galena Chamber of Commerce/Visitor Center.

Many-sided golf and cross-country ski resort in gorgeous natural area not far from town

Felt Manor Guest House. *(800) 383-2830. (815) 777-9093. 125 S. Prospect, 3 blocks uphill from downtown. Access off High St.* 5 guest rooms, 3 with private baths (to $85), two share a bath ($70). off-season, midweek, multiple-day discounts. No smoking. Air-conditioned rooms. Continental breakfast, high tea in afternoon. 24-room mansion on 2 1/2-acre grounds overlooks downtown Galena, has 25-mile view. Guests have exclusive use of 2 downstairs parlors, grand piano, pump organ, library with VCR, dining room, except for occasional weddings, meetings. Biggest home in town, on street of impressive homes. Greek Revival with mansard roof, many additions. Steep hills and stairs mean a walk from town is real exercise. Owners live on 3rd floor.

Grand house on Quality Hill with remarkable view

Park Avenue Guest House. *(800) 359-0743. (815) 777-1075. On east side of Galena River at 208 Park between Jefferson and Adams, 3 blocks northeast of Grant's Park.* 4 rooms, all with shower-only bath, on 2nd floor. $70, $95 for suite. $10 off for midweek, off season.

Air-conditioned. Smoking OK in common rooms (owners smoke). Hearty continental breakfast. Elaborate Queen Anne house with wrap-around screened porch, side garden and gazebo. Guests can use parlors, VCR. Furnished with antiques. On quiet street of older homes, walking distance to downtown.

Victorian painted lady with big yard and porch

Pine Hollow Inn. *(815) 777-1071. 4700 North Council Hill Rd, 3/4 mile northeast of city limits. (Road is the eastern continuation of Main/Broadway/Dewey.)* 5 rooms with private baths. $85 for standard room, $95 for 2 with Jacuzzi. $10 off for weekdays. May be more June-Dec. No smoking. Continental breakfast. Air-conditioned. Wood-burning fireplaces. Old-looking new house on 110-acre Christmas tree farm with creek. Informal country furnishings. Guests can use large, eat-in kitchen, microwave, fridge, long front porch, walk on far. No other common rooms. Guest rooms have loveseat or sofa. Owners live in nearby house.

Country setting close to town

Triangle Motel. *(815) 777-2897. On U.S. 20 1/2 mile east of intersection of Hwy. 84, 1 mile east of downtown Galena.* 20 rooms on 1 floor. Weekend rates: $38-50. 10% discount Sun-Thurs with cash. Clean older motel. Cable TV, Showtime. Coffee in office. Swing set, play area, picnic tables. On highway strip near McDonald's.

Only budget motel in town

See also: **Hazel Green**, p. 69, and **Platteville**, p. 70.

WARREN (population 1,600) An old country town 35 minutes east of Galena via the scenic Stagecoach Trail. Cheese plant tours. Nice park with pool. Near interesting bluffs and trails of Apple Canyon State Park and the old mining town of Shullsburg, Wisconsin. Good bicycling area.

Frontier Inn. *108 Railroad Street (Stagecoach Trail) north of tracks from downtown. (815) 745-9613. Mon-Sat 8 a.m.-1 a.m. Dining room open Mon-Fri 11-1:30, Tues, Fri & Sat 5-10. No credit cards. Out-of-town checks OK. Full bar.*

Popular cafe and supper club in old hotel. Lunch specials (always under $4) may include broasted chicken, roast beef, BBQ ribs. Cup of soup and sandwich: $2.50. Homemade pies $1/ slice. Complete menu with salad bar served 3 nights a week, $5.50-$7. Fresh catfish on Fridays, ribs or steak special Saturdays. Occasional live music Sat. Juke box, darts, pinball.

Noni's Bed and Breakfast. *(815) 745-2045 (nights, weekends). (815) 745-2000 (days). 516 W. Main (Stagecoach Trail) 5 blocks west of downtown. 2 rooms share a bath. Will rent 1-2 more rooms to entire families. $40 weekends, $35 midweek, $5 off each night with 3-night stays.* Full breakfast. Big old house. Owner a longtime resident in tourism industry. Guests may use living room, sun porch, study, dining room, kitchen, fridge, patio, picnic tables, grill. Shady yard. Park with pool within walking distance.

Big, homey house in farm town.

Southwestern Wisconsin

Combining back road adventures and old mine towns, excellent sausage and Camembert makers, Shakespeare, a terrific lead museum, and the Chicago Bears.

THE HILLY SOUTHERN PART of the old Wisconsin Lead Region is the natural vacation hinterland for anyone visiting Galena, Dubuque, New Glarus, Spring Green, or Mineral Point. It's out of the way yet convenient, and not usually overrun with tourists — a fine place for leisurely country drives to visit an ornate old mining town like Shullsburg, or a top-notch small sausage maker, or a cheese factory that makes French-type Brie and Camembert.

Lead mines in Platteville (p. 61) and Shullsburg (p. 59) can be toured — a cool treat on a hot summer day. The **mining museum** (p. 61) next to Platteville's lead mine has the best displays anywhere on the area's unique geology and mining history. A visit to Platteville and the Chicago Bears summer training camp (p.49) or the fine Wisconsin Shakespeare Festival (p. 60) can be a memorable vacation highlight.

Lead was formed here in the southern part of that ancient limestone plateau known as the Driftless Region (p. 62). Its uplands and ridgetops have straighter roads and treeless fields, where vistas of farms and silos unfold for many miles. Winding roads and pockets of wildness are tucked down in the deep, V-shaped hidden valleys. The center of the Wisconsin Lead Region was **Mineral Point**, 20 miles east of Platteville, today a delightful town known for its many resident craftspeople and its unusual stone architecture brought by Cornishmen. Mining sophistication in the entire area was enormously advanced by the arrival in the 1830s of Cornish miners skilled in techniques of hard-rock mining. Early miners had just picked at

Distances from Platteville

Chicago	203 miles
Twin Cities	289 miles
Madison	67 miles
Milwaukee	124 miles
Dickeyville	11 miles
Dubuque	22 miles
Galena	21 miles
Belmont	7 miles
Mineral Pt.	20 miles
Shullsburg	22 miles

Other distances:

Dickeyville-Cassville 29
Galena-Hazel Green 9
Galena-Shullsburg 18
Shullsburg-Darlington 11

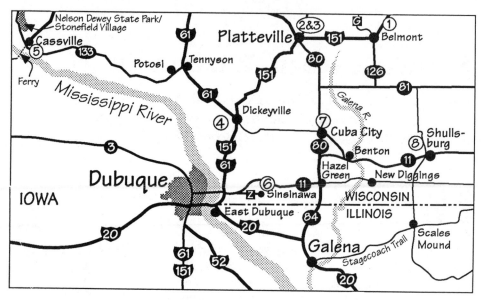

Southwest Wisconsin & Vicinity

① Besnier. Brie & Camembert made in Belmont by leading French cheesemaker. Sold at half retail price.

② The Mining Museum/Rollo Jamison Museum. 2 fun museums. One has the best lead mine tour & exhibits on Lead Region geology & history. The other's a brisk spin through highlights of an inveterate collector's old roadside museum.

③ The Timbers. Outstanding international dishes — over 100, all individually prepared, like medaillons of pork Baden-Baden (with cognac, mushrooms). Dinners $12-14, lunches $4-7. Theater organ played at 7:15, 8:15. Interior by Wright pupil.

④ Dickeyville Grotto. Colorful folk art mosaic of rock, shells on shrine, garden walkway with niches.

⑤ Cassville. A most picturesque 1840s town between rocky bluffs and Mississippi. Great bird-watching, camping at state park. Stonefield a recreated 1890s farm village. Quaint ferry to Iowa.

⑥ Sinsinawa. Experience Dominican hospitality on tour of beautiful, historic motherhouse complex of active, outreach order of nuns. Art & history exhibits, sustainable agriculture featured.

⑦ Weber Bros. Processing. Outstanding sausage, bacon, hams, meats. Super-personal service. Worth taking an ice chest for.

⑧ Shullsburg. Town of faded mining grandeur reached on interesting backroads drives. Pleasant little restaurant (The Lobby), nifty antique shop, summer lead mine tours, streets named Peace and Hope.

surface deposits of lead. (Mineral Point and Pendarvis are covered in a 1993 companion volume to this book, *Hunts' Getaways in Southern Wisconsin*.)

Except for the college town of Platteville and some other stretches of busy U.S. 151 between Madison and Dubuque, much of the entire area has the quaint, rural appearance of having escaped the stress and strain of modern life. The silos of dairy farms stand out like church steeples on the rolling ridges; country crossroads are often marked by cheese factories, some still in use, others closed. Isolated by being in the extreme corner of the state, the backroads areas here have a get-away-from-it-all quality that can leave you feeling you've been far, far away from the contemporary world.

The Wisconsin lead boom

By 1827, news of lead deposits around Galena, Illinois, had attracted so many fortune-seekers that prospectors were spreading north, beyond the federally authorized lead district, into lands of what was then still Michigan Territory to the north. The federal government still reserved these lands for Indians. Most prospectors were from frontier areas where Indian-fighting was a way of life, a defense of hearth and home, and an avenue to glory. They felt entitled to claim lead diggings simply by virtue of being Americans. Lack of paper treaties with Indians was a fine point valued only by Easterners; it did nothing to hold back these western frontiersmen.

The Wisconsin lead boom is recounted in vivid detail by Marie Dieter in *The Story of Mineral Point*:

The white men came for lead and the profits of the lead industry; they planned to get rich quick, strip the region of its wealth as long as the Indians were quiet, and flee when trouble threatened. Consequently, life was unstable. Towns appeared wherever strikes were made and disappeared whenever the lead veins ran out. Miners migrated freely from one digging to another. Whole families lived for years in tents, wagons, or dank, unhealthy dugouts, caves, and sod huts, waiting for the lucky strike that would quickly give them wealth.

Many early Wisconsin pioneers didn't stay long enough to leave much in the way of a historical record about themselves. Two politically ambitious

The Chicago Bears' summer camp draws fans to Platteville each summer from mid-July through the first week of August. Visitors are welcome to watch; bring a lawn chair. To get from U.S. 151 to the practice field on the U-W/Platteville campus, turn north at McDonald's onto Staley Ave. In 2 blocks turn left onto Gridley, and go past the stadium to the field. Be prepared for crowds; Platteville is packed at this time!

The oldest settled part of Wisconsin, the Lead Region dates back to the 1820s, when many now-sleepy towns like Benton, New Diggings, Hazel Green, and Calamine were rousing mining camps full of frontiersmen who largely came from Missouri, Kentucky, and Tennessee.

The Black Hawk War: Celebration and Shame

A large Fox-Sauk tribe had long lived and farmed in the fertile land of the lower Rock River valley in Illinois. In the 1820s, settlers began squeezing them out from the east, and by 1827 and 1828, lead miners kept them from moving north. Their leader, Keokuk, decided to move them all west of the Mississippi. But Black Hawk, who had been a British-backed Indian hero of the War of 1812, led a band back to their ancestral lands along the Rock in spring, 1832.

Black Hawk unrealistically hoped for aid from the British and other Indians. The Illinois and Wisconsin militia pursued his band across southwest Wisconsin in a series of bloody, ugly skirmishes that resulted in the deaths of nearly half its original number, including many women and children. Many militiamen were untrained and undisciplined troops brought up with a visceral hatred of Indians, and they did not fight with much honor or compassion. Black Hawk's defeat deterred other nearby Indian leaders from considering resistance. They soon ceded their lands and signed all the treaties the federal government requested.

The Black Hawk War resulted in celebrity heroes on both sides. Henry Dodge, leader of the Wisconsin militia, became the idol of the southwestern lead miners, and was made territorial governor by his friend, President Andrew Jackson. In defeat, the captured Black Hawk was widely celebrated as an Indian leader who stood up for his people's right to stay on their ancestral land. In his remaining years he became a star on the national lecture circuit; Prairie du Chien's main business street is one of many place names that honor him.

The war also drew regional attention to southwestern Wisconsin and its farming potential. Unlike most mining areas, the lead district in Wisconsin and adjoining Jo Daviess County, Illinois, enjoys good soil with a limestone base, much like the Kentucky bluegrass region. It is ideal for livestock and dairying, with crops on level valley floors and ridgetops, and pasture or woods on the steep hillsides.

lead miners who *are* well-known in history were Henry Dodge, Wisconsin's first territorial governor, and William Hamilton, fifth son of the famed federalist Alexander Hamilton.

The young Hamilton had come west as a surveyor to earn his fortune and win a place in the emerging frontier society. Well-educated and gracious, a darling of Illinois society, he had already won political prominence when he came to Wisconsin looking for lead. In 1828 he found it at Hamilton's Diggings, now called Wiota, east of Shullsburg and Darlington.

Dodge, raised in Kentucky, was a western man of the people in the populist mold of Andrew Jackson. He typically favored buckskin frontier garb on occasions when more formal attire was the rule. Dodge had already prospered in lead mining in Ste. Genevieve, Missouri, nearly joined in Aaron Burr's conspiracy, and distinguished himself for audacity as a Missouri militia general in the War of 1812. When he was 45, Missouri lead mining was so clearly being eclipsed by richer discoveries near Galena that he came north with his family and his freed slaves. (Slaves in Illinois and Wisconsin were freed by law.)

Eventually Dodge found lead at the site of Dodgeville, started a community, built a stockade, and "defied the Indians or government to move him," according to historians Robert Nesbit and William Thompson. Spoiling for a fight, he was perfectly positioned to become the miners' defender and hero at the first sign of Indian resistance to miners' incursions — an opportunity soon offered by the Black Hawk War in 1828.

How Wisconsin became "The Badger State"
"Many miners came north in spring, mined through the summer, and returned south [usually to Illinois] in fall; these men were called **'Suckers,'** after the migratory fish. Others stayed the year around, living in burrows in the hillsides [in order to guard their remaining lead diggings]; these men were called **'Badgers,'**" explained Marie Dieter in The Story of Mineral Point, because they lived in holes like that burrowing animal.

WHEN TO VISIT

Spring: Outstanding bird-watching at Nelson Dewey State Park during spring migration (March & April). Wildflowers there and at Belmont Mound.

Summer: All historic sites open. Cassville's Stonefield Village, First Capitol, Mitchell-Rountree Stone Cottage, Rollo Jamison Museum. Berries on Belmont Mound trails. Prairie remnants bloom late summer. Summer theater at Shakespeare Festival, Main Street Players. Chicago Bears training camp. Mine tours at Shullsburg, Platteville are cool on hot days. Nelson Dewey State Park on Mississippi is relatively uncrowded. Cassville ferry operating. Flowers bloom at Dickeyville Grotto. Group tours of Sinsinawa sustainable agriculture farm.

Fall: Great fall color, bird-watching, few crowds at Cassville's Nelson Dewey State Park. Cassville ferry permits crossing to picturesque Guttenberg, Iowa. Fall color also at Belmont Mound, Stagecoach Trail. UW/Platteville college events.

Winter: At Sinsinawa, sing-along Messiah, Madonnas in art. Excellent mining museum indoor exhibits open all year. Period Christmas displays at Jamison Museum. Eagles at Cassville power plant late Jan. & Feb. UW/Platteville college events.

ANNUAL EVENTS

July 4 celebration: Shullsburg. **Heritage Day:** at Jamison Museum, July 4, lots of demos. **Mine Day:** at Mining Museum last Sat. in July. **Shullsburg Historical Pageant:** first weekend August. **Christmas show**: at Jamison Museum most of December.

ENTERTAINMENT

Main Street Players: high-caliber local theater from Galena in excellent, air-conditioned space at beautiful Sinsinawa Mound. Every weekend, June-Oct. $8. (815) 777-0410.
Wisconsin Shakespeare Festival: July & early Aug. Highly regarded. Each season offers a tragedy, history, and comedy in repertory, so all 3 can be seen within 3 or 4 days. Weekly: 3 matinees, 5 8 p.m. performances, dark Mondays. $12-$13, $7 students. (608) 342-1298. Limited space; reserve early. **Sinsinawa Strings:** chamber music at Sinsinawa. (608) 748-4411. **UW/Platteville Campus Events:** visiting performers during the school year. (608) 342-1298. **Chicago Bears Summer Camp:** see p. 49 for directions. Visitors welcome to watch. Bring a lawn chair. No charge. **Live music:** (bluegrass, cajun, rock) at the Hoist House in Platteville, (608) 348-7819.

POINTS OF INTEREST

Dickeyville

This German Catholic village of under 1,000 is midway between Dubuque and Platteville, about 10 miles from each on U. S. 151.
Its highlight is:

Dickeyville Grotto

Shrine always open. Donations for upkeep are $2/adult, $1/child. Tours 10-6 daily in July & Aug., weekends only in May, June, Sept. & Oct. Gift shop open May-Oct. daily 9-6.

305 W. Main, 1/2 block north of U.S. 151. (608) 568-7519.

Folk art has flowered in Wisconsin, where a good number of creative people seem comfortable enough with themselves — and oblivious enough to outside notions of sophistication and taste — to follow their own artistic impulses or those of their ethnic cultures.

Perhaps the best-known folk-art creation is this

A colorful mosaic of rocks, glass, and shells encrust every surface on the Dickeyville Grotto and adjacent garden walk of shrines. It's best seen up close, with plenty of time to linger on fanciful details. ▼

elaborate grotto and garden walk, created by
Father Mathias Werner alongside his Holy Ghost
Church in the 1920s with the help of his house-
keeper cousin. It's a colorful, energetic creation,
well worth a detour if you're near Galena, Dubuque,
or Platteville. Into the cement surface of the grotto
has been set a fascinating, bristling mosaic of local
rocks, broken china and glass, shells, stones, and
petrified wood from all over the world. Inside the
little grotto building, a ceiling of crystals and stalactites hovers above the Virgin and Child.

You have to get up close to appreciate the effect;
it works better as a decorative surface than a spa-
tial environment. The mosaic surface extends out
into a walkway with sculptural niches, and onto
fanciful cement plants and animals in the garden.
It ends at the gate of the church cemetery.

Father Werner says the grotto was meant to in-
spire devotion to God and country. Statues of the
Holy Family, the Apostles, and Jesus are in one
area, figures of Columbus, Lincoln, and Washington
in another.

For people who are into religious art — and
more and more youngish, art-minded people are —
the **gift shop** has figures of hundreds of different
saints, along with souvenirs of the grotto itself.

Hazel Green

This country town of 1,200, nine miles north of
Galena, 11 miles east of Dubuque, and 14 miles
south of Platteville, makes a nice stop between
those points. It was one of the first permanent
settlements in the Wisconsin Lead District. In
1824, lead deposits were discovered here that
were so rich, one miner took out 17,000 pounds
in one day. Not all miners were so lucky — hence,
Hazel Green's original name: Hardscrabble.

Hazel Green's main feature was and is its location on the main road through the lead region
from Galena to Mineral Point. The **Wisconsin
House Stagecoach Inn** (see p. 69), built in 1846,
looks much as it did when U.S. Grant visited on

*Inspired by the
Dickeyville Grotto,
Paul and Matilda Wegner
created the Glass Church,
Peace Monument, and
Prayer Garden, and much
more a few years later at
their farm north of Sparta.
Pieces of glass and broken
china turned concrete
structures into fantastic
visions. Open to the public.*

*The lead road from
Galena to Platteville
and Mineral Point,
now highways 80 & 151
was an 1837 spur to the
important Military Road
between Prairie du Chien
and Lake Winnebago. The
Mineral Point-Galena road
was long one of the most
traveled in Wisconsin,
wrote Marie Dieter in The
Story of Mineral Point.
"Traffic was a confused
and noisy mass of oxen,
cattle, horses, and mules;
huge swinging Concord
coaches, lumber wagons,
ox-carts, carriages, and
prairie schooners; jobless
men, adventurers,
criminals, editors, gam-
blers, lawyers, farmers,
miners, professional men,
and artisans."*

frequent business trips for his father's leather business. Today it houses an antique shop, a highly-regarded restaurant (p. 69), and a bed and breakfast inn (p. 69). It and other **antique shops** on Hazel Green's main street are worth a look.

Cuba City

Five miles north of Hazel Green, also on the old lead road between Galena and Mineral Point, is this plain town of 1,870 in the corn-hog area of extreme southwestern Wisconsin. It was developed by a family who built a roadside inn and sold off surrounding town lots. Later, residents success- fully induced a railroad to come through town, in- suring Cuba City's survival after lead ran out. They wanted to call their newly incorporated place Yuba City, the story goes, after a mining strike in Cali- fornia, but, finding Wisconsin already had a Yuba, decided on Cuba City instead.

Weber Brothers Processing

Mon-Sat 7:30-5:30, Wed & Fri to 9.
725 N. Jackson (Hwy. 80) at the north edge of Cuba City, 9 miles south of Platteville and 14 miles north of Galena. (608) 744-2159.

To discriminating food-lovers from Galena and Dubuque, Cuba City is known as the home of Weber's, the award-winning maker of home-cured ham, bacon, and sausage. It's one of those plain, gleaming white places where the visual attraction is meat in myriad forms: 145 kinds of sausage, prize-winning bacon, smoked ham, summer sau- sage, dried beef and beef jerky, ring bologna, brats, liver sausage, and beef loaf — plus special cuts of roasts, chops, steaks, ribs, and more. The walls are cov- ered with awards from many state and national meat-judging contests.

Meat runs in the Weber family. Their

Why you can't buy Weber's meats in Galena or Chicago

The heavily regulated meat business involves a decision point that forces processors like Weber's to stay small or invest in expensive new equipment to gain USDA certification and sell across state lines. Meeting the U.S. Department of Agriculture's very, very particular specifications for cross-state marketing is difficult for non-USDA plants built according to state specifications. So a totally sanitary operation like Weber's can't be USDA-certified if it includes older non-conforming equip- ment — like narrower doors on meat lockers.

grandfather, a butcher, emigrated from Switzerland; their father set up shop in Cuba City and started this plant in 1945. At that time, custom-slaughtering and processing for area farmers was the big thing. Now, with the declining number of farm families, plants like Weber's are focusing on developing their retail and wholesale business so they will draw customers from a wide radius. (Weber's also sells at the big Madison farmers' market.) Special requests are welcome, whether for four nice T-bone steaks cut just the thickness you ask for, or for three slices of bacon wrapped for a senior citizen living alone. You could get meat for a terrific mixed grill on a picnic here, or create a sub sandwich with 10 kinds of cold cuts.

Weber's offers excellent quality without demanding premium prices. The ring bologna, for instance, is $2.25 a pound, and it has a little over half the fat of most commercial bologna.

Sinsinawa

Sinsinawa is the westernmost of southwestern Wisconsin's five striking mounds of resistant rock that begin with the Blue Mounds near Madison. Here Father Samuel Mazzuchelli, the indefatigible frontier missionary priest, established an academy for daughters of lead miners in 1847. It was the first secondary school in Wisconsin that girls could attend.

"Sinsinawa"
(pronounced "SIN-SIN-uh-wuh") means "home of the young eagle." Indians farmed the mound and regarded it as a spiritual place.

Sinsinawa is not so much a settlement as an institution with a quaint **post office** (and a nifty **philatelic center** where you can buy previously issued U.S. stamps).

Sinsinawa Conference & Retreat Center/ Motherhouse of Sinsinawa Dominicans

Visitors welcome. (608) 748-4411. Call ahead to arrange a tour about the history and current nature of the Sinsinawa Dominicans' educational missions.

$8.50 includes midday meal.

From Hwy. 11 between Hazel Green & Dubuque, take County Rd. Z from either direction to Mound.

The limestone building of Father Mazzuchelli's girls' academy and the religious community he founded became the nucleus of today's large complex of old and new buildings that houses the headquarters of the Sinsinawa Dominicans, a teaching and preaching order of some 1,050 sisters. They are active in many schools, professions, entrepreneurial ventures, and artistic endeavors in the United States, South America, and Europe.

Openness and hospitality are Dominican hallmarks. Tour visitors learn about the mound itself, its geology and history, and the Sinsinawa Dominicans and their cultural and artistic activities. They see the books Father Mazzuchelli brought — books which had a considerable impact on science education in 19th-century Wisconsin.

Tour visitors are invited to share the **noonday meal** with the 200 resident members of the Sinsinawa community. Visitors are welcome to stay and walk through the landscaped grounds to **devotional grottoes** for contemplation, and also to join the sisters in their daily **mass** and **morning and evening prayers.** (The 19th-century academy buildings and chapel are closed for renovation until 1993, but the historic exhibits are open.)

Art exhibits range from huge copies of Madonnas and other Italian paintings (done by sisters sent to study art on the Continent in 1900), to a recent show, "Watercolors of the Mother God," depicting God in the female sense. Christmas exhibits feature Madonnas, old and new, and a sing-a-long Messiah. The Sinsinawa Strings, a chamber orchestra of sisters and other area musicians, is based here; the 750-seat theater is the home of the Galena's Main Street Players theater.

Group tours of the **Sinsinawa farm** include dairy and hog operations, orchard, vineyards, vegetable, and butterfly gardens. The farm is managed as a model of sustainable agriculture using as little chemical ferilizer and fuel as possible.

Humane and multi-talented, Father Samuel Mazzuchelli (pronounced "MAZ-ooo-KEL-ee"), came from a wealthy family in Milan. As a teenager he joined the Dominicans. At 22, Father Mazzuchelli came to Cincinnati to study English and become ordained as a priest. From 1830 to his death in 1864, he worked on the frontier of the Old Northwest, among fur traders and Indians, soldiers, and later among miners and Irish and German settlers in the Upper Mississippi. He designed and constructed many attractive churches for the over 30 parishes he founded, (the Lead Region is full of them), pioneered liberal education for girls on the frontier, and advised many early political leaders (mostly Protestants) in Iowa, Wisconsin, and Illinois. His admirers are working to beatify him — the first step to sainthood.

Shullsburg

Shullsburg (population 1,200) is a pleasant place to visit if you enjoy getting *way* off the beaten track. It's isolated by its location five miles north of the Illinois border and over 20 miles from places of any size. Shullsburg's touristic assets consist of an old **lead mine** (open for summer tours) and an attractive aura of faded grandeur. Fortunes made in lead and zinc built a number of **stately homes and commercial buildings**, many made of limestone in Greek Revival and Federal styles of the 1830s and 1840s, others in later Victorian styles. Unusual architectural details reward the observant visitor.

Once Shullsburg was the metropolis of Lafayette County, with some 11,000 residents. In 1861 it lost the county seat to more centrally located Darlington. Since its long-lived zinc smelter closed in 1979, the population has decreased by a sixth.

A few enthusiastic Shullsburg residents have devoted themselves to attracting visitors from Galena, a beautiful 23-mile drive away via the **Stagecoach Trail** (p. 42). Turn north at Scales Mound, Illinois. That road becomes County Road O which takes you into Shullsburg. If you take this drive, be sure to look around **Scales Mound** itself. It's another old lead town built near two striking mounds. Capped with especially resistant limestone, these and similar mounds escaped being eroded away by water the way the surrounding area was. **Charles Mound**, north of town and almost in Wisconsin, is the highest spot in Illinois. Today Scales Mound has under 400 people, but it was once a bustling railroad town with several hotels. Most of its buildings have been included on the National Register of Historic Places.

In Shullsburg, the ornate old hotel is now a restaurant and cheese store known as the **Shullsburg Creamery** (see below). **Tailings**, an attractive antique and gift shop, is west of the creamery on Water Street. Remodeling has deprived the **Jackson Confectionery**, an old down-

▲ **Simple windlass hoists dropped buckets carrying miners or ore into early mine shafts.**

town soda fountain, of its vintage charm, but it still makes a nice snack stop. **Badger Park**, south of downtown and up the hill, has a swimming pool, tennis courts, and picnic facilities.

Shullsburg's points of historic interest are highlighted in a **six-mile self-guided auto tour** available at local stores. (It's also suitable for bicycles; the roads are paved, and there's not much traffic.)

Shullsburg Creamery

Mon-Fri 9-9, Sat 6 a.m-9 p.m., Sun. 9-9. 208 W. Water, downtown Shullsburg. (608) 965-4485.

Some 20 years ago, when Art Stocker, a dissatisfied Chicago businessman, came upon this cheese store in a grand old hotel, it seemed so appealing that he bought it and the adjacent dairy plant. With the help of sons Scott and Bill, the business grew into a sizable wholesaler of **cheeses and deli items.**

But the simple life Stocker sought in Shullsburg turned out to be as grueling as his Chicago job. He succumbed to a heart attack in 1990. The creamery plant is now a warehouse where cheese and meats are repackaged and stored; the store showcases their deli line. A **video** highlights the cheese-making process at their Ferryville plant. (Colby longhorn is its specialty.) The lobby of the landmark hotel here has been attractively renovated to include **The Lobby** restaurant.

Badger Mine & Museum

Open daily, Mem.-Labor Day, 9-5. $3/adults, $2/children.

In Badger Park on County Rd. O (Scales Mound Rd.) just south and up the hill from downtown Shullsburg. (608) 965-4860.

High school students take visitors down a spiral staircase 47 feet to the main drift of this old lead mine, operated from 1827 to 1856. Tools and ore specimens illustrate early mining methods, while exhibits and recreated shops (druggist, blacksmith, etc.) give an idea of the mining era.

Three historic routes from Galena to Shullsburg go over back roads through old lead-mining towns. Request an attractive map/brochure from Shullsburg Community Development, Box 3, Shullsburg, WI 53586-0003.

In Shullsburg, Father Samuel Mazzuchelli, the tireless Dominican missionary priest from Milan, built one of the trim neoclassical churches he designed and erected in so many of his frontier parishes. (See p. 57.) Since St. Matthew's was in a new part of town, he also had streets named after virtues. You may even want to pose for a photo in front of one of these wonderful street signs — say, at the intersection of Happy and Goodness or Judgement and Truth, Wisdom and Peace or Friendship and Mercy. Judgement is the main drag of churches, public buildings, and impressive homes, including two funeral homes.

Platteville

This old lead-mining town has become one of the few places in southwestern Wisconsin that are in any way cosmopolitan, thanks to the presence of the University of Wisconsin/Platteville. It's the successor to Wisconsin's first normal school and the old school of mining. Of its over 5,000 full-time students, nearly all are undergraduates. Strengths are engineering, agriculture, business, theater, and education.

Platteville's sizable population (9,700) and good accessibility on U.S. 151 and state routes 80 and 81 make it a natural for franchise restaurant chains, a K-Mart, and a Wal-Mart. There's a good sampling of cultural events throughout the year.

Superb Shakespeare at incredibly low prices
The Wisconsin Shakespeare Festival, run by the UW/Platteville theater department since 1977, has won national acclaim. The air-conditioned, 238-seat theater is so small that every word can be clearly heard, every expression seen. Tickets are only $12-$13. Most actors are professionals. Some have gone on to star at Stratford.

Hamlet and the ghost, in a past production. ▼

The Mining Museum

Museum with self-guided displays: open daily, May-Oct., 9-5. Nov.-April open Mon-Fri 9-4. Free admission. **Guided mine tour:** *Open daily, May-Oct., 9-5. Adults $3.50, ages 5-15 $1.50 (also includes ticket to Rollo Jamison Museum on whatever day you choose).*

405 E. Main at Virgin Ave. From U.S. 151 on southeast side of town, turn north onto Virgin 2 blocks east of the Hwy. 80/81 intersection. From the north on Hwy. 80 or 81, turn east onto Main in the historic downtown, continue up to 405 E. Main. (608) 348-3301. Air-conditioned.

It's worth a trip to Platteville just for the dramatic, fun trip down into the **1845 Bevans Lead Mine,** and for the adjacent museum, which offers a very interesting overview of the history and geology of area lead mining. Well-informed, entertaining college students take visitors on a short, bumpy ride on a 1931 **mine train** to a recreated head-frame or hoist house. There you take 90 stairs down into the mine and go along tunnels through the horizontal drift.

What with the dim light and realistically dressed and posed figures of miners, it's not too hard to imagine what it was like to work in a mine. The tour progresses from the 1850s era of hard-rock mining to the 20th century-era of mechanized zinc mining. The mine stays 52 degrees year-round, so the mine tour is well-suited to hot summer days. Sweaters and walking shoes are advised.

A most interesting tour through an old lead mine is a highlight of Platteville's excellent Mining Museum. ▼

The excellent **Mining Museum** was founded by alums of the old school of mines here. Models, dioramas, and historic photographs vividly tell the story of lead and zinc mining in the Driftless Region. Mining tools and minerals of the lead region, and mine safety apparatus are appealingly arranged to get across big-picture ideas. Huge **three-dimensional displays of the Driftless Region's topography,** underground rock formations, and representative mines are quite fascinating to anyone familiar with that beautiful area.

Rollo Jamison Museum

Guided tour: Open daily, May-Oct., 9-5. Adults $3.50, ages 5-15 $1.50 (also includes ticket to Lead Mine Tour on whatever day you choose. **Self-guided exhibit on agriculture** *open daily, May-Oct., 9-5. From Nov.-April open Mon-Fri 9-4. Free admission.*

Location and directions: see Mining Museum. Neither section is air-conditioned.

For some people, collecting things is the organizing principle of their lives. Rollo Jamison became hooked on collecting at the age of five, when he followed behind his father at plowing time and found arrowheads in the early 1900s. Eventually he established a museum as an adjunct to his Spring Valley Tavern in Beetown. He had collected so much stuff — kitchen gadgets of yesteryear, old dental drills, a Simplex cash register that used marbles instead of keys, squirrels in boxing gloves mounted by a taxidermist friend — that he claimed to have "over 100,000 items." (It turned out to be more like 20,000.)

When motor touring became popular in the 1930s, crowds descended on the country tavern to see Jamison's stuff. He continually added to the collections, digging through dumps for old player piano rolls, buying up old irons and shaving mugs, and following up leads like another tavern owner selling black-painted monsters billed as "bronze temple guardians from Japan." Actually, they may

Special museum events
Heritage Day.
July 4. Lots of demos on a selected theme from Rollo's huge collection.
Mine Day. *Last Sat. in July. Real-life demos of drilling, hoisting buckets, tramming & sorting ore.*
Christmas Show.
Celebrations from different time periods, focused on Rollo's collections — maybe 1941 with electric trains, or country Xmas of 19th century. Most of Dec.

have been displays made for the 1893 Chicago World's Fair.

Declining health led Jamison to give his collection to the city of Platteville on the promise that it wouldn't be dispersed. Now it occupies most of a large old school building next to the Mining Museum. Old photos of Jamison and his Beetown museum convey the improvised spirit of that old-fashioned commercial roadside attraction.

The room displays (old-fashioned kitchen, barbershop, beauty parlor, etc.) are very much like many similar "community attic" local history museums. Many collections of coin-operated music machines and penny arcade games are more impressive. This museum's charm is its straightforward focus on Rollo Jamison's passion for collecting. A brisk-paced tour by college-age guides includes lots of quick demonstrations that kids and adults enjoy, interspersed with unexpected comments. After hearing the tinkling tune of the Regina music box with its huge, punched disk, our guide commented, "You couldn't sing or dance to it, so people got tired of it quick!"

▲ Musical devices from huge music boxes to gramophones and player pianos are a highlight of Rollo Jamison's onetime roadside museum. This depiction of the delights of the graphophone is from the 1902 Sears & Roebuck catalog.

Mitchell-Rountree Stone Cottage

Open daily May-Sept, 12-5. $1/person.

U.S. 80 (Lancaster St.) at Madison, about 8 blocks northwest of downtown Platteville. (608) 348-5196.

This charming colonial-style house, built in 1837, was the first permanent house in Platteville. (That is, it was not a temporary sod or log house.) It was consciously designed to resemble the houses its builders, Methodist minister Samuel Mitchell and his wife, had known from their original home in Virginia. They sited it on spacious grounds on a salubrious hillside and oriented it to enjoy the setting sun.

Remarkably, the house and its furnishings remain much as they were in the decades after 1868, when Major John Rountree, a lead investor and Platteville's co-founder, bought it as a wedding present for his son and daughter-in-law. Their daughter Laura lived in the "cottage" (by then a six-room house) for all her 94 years. When she died, in 1966, she gave the house and all its contents to the Platteville Historical Society. Her own landscape paintings and knowledge gleaned from her diaries add to the interest of the house tour.

Ipswitch prairie natural area

From U.S. 151 about 3 miles east of Platteville, go south on Ipswitch Rd. After about 1 1/2 miles south, the prairie parallels the road along an abandoned railroad bed. For information about other prairies, contact Southwestern Wisconsin Prairie Enthusiasts, c/o Gary Eldred, 1492 Sleepy Hollow Rd., Boscobel, WI 53805.

Wisconsin prairie enthusiasts treasure any remnants of the native prairies that once covered a good deal of southwest Wisconsin (p. 12). They value the biological diversity of these self-renewing ecosystems and love the subtle beauty of prairie wildflowers and grasses. This prairie remnant is much easier to see than most. It's conveniently located alongside Ipswitch Road, which bypasses Platteville between U.S. 151 and Mineral Point and Highway 80, heading for Cuba City and Galena. A mile long by 100 feet wide, it lies along an abandoned railroad right-of-way.

Walnut Ridge

Tues-Sat 9:30-5:30, Sun 11:30-5. Also open by appointment. Closed Sundays Jan-March, call to confirm Sundays in off-season.
2238 County A, 7 miles, 10 minutes north of

The world's largest M *was created on the side of Platteville Mound by students at the School of Mines in 1936. Wanting a mark of distinction for their school, they studied other large limestone letters and settled on a huge M. They hauled some 400 tons of crushed limestone to make the giant letter, about 236 feet on each side.*

Railroads saved native prairie grasses *from the relentless subjugation to the farmer's plow. Railroads cut narrow rights of way through land that would otherwise have been cultivated and worn out by wheat, the favorite early cash crop of the Midwestern frontier. Furthermore, the engine's cinders started the occasional small fires necessary to keep out woody plants.*

*Platteville. From town, take
Hwy. 81 2 miles to D. Go right
on D, continue north 6 miles. At
A, turn left. House and shop are
4th house on left.
(608) 348-9359.*

This rustic antique shop
makes a fine destination for a
backroads drive. Jill and
Chuck Staab are fascinated
with the primitive, handmade,
preindustrial side of country
living. That's what's featured
in their antique shop, in a
hand-hewn log building by
their house on a wooded ridge. Jill's idea of
country crafts consists of soaps a neighbor makes
and pillows and teddy bears made of old quilt fabric. Wreaths are made of herbs and flowers grown
in two large **gardens** which visitors are welcome to
see. Antiques are primitive, not the popular oak
furniture mass-produced at the turn of the century. Within a year or so, the Staabs hope to open a
bed and breakfast inn on the property.

Belmont

An unassuming town of 750. Belmont was chosen the temporary site of Wisconsin's first capital
by territorial governor Henry Dodge because it was
close to Iowa, then still part of Wisconsin Territory. The capitol's modest official buildings were
provided by Belmont's speculator-founder, in
hopes that his townsite might become Wisconsin's
permanent capital. But Belmont and its lack of accommodations proved so unpopular that the new
territorial legislators immediately voted to locate
the permanent capital at a virtually uninhabited
townsite called Madison. It didn't hurt that James
Doty, who had bought up and laid out the townsite
on an isthmus between two large lakes, had given
choice Madison lots to key legislators.

When a branch of the Mineral Point Railroad was built to Platteville in 1870, Belmont's business district moved three miles southeast from its original site to be on the rail line, now the Pecatonica State Trail that goes to Mineral Point. (It's included in *Hunts' Getaways in Southern Wisconsin*.)

Belmont Mound State Park

No posted hours. No admission fee.
(608) 523-4427.

This wooded mound is a surprising mountain island of wilderness, over a fourth of a mile long, in a grassy uplands sea of pastures and grazing dairy cows. Belmont Mound makes a worthwhile stop on any drive — especially if you have cheese, fruit, and bread along for a picnic.

You can drive to the mound's top and climb a tower to take in the splendid view. But why not park down below and hike up to earn your view and enjoy the forest along the way? A 256-acre park covers most of the mound, which is 1,400 feet above sea level, 160 feet above nearby Highway G, and nearly 400 feet above the nearby village of Belmont. The **hiking trail**, a 1 1/2 mile loop, is between the water pump and **picnic/playground area**. It passes alongside the remains of old kilns probably used to make lime. **Morels, raspberries, and blackberries** can be found here in season.

From the 64-foot **lookout tower** you can see north across to the Wisconsin River valley (30 miles), east to Blue Mound (the highest point in southern Wisconsin, also 30 miles away), and southwest to other sister mounds, the Platteville Mound (8 miles distant) and Sinsinawa Mound near Dubuque (now a Dominican convent and retreat center, 20 miles away). At night the lights of Dubuque are clearly visible.

Three dramatic rock formations are some 100 yards north of the park drive on the mound's north side. The **"Devil's Dining Table"** and **"Devil's Chair"** each sit on a narrow rock base. North of the dining table is **"The Cave,"** a dark passageway eroded by wind and water along a cleft

The geology behind the striking mounds of southwest Wisconsin
In the Silurian period some 400 million years ago, warm, shallow seas covered most of the Midwest and left deposits of animal shells. Compressed with time, they became a hard, resistant limestone layer over softer layers of sandstone and limestone.

Since then, down-cutting streams have eroded away the hard Niagara dolomite nearly everywhere in southwestern Wisconsin. Only small areas remain, capping the string of mounds from the Blue Mounds to the Belmont and Platteville mounds and Sinsinawa near Dubuque.

through a huge rock. Past them is a 40-acre virgin woods that has never been cultivated or logged.

First Capitol State Park

Open daily Mem.-Labor Day 9-5. Free.

At the intersection of county roads G and B. From U.S. 151 at Belmont, take G 3 miles northwest to park. (608) 523-4427.

Two buildings from Wisconsin Territory's short-lived first capitol had become barns when they were restored as simple museums by a citizen campaign. The **Council House** looks much like a very old, two-story general store without the porch. It is furnished much as it was when the territorial legislature met here in the fall of 1836, down to the ink bottles and spittoons. Inside the house-like **Supreme Court Building** are models of a lead mine and of Belmont in 1836, along with displays on frontier agriculture, crafts, and every-day life. A **picnic area** with hand pump, pit toilets, and parking lot has been built for visitors.

The first capitol's buildings you see today event-ually became barns. But the persistence of a Platteville newspaper editor and Wisconsin wo-men's clubs did eventually result in their eventful acquisition and restoration.

Besnier America

Mon-Fri 8-4:30.

330 Penn St. near the center of Belmont, which becomes Hwy. G. Stop at the office in the house next to the big, white plant. (608) 762-5173.

You can buy authentic French-type Camembert and Brie cheeses straight from the factory here. Large European cheese manufacturers have been establishing American plants as food production and marketing becomes increasingly international. Besnier, the largest French manufacturer of dairy products and #1 maker of Camembert, wanted to increase American sales of its soft-ripened cheeses. Such cheeses are quite perishable, so it makes sense to produce them in North America

Bicycle trails from Belmont to Mineral Point and Monroe
These beautiful trails on abandoned rail beds go through dairy country, wooded valleys, and marshes, connecting small towns like Calamine, Dar-lington, Gratiot, and Browntown. For more information, contact: Steve Hubner, Ag Center, Dar-lington, WI 53530. (608) 776-4830. He handles the Cheese Country Trail from Monroe to Mineral Point. For info on the Pecatonica State Trail from Belmont (and eventually Platteville) to Calamine and the Cheese Country Trail, call (608) 523-4427 or write Yellowstone Lake State Park, 7896 N. Lake Rd., Blanchardville, WI 53516.

A bicyclist's paradise if you can handle the hills
Traffic on the Driftless Region's county roads is seldom a problem. It's mostly dairy country, and most county roads in Wisconsin are paved to permit year-round access to milk trucks. One excep-tion: the hog and corn country around Hazel Green and Cuba City, extending into Jo Daviess County, Illinois.

rather than shipping them from Europe.

To establish its first North American plant, Besnier S.A. chose Wisconsin due to its plentiful supply of high-quality milk. Two Normandy cheesemakers with limited English-speaking ability came to set up the new plant, develop marketing in America, and make Wisconsin their new home. The big, white Belmont factory went into production in 1981. It employs about 40 and can make 15,000 pounds of Camembert and Brie a day. That's a lot, considering the small size of each cheese and large amount of hand labor involved in making soft-ripened cheeses.

It's a happy coincidence that the town of Belmont has a French name. (It means "beautiful mountain.") "Tradition de Belmont" is the brand used for marketing all Besnier America's soft-ripened cheeses. New plants have also been opened in California.

Factory prices are about half of retail, as at most cheese factories: $1.55 for 8 oz., $2.60-$2.80 for 15 oz., and $5.50-$6 for 1 kilo (2.2 lbs.). Shipping via UPS costs an extra $5 per order. Brie comes in flavors: herb, onion, bacon, and cracked pepper.

Knebel's Meats

Mon-Fri 7-5:30, Sat 7-5.

115 S. Mound (U.S. 151) in downtown Belmont. *(608) 762-5197.*

A regionally well-known maker of hams and sausages, Knebel's makes a fine stop for stocking up on picnic provisions. The natural-casing wie-

▲ **French gastronomic mystique meets America's Dairyland in Belmont, Wisconsin, home of the first North American plant to produce authentic French soft-ripened cheesee.**

An idyllic getaway destination
*for a pokey day's drive through the Lead Region is the tucked-away Mississippi River town of **Cassville** (p. 69), 29 miles west of Dickeyville. The Mississippi is many-channeled here, with the fabulous bird-watching and good fishing that goes with that complex natural environment. Once you get to Cassville, plan to stay put and enjoy the scenery, Stonefield Village, and Nelson Dewey State Park. Winding roads make it too much trouble to take many side trips.*

ners have far less fat than most national brands. Their brats and Landjaeger snack sticks are also popular. You can get their famous boneless ham and some 50 kinds of lunch meats, sliced in just the amount you want — smoked turkey breast, Dutch pork loaf, honey loaf, ring bologna smoked or plain, with or without garlic, beef and pork or just beef. Plus, there's good, chewy sandwich bread and sweet baked goods from Platteville's Hometowne Bakery and deli items like coleslaw and potato salad.

Discovering
the scenic routes
Get DeLorme's wonderfully detailed Wisconsin Atlas & Gazetteer ($14.95). Locate the river valleys and you'll discover the prettiest, least direct country drives.

RESTAURANTS & LODGINGS

CASSVILLE (population 1,300) This 1840s town 40 minutes fronm Platteville is one of the prettiest places on the Upper Mississippi, with a beautiful blufftop state park. **Stonefield Village**, a recreated farm hamlet of the 1890s, is Wisconsin's state agricultural museum. **Twin-O-Rama** is an infectiously corny festival started by twins in 1929. For more info, write Tourism, Box 576, Cassville, WI 53806 or call (608) 725-5180.

See also Breitbach's Country Dining in **Balltown**, p. 109. If the Cassville ferry is operating, Balltown is about 10 miles south of it on Iowa's Great River Road.

Geiger House. *(608) 725-5419. 401 Denniston, a block east of Hwy. 133.* Three rooms share 2 baths. $50. 1855 Greek Revival house has beautiful views of bluffs that are practically in the back yard. Full breakfast. Guests can use library, dining room with fireplace, sitting room. Bikes available.
Gracious old house in a very pretty town

HAZEL GREEN (population 1,300) For more info, see p. 54.

Wisconsin House Stagecoach Inn. *2105 Main, at the south end of Hazel Green's downtown, 1 block east of Hwy. 80/84. (608) 854-2233. Reservations essential; advance reservations suggested. Dinners on Friday and Saturday evening only, seating at 7:30, cocktails at 7.*

$15 includes hors d'oeuvres and everything except for dessert. Guests (up to 26 of them) sit at a single table in dining room of historic inn. Menu is fixed, with entree such as marinated pork or pot roast. Under new owners, inn is a little more upscale, without previous owners' yodeling and accordion entertainment.

Wisconsin House Stagecoach Inn. *(608) 854-2233. 2105 Main, at the south end of Hazel Green's downtown.* 6 rooms with private baths, $65 and (for suites) $85. 2 rooms share a bath, $40 and $50. Midweek senior discount 10%. Jan-March: 10% discount for 2 nights' lodging and 1 dinner. Full breakfast. Air-conditioned. New owners have replaced some of the previous owners' primitive antiques with more comfortable seating, but many antiques remain. A little more upscale, but still an informal country inn. Cable TV can be taken to room. Parlor, pub, library with games open to guests at any time. Two-story front porch extends width of inn. Bumper pool, billiards. Shady garden, gazebo. Grill. Guests may borrow bikes. 1846 stagecoach stop on old lead road has been featured in *Country Living*. Hazel Green's retail district has a couple of antique shops, old buildings from lead rush days, the expected small-town tavern.

Small-town inn 15 min. from Galena, Dubuque, Platteville, with many amenities.

PLATTEVILLE (population 9,700) This pleasant old mining town/college town is overloaded during Chicago Bears summer camp in late July and early August. Reserve early!!

Gadzooks. *On Pine at Water (also routes 80 & 81) at the southeast side of downtown Platteville, in the strip mall next to Dick's Supermarket. (608) 348-7700. Mon-Thurs 11-9, Fri 11-10, Sat 8 a.m.-10 p.m., Sun 8-5. Visa, MC, Disc. Full bar.*
Cheerful spot with cozy little bar, booths. Good service. Varied menu prepared to order appeals to many tastes (Italian stuffed shells, Greek salad and more, Mexican enchiladas, Cajun fish and chicken, country, low-fat chicken dishes). For lunch, $3.25 soup, salad, and half sandwich special, daily specials. All-day sandwich menu, served with potato, slaw, pickle) includes big $3.50 burgers, popular $6 Platteville sandwich (variants on Philly cheese steaks). Full slab BBQ ribs at $11 is top of dinner menu. Dinners include potato, salad, vegetable, roll.

Pizzeria Uno. *On U.S. 151 a little west of intersection with Hwy. 80, on south side of road east of McDonald's. Look for the alligator. (608) 348-7808. Tues-Sun 4-11, Mon 5-9. No credit cards. Out-of-town checks OK. Full bar.*
Good food beyond pizza. Lots of fun not just for college students. Unrelated to Chicago-based Pizzeria Uno chain except through inspiration. (Chicago founders borrowed name, cornmeal crust for deep-dish pizza before Uno went national.) Favorites include huge chef and Italian salads ($4.25), veggie lasagna with salad ($5.50; 75¢ more with meat sauce), Mel's secret recipe Italian beef sandwich ($4.75). Daily specials range from Friday fettucine to Wednesday rye-crust Wisconsin bratwurst pizza. Pizza prices: medium deep-dish deluxe (feeds 3) $14, medium deluxe thin-crust in whole wheat or regular $12.50. Many imported beers. Video games.

The Timbers. *Entrance off U.S. 151 just east of intersection with Hwy. 80 and 81. Drive goes up a hill on north side of 151. (608) 348-2406. Mon-Sat 11-1:30, 5-10, Sun 10:30-2 (brunch), 2-9 (dinner). Major credit cards. Full bar.* Supper club with interior designed in Frank Lloyd Wright vein by his student. **Theater organ**, built for previous owner, is played at 7:15 and 8:15 nightly, Sundays at 1 and 7. Much-praised international menu of some hundred items, individually prepared. Samples at dinner: medaillons of pork Baden-Baden in mushroom cognac sauce on noodles ($12.75), haddock Neapolitan, sauteed in olive oil with mushrooms, olives, tomato and garlic ($12.25). Dinners come with relish tray, salad, starch. Friday-night fish fry, Saturday prime rib. For lunch, changing daily specials ($6-$7), burgers, sandwiches, salads. A special favorite: crab and shrimp broiled on toast with tomatoes and cheddar cheese ($7.25).

Best Western Governor Dodge. *(608) 348-2301. On north side of U.S. 151 a few blocks west of 80/81 intersection.* 74 rooms on 2 floors, $59-$65. Cable TV, Showtime. Family restaurant with bar on premises. Indoor pool with outdoor sun deck. Whirlpool. Men's and women's saunas. Video game room. Half-mile south of U-W/Platteville campus, set back from road on commercial strip.

Top of the line in Platteville, with town's only indoor pool

Cunningham House. *(608) 348-5532. 110 Market 1 block north of Main, close to downtown Platteville.* Homestay bed and breakfast. 3 rooms share 2 baths. $45. Ample, solid brick house from 1907 faces city park with huge old trees. In residential neighborhood. Hosts almost all celebs speaking at the college; Ralph Nader loved it. Full breakfast. Air-conditioned. No credit cards. Guests can use living room with big-screen TV, VCR, dinig room, kitchen with microwave, deck and grill, big front porch. Enthusiastic innkeeper active in local affairs.

Comfortable B&B with nice in-town location, attractive rates

Mound View Motel. *(608) 348-9518. On U.S. 151 a mile west of Hwy. 80/81 intersection.* 16 rooms on 1 floor. $35-$43. Sits back from commercial strip in front of K Mart. Good-size rooms for older motel. Extremely well maintained. Views of Platteville Mound. Cable TV, Showtime. Picnic tables in front.

Very pleasant ma-and-pa motel with moderate prices

Dubuque

Few American cities have kept their 19th-century look better than this old river town. Extra attractions are riverboat gambling, dramatic bluffs, and a great river museum.

Dubuque is one of those Midwestern cities whose name is used, along with Peoria and Toledo, as a synonym for a bland, homogenized, utterly predictable, boringly normal, vanilla-pudding way of life. But this stereotype, like so many others, doesn't jibe with the real world. As it turns out, Dubuque is one of the most unusual cities of the American heartland. Many parts of the city look so old that it often fills in for Boston as a movie location. (All of *Field of Dreams*. even the Boston scenes, was shot in and near Dubuque.) In the old part of Dubuque below the bluffs, neighborhood after neighborhood looks much as it did 40 or 50 years ago. Many streets consist of simple 19th-century brick row houses, while a few are show streets of Victorian mansions.

Dubuque's rich variety of 19th-century architecture and splendid historic houses have become quite a visitor draw for lovers of Victoriana. Several opulent old mansions are now remarkable bed and breakfast inns. Four grand houses hold an elegant **progressive dinner/homes tour** for the general public every Friday and Saturday in season. And the **Fenelon Place Elevator**, one of the very few hillside cable railways remaining in the United States, is great fun for everyone, with a spectacular view from the top.

Old house buffs visiting Dubuque are no match in numbers for sightseer-gamblers attracted by the **Casino Belle**, one of the very biggest of all the floating casinos now plying the Mississippi. Dubuque's outstanding **River Adventure** museum is geared to both groups; it's located right by the Casino Belle dock. Combining dramatic indoor displays with two actual riverboats, it's far and away the best Mississippi River museum above

Miles from Dubuque to

Chicago	183
Twin Cities	260
Madiso	90
Milwaukee	173
Decorah	110
Waterloo	90
Cedar Rapids	60

To find out more

*Stop at the **Iowa Welcome Center** at the Ice Harbor (p. 84) or contact the **Dubuque Convention and Visitors Bureau**, Box 705, Dubuque, IA 52004-0705. (800) 798-4748 (recording) and (319) 557-9200 (direct line). The Visitor's Guide is concise and useful.*

Memphis.

For the history-minded, however, what's most compelling about Dubuque is the sense that much of this city of 60,000 has stayed in an unexpected time warp. Almost everything you see on the flatlands below the bluffs dates from 1910 and earlier. It's entirely possible to live in a wonderful old house from the 1850s or 1890s, in a settled neighborhood, and ignore the modern world of subdivisions, shopping malls, and drive-ins up atop the bluffs. In the compact, pedestrian river city down below, you can walk everywhere you need to go — downtown, the farmers' market, the Oky Doky convenience store, the natural food store, the art museum, the palatial library, the theater. Dubuque has *two* old theaters from the Gilded Age. The **Five Flags Civic Center** is the home of Dubuque's excellent symphony and many touring productions, while the local civic theater occupies the **Grand**.

▲ **When river transportation lost out to rail, most river cities lost out, too. Dubuque made the transition, thanks to excellent east-west and north-south rail connections.**

The old part of Dubuque is full of interesting architectural details: unusual chimneys, beautiful doorways, over a dozen styles of shutters, terra cotta decorations in relief, sheet metal cornices that haven't fallen victim to modernization. Dubuque's roofscape of towers and steeples is striking, viewed from the U.S. 151 bridge from Wisconsin or from Dubuque's blufftop streets.

Movie producers first discovered Dubuque's unusual state of preservation when The *Pajama Game*, written by native son Richard Bissell, was shot here. But things really got going in the late 1970s when Sylvester Stallone filmed *F.I.S.T.* here. Art directors in search of period backlots loved it that not a TV antenna was to be seen. (TV reception here in the valley was so poor that Dubuque got one of the first cable TV systems in

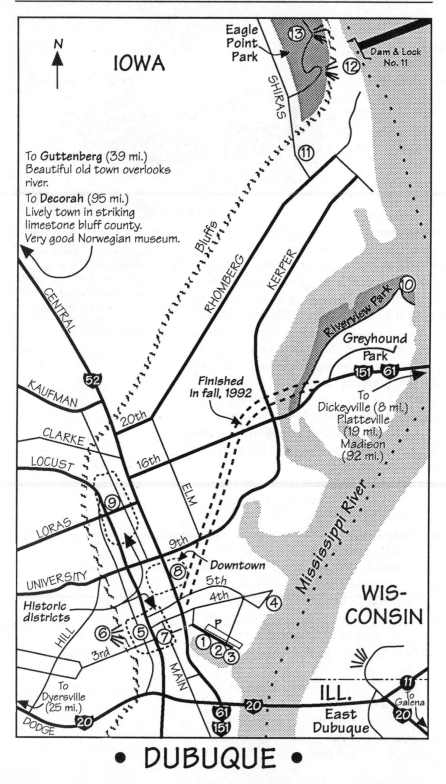

N

IOWA

Eagle Point Park

⑬

⑫ Dam & Lock No. 11

SHIRAS

To **Guttenberg** (39 mi.) Beautiful old town overlooks river.

To **Decorah** (95 mi.) Lively town in striking limestone bluff county. Very good Norwegian museum.

⑪

Bluffs

RHOMBERG

KERPER

CENTRAL

Riverview Park ⑩

Greyhound Park

⑮ 151 ⑥ 61

To Dickeyville (8 mi.) Platteville (19 mi.) Madison (92 mi.)

KAUFMAN

52

20th

CLARKE

LOCUST

16th

ELM

Finished in fall, 1992

Mississippi River

⑨

LORAS

9th

UNIVERSITY

Downtown

⑧

5th

4th

④

WIS-CONSIN

Historic districts

HILL

⑥

⑤

⑦

3rd

MAIN

① ② ③

P

To Dyersville (25 mi.)

DODGE

20

61

20

151

ILL.

East Dubuque

⑪ To Galena

20

• DUBUQUE •

DUBUQUE MAP NOTES

①River Adventure museum. Best interpretation of Upper Miss river life. Engaging life-size dioramas of clamming boat, lead mine, much more in Riverboat Museum. On a huge steam dredge, visit crew quarters, pilot house, take sounding. P. 85.

②Casino Belle. Vast 2,000-passenger pioneer of riverboat gambling. Offers lunch, 3-hour cruise & loads of song & dance for $30, dinner (nice at sunset) for $40. P. 88.

③Iowa Welcome Center. Info source for varied attractions in scenic northeast Iowa: outstanding Vesterheim Norwegian museum in delightful Decorah; Dyersville's Field of Dreams; charming old river towns of Bellevue & Guttenberg. P. 84.

④Old Shot Tower (1855) dropped molten lead to form shot. In old industrial area next to Star Brewery.

⑤Fenelon Place Elevator and Cable Car Square. Specialty shops along Fourth and Bluff at base of quaint funicular railway up the bluff. P. 91.

⑥Fenelon Place. Don't just go up & come down the cable railway. Stay & enjoy the spectacular view of city & river; stroll by old homes. P. 91.

⑦Cathedral Square & South Main Street Historic District. A stately church and mix of 19th c. architecture makes a nice walk. P. 93.

⑧Old Jail/Dubuque Art Museum. Surprising combination of lively small museum in impressive 1857 jail, renovated with respect. See dungeon, furnished cell. Good local watercolors in museum shop. P. 97.

⑨Mansion Row and Jackson Park Historic Districts. On Locust, 19th-c. Dubuque's show street, mansions compete for ostentatious splendor. Dramatic public stairways, fanciful houses climb steep bluffs. Pp 95, 98.

⑩Riverview Park. Undeveloped park behind greyhound track is best local place to get close to river away from industry.

⑪Mathias Ham House. Grandly furnished home of real estate developer who hoped to establish his own city at Eagle Point to rival Dubuque. P. 100.

⑫Lock & Dam # 11. See the slow-moving, deliberate drama of huge barge tows being broken in two and locked through. Free guided tours Sundays at 2, Mem.-Labor Day.

⑬Eagle Point Park. Open May-Oct. Dubuque's prettiest park. Great view of river, lock & dam. 164 acres on wooded bluffs have BBQs, playground, wading pool, horseshoes. Band concerts.

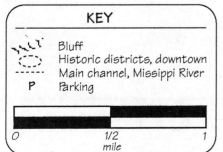

KEY

〰	Bluff
⬚	Historic districts, downtown
- - - - -	Main channel, Missippi River
P	Parking

0   1/2   1
            mile

the nation.) The Chamber of Commerce's Movie Bureau puts out a glossy brochure for movie producers highlighting diverse scenes such as the bleak back of a tenement and a skyline shot that could have been taken 90 years ago.

The story behind the time warp

Dubuque is an example of what can happen to old river cities that didn't fully link up with modern networks of transportation. Excellent rail connections enabled the city to thrive in the late 19th century, but local industries faltered between 1900 and 1930, when most Midwestern cities experienced rapid growth. Dubuque remained relatively small and became more isolated after railroads declined. Its population is 60,000 today, with no adjacent incorporated suburbs.

Economic stagnation in the early 20th century meant few buildings were torn down for newer, bigger downtown structures in the early age of the automobile. And it meant that Dubuque didn't gain those American immigrant groups of the early 20th century, so often found in Midwestern cities. Here there are no Polish, Italian, or Bohemian neighborhoods, no legendary Coney Island founded by a Greek, no Jewish delis or fresh bagels (there is a synagogue, however), no smattering of Lebanese Arabs or Serbs, no sizable contingent of Scandinavians off the farm, and no black community dating back to World War I. In fact, there are hardly any African-Americans at all, and very few

Why movie producers love Dubuque

◆ *"In so many other locations, you find sky-scrapers in the background, or one new building in the middle of a neighborhood. Dubuque is just right," commented the production manager of F.I.S.T.*

◆ *"In some ways, there's been a time warp here," said the art director of Take This Job & Shove It.*

◆ *Right-to-work laws, low hotel rates, and helpful extras are other production plusses.*

The film bureau of Dubuque's chamber of commerce plays up Dubuque's lack of TV antennas and its diverse streetscapes and views in its successful bid for film locations. Scenes of urban squalor and Victorian grandeur can be found blocks apart. ▼

Mexican-Americans, either. (That settled quality of old Dubuque has, however, apparently enabled the city to nurture a lot of vivid personalities and characters. Storyteller Mike Ryan says he's found far more ghost stories here than anywhere else.)

Dubuque's lack of ethnic diversity is well known in the region and goes back much farther than the much-publicized spate of recent cross-burnings. "Dubuque is a really strange place," people from Galena or Platteville or Iowa City will tell you. "It's all white and 90% Catholic, and the Irish Catholics and German Catholics don't get along with each other."

That's a stereotype, it turns out — the percentage of Catholics is more like two-thirds, and there's now quite a bit of intermarriage between Irish and Germans. But like many stereotypes, it has elements of truth.

Julien Dubuque, Indians, and lead mining

Dubuque's namesake and most famous historical figure was Julien Dubuque, a clever and enterprising French-Canadian fur trader who came to Prairie du Chien when the Upper Mississippi was still part of Spanish Louisiana. He heard about Indians digging lead near where Dubuque is today, and soon worked out a deal in which Indians mined lead for him to smelt and trade downriver. Like many French traders, he took an Indian wife.

Legends abound of the ways Dubuque impressed and gained power over the Indians, such as spilling

Movies filmed in Dubuque
Pennies from Heaven
Take This Job & Shove It
Miles from Home
Field of Dreams
F.I.S.T.
Gaily, Gaily
The Pajama Game

19th-century row houses and New England-looking rural scenes are a few miles apart in Dubuque County. ▼

oil on water and lighting it. He continued his lead
operation for over 20 years, remaining shadowy
and secretive about details, until his death in
1810. His Indian relatives and followers erected a
lead-covered monument on his grave, replaced by
a romantic, medieval-looking stone tower in the
1890s. The beautiful blufftop area of his mines,
smelter, and grave is today the **Mines of Spain
State Recreation Area** just south of town. (See p.
103.)

Today's settlement of Dubuque, north of the
Indian village where Dubuque lived, wasn't founded
until 1833, when Indians ceded their territory after Black Hawk's defeat (p. 50). As in Galena, its
early economic basis was lead. Merchants supplying miners also prospered. Steamboat ventures
soon followed. Dubuque, on the Mississippi's west
bank, was a natural commercial center for the new
Iowa territory being settled.

▲ **The grave site of
secretive trader Julien
Dubuque is commem-
orated by a stone tower
from the 1890s.**

Dubuque became an educational and religious
center on the frontier as well. It was a base for several denominations in the Upper Midwest. In the
1850s, Presbyterians established what is now the
University of Dubuque, and Lutherans founded
Wartburg Theological Seminary. Its buildings are
modeled on Wartburg Castle, where Luther sought
refuge and began his German translation of the
New Testament.

How Dubuque became so Catholic

The efforts of the energetic Catholic bishop,
Mathias Loras, a Frenchman, soon turned Dubuque
and the area around it into a center of Catholicism
on the mainly Protestant frontier. Loras's contacts
with Catholic clergy in Europe resulted in much
immigration from Ireland, Germany, and Luxem-
bourg, beginning in the turbulent 1840s, when
crop failure and industrialization wreaked havoc on
the old European order.

Today an estimated 65% of Dubuque's population is Catholic. More students are in the parochial
school system than the public school system. It's
not uncommon to meet young adults from Dubuque

and outlying communities who will tell you they had never met a person who wasn't Catholic until they were out of high school. Catholics around here come in mainly two kinds: Irish and German. All others are considered somewhat exotic. In Dubuque there are two Catholic colleges, **Loras College** and **Clarke College**, and motherhouses of three religious orders: the Sisters of Charity at Mount Carmel, the cloistered Trappestine nuns at Our Lady of the Mississippi, and, across the river in Wisconsin, the Sinsinawa Dominican Sisters.

During the railroad age of the late 19th century, many river towns withered. Instead, Dubuque prospered. The important Illinois Central Railroad from Chicago developed the town of Dunleith (now East Dubuque) as the site of its repair shops in 1857. Supplying Union troops in the Civil War was a boon to both industry and agriculture, in Dubuque as in so many other growing manufacturing and trading centers in the new West. Lumbering became the leading local industry and the main stimulus to Dubuque's showy architectural styles. Vast log rafts were floated down the river to be

Dubuque in 1854 *was a prosperous whole-sale and retail center serving an extensive area. It was a dignified place with gaslights, paved streets, and horse-drawn omnibusses — quite metro-politan and up-to-date for a frontier city. Its port handled a dozen steamer landings a day.*

To staff the gaming tables on the Casino Belle, the local com-munity college trained hundreds of Dubuquers. Getting into river gam-bling early has paid off for Dubuque—so far. ▼

turned into railroad ties, doors, and windows here. Dubuque also became the boatbuilding center of the Upper Mississippi.

After decades of prosperity, unusual decline

But after the turn of the century, the lumber ran out, the wheat belt moved west, and not enough new industries developed to take up the slack. Dubuque entered a period of stagnation. If, after 1900, Dubuque had developed like other cities of its size in the Upper Midwest, today it would be more like Cedar Rapids, with a population of 110,000 people, instead of 57,000, as it is today. It would have far fewer old buildings and more kinds of people who moved to Midwestern cities for the kinds of jobs that opened up after 1900.

If Dubuque had grown larger, it would be on an interstate. Dubuque's highway connections to the outside world are an index of its isolation and a matter of great local concern.The recent widening of U.S. 151 to Madison is a welcome event.

America's weakening industrial base within the past 20 years has jolted the old status quo of Democratic, conservative, blue-collar Dubuque. Many of its people grew up in an unusually traditional, isolated world, in which sons followed their fathers into the John Deere factory or meat-packing plant. In the 1980s, the John Deere tractor works shrank from employing over 6,000 to 2,500. Dubuque Packing was bought out by an outside firm, with loss of more jobs. The city's population shrank from 62,400 in 1980 to 57,500 in 1990.

Gambling and tourism: responses to crisis

Gambling-based tourism has been the first and most visibly successful local initiative to diversify Dubuque's economy. You can hardly drive anywhere in northern Illinois or southern Wisconsin without seeing billboards for the Casino Belle, the gigantic, locally owned pioneer of riverboat gambling. In 1991 hundreds of local people were trained to become gambling dealers in a five-week crash course taught at the local community college by veterans of Las Vegas and Atlantic City. Du-

One of America's three best river museums is the River Adventure museum complex in Dubuque. Others are the Ohio River Museum in Marietta, Ohio, and Memphis's Mud Island River Museum, devoted to the Lower Mississippi.

Seeing riverboats in action

♦ *It's fun to see huge barge tows locked through at a dam. Dam #11 beneath Eagle Point has an elevated observation deck and picnic area.*

♦ *At the Ice Harbor, you can see towboats of the local fleeting service taking individual barges out to big barge tows. At the Coast guard station on the harbor's south side, Coast Guard towboats sometimes dock to take on water.*

buque's Casino Belle and River Museum on the old winter Ice Harbor have upstaged Galena as the major destination for tour buses.

The idea of legalized gambling comes as a shock to outsiders whose image of Iowa is based on straight-laced Protestant communities like the one in *The Music Man*. But Catholics have never been averse to a little controlled gambling for a good cause. Bingo and raffles have helped finance many a church. Yet even some blue-collar residents regard gambling as "a desperate move." With so many other hard-pressed states legalizing riverboat gambling, it's hard to tell how long Dubuque will maintain its early edge.

In today's changed world, Dubuque's homogeneity and isolation have increasingly become a big recruiting drawback for the colleges, the important hospital sector, and firms like the Dubuque area's software and systems designers that must attract new talent to the area. No matter how beautiful Dubuque's scenery and how remarkable its stock of historic housing, professors and computer professionals also want simple things like a congenial variety of people in the workplace, and everyday food like a fresh bagel or a good Chinese restaurant or BBQ joint. The only trace of a Jewish deli in Dubuque turns out to be signs painted on storefronts used in filming the scene in *Field of Dreams* in which Kevin Costner goes to an old Jewish part of Boston to look up James Earl Jones.

The story behind the cross burnings

An enthusiastic citizens' group was determined to make Dubuque more cosmopolitan and attractive to outsiders, and to expose its young people to other kinds of people. It came up with a diversity plan to attract more people of color, and the city council approved it. Firms and organizations that hired minorities would be given awards. Almost as an afterthought, a numbers goal was agreed upon in order to measure progress: to recruit 20 families a year for the next five years.

What happened, not surprisingly, was that re-

Celebrated candies from Dubuque

They can be found at most local gift shops, or shipped direct or ordered by phone through Hartig-Snyder Drugs, 703 Main, Dubuque IA 52001. (319) 556-3092.

♦ *Trappestine Creamy Caramels. Cloistered sisters at Our Lady of the Mississippi Abbey on U.S. 52 south of Dubuque produce "some of the best handmade caramels ever made," say Allison and Margaret Engel in* Food Finds. *Buttery rich and not painfully sweet, they melt away and come in many kinds, with wonderful chocolate coating an option in cool months. No preservatives; they turn into rocks with time. They can also be purchased at the candy shop at the delightfully serene abbey. Call for details. (319) 556-6330 or 582-2595.*

♦ *Betty Jane's Gremlins. They're like turtles but smaller, which makes for a higher ratio of pecan and chocolate to caramel. The Trappestine Sisters set a high local standard for caramel, so gremlins stand out way above typical turtles. Downtown location: 965 Main. (319) 582-4668.*

sentiment and fear spread among the large and
economically stressed working-class population.
That fueled isolated cross-burnings, along with
rumors, anger, and fears among people whose
direct experience with black people was generally
nonexistent. Stereotypes based on movie and TV
images of a drug-plagued inner-city underclass
came into play. Spending tax dollars to import minorities for already scarce jobs fueled resentment.
The goals were viewed as quotas, and carried all
their political baggage. The diversity plan was
"motivated by good intentions but naïve and
marred by limited exposure," says an observant
transplant. "That's typical of a lot that goes on in
Dubuque."

Now there's a new Council for Diversity charged
with working for a broader definition of cultural
diversity, emphasizing openness and not social
engineering. Numbers goals will be eliminated.

The cross-burnings seem to have stopped, now
that five participants have been apprehended and
charged. Four of the men were under 20. Most
people you meet in Dubuque view the cross-burnings with great embarrassment, as attention-get-
ting teen pranks of bigoted, ignorant people.

In any case, Dubuque is becoming more white-
collar and more cosmopolitan, however slowly.
The software companies attract outsiders, and the
colleges have started to think of themselves as the
tri-college community. The growing community of
urban refugees and second-homeowners in and
near Galena has benefited Dubuque, and the services and cultural institutions available in Dubuque
have benefited Galena. It's still not a great area for
singles. (The men in Dubuque are all married, and
the single men in Galena are mostly gay, according
to a young and frustrated single faculty woman who
came to teach in Dubuque and ended up finding a
mate near Madison.)

For most visitors, Dubuque is gambling and greyhound racing and Victorian homes. For inquisitive
outsiders, it's a lot more: a chance to see first-
hand the way it really used to be in many settled

old American cities. It's easy for many of us to idealize the days of yesteryear, when old neighborhoods were intact and there was a place for everybody. Such nostalgia appeals especially to people who dislike the depersonalized lifestyles of new suburbs organized around automobiles. But Dubuque shows how the old sense of belonging and order came with a certain cost in isolation and homogeneity.

WHEN TO VISIT

Spring: Wildflower displays at Mines of Spain, Swiss Valley nature areas. Pleasant hiking, more open bluff views on Mississippi. Some spring flowers at Dubuque Botanical Gardens. Cool weather for in-town walks, biking on Heritage Trail. Hotel occupancy not yet full with gambling tourists.

Summer: Hot, muggy weather may limit outdoor activity except in early morning. Botanical Gardens, Farmers' Markets are at their best into September. Pool and water slide by dam is a treat; so is Eagle Point Park. River museum, art museum, Casino Belle, other cruise boats are air-conditioned. Great River Road good for touring in air-conditioned cars.

Fall: Great time for biking and hiking (see spring), walks through historic areas. Fall colors on bluffs make river cruises most beautiful.

Winter: Downhill skiing at Sundown, cross-country at Swiss Valley and Eagle Point.

ANNUAL EVENTS:

Dubuquefest: 3rd week in May, Wed-Sun. All-arts fest (mostly free) with music, dance, puppets, poetry, drama, arts fair, historical presentations of Rivers Hall of Fame. **Fourth of July:** Ham House Ice Cream Social, fireworks by Lock & Dam #11, pops concert with drum & bugle corps. More fireworks in Dyersville. **Mississippi River Revival Folk Festival:** sometime in August. Live music, environmental exhibits, kids' fair. **Riverfest:** 2nd weekend in Sept. Biggest local street parade, continuous music, boat parade, carnival & art fair, street dance, historic demonstrations and displays, more. **Dragon Boat Festival:** month varies. 1992 with Riverfest. Bright carved Chinese dragon boats race on Mississippi.

ENTERTAINMENT

See also: **Galena** (p. 207) and **Southwest Wisconsin** (p. 52), just 20 minutes away.
Five Flags Theater: home of the high-quality **Dubuque Symphony** and venue for many touring performances. An opulent 1910 theater at 4th and Main is the centerpiece of Dubuque's civic center. (319) 589-4254. **Grand Opera House:** 1890 theater is home to an accomplished civic theater with summer repertory productions. (319) 588-1305 (tickets), 588-4356 (business). **Dubuque County Fairgrounds:** hosts **NASCAR Winston Racing** every Sunday, April-Sept., **dances** every weekend, rodeos, truck pulls, gun shows, etc. (319) 588-1406. **Greyhound Park:** see p. 99. **Sunday summer concerts:** at the botanical gardens. (319) 556-2100. **Friday noon summer concerts:** at Washington Park, 6th and Locust. *For more information,* call (800) 798-4748 and (319) 557-9200.

POINTS OF INTEREST

The Ice Harbor —
Dubuque's tourism hub

The Ice Harbor is well signed from all major entries into Dubuque. It's just south of downtown on East 3rd at the river. From Central, take the 5th St. entrance. (3rd St. passes over Central but connects with Locust and the Fenelon Place Elevator.)

The focal point of Dubuque's new tourism thrust is the city's old Ice Harbor, originally constructed by an act of Congress in 1885 to provide a protected winter harbor on the Upper Mississippi. The river history museum is in an old freighthouse next to their excursion boat dock, forming the nucleus of this one-stop tourism center.

The Ice Harbor provides practically unlimited **free parking** for crowds of gamblers and museum visitors. A big, multipurpose new **visitor complex** is by the **Casino Belle docks**. There the **Iowa Welcome Center** is a useful first stop for all visitors, with loads of information about a surprising variety of sights within an hour or two of Dubuque. Ask to see a **video introduction** to Dubuque.

On the uppermost floor, an observation deck provides an elevated vantage point for seeing the Mississippi's main channel.

Off the Casino Belle ticket area and also above it are automatic teller machines (they make gambling so convenient!) and mostly ordinary tourist shops. An engaging exception: the **Hall of Names** (319-588-9050), where for $10 you can get a printout about your family name and its history, now done for nationalities from Afghan to Lithuanian to Japanese.

Toward the Ice Harbor's end is the dock for **Roberts River Rides'** non-gambling excursion boat (p. 90) and the rest of the **River Museum** complex (two outdoor boats and two museum buildings). **Harbor Place Mall** has booths of unremarkable antiques and gifts, country and Victorian crafts,

"Trolley" tours of Dubuque
leave from the Welcome Center. In a little over an hour, they tour major landmarks and historic districts, then go to the lock and dam or the arboretum, according to participants' interests. The schedule changes; call (319) 582-0077 or ask at the Welcome Center.

plus a fudge shop with pretty good soups and sandwiches. Some picnic tables overlook the harbor.

The River Museum Complex at the Ice Harbor

May-Oct: open daily 10-6:30. Nov-April: open daily except Mondays & holidays, 10-4. Combined ticket for all museums, good for 2 consecutive days: $7 adults, $3.50 ages 7-15. Entire family; $20. For riverboat museum, boathouse & boats only, $5 adult. For Dubuque Heritage Center & National Rivers Hall of Fame only, $3 adult.

The Ice Harbor is just south of downtown on East 3rd at the river. From Central, take 5th Street entrance. (3rd St. passes <u>over</u> Central but connects with Locust and the Fenelon Pl. Elevator.) (319) 557-9545.

For anyone with even a passing interest in the fascinating history of the Mississippi River, it's worth a trip to Dubuque just to see this remarkable river museum complex. The spotlight is on Dubuque's past as the Upper Mississippi's boat-building center, but the museum complex illuminates things seen all along the upper river. The complex consists of two boats and four indoor mu-

"The River Adventure" *is a collection of four indoor museums and two boats, focused on riverboats in all their many forms, from dugout canoes and homemade clamming and fishing craft to small pleasure craft to luxury passenger steamboats and giant steam dredges like the 227-foot William M. Black, permanently docked here.*

River life is the focus of Dubuque's excellent Woodward Riverboat Museum. A huge old steamboat paddlewheel is at the left. ▼

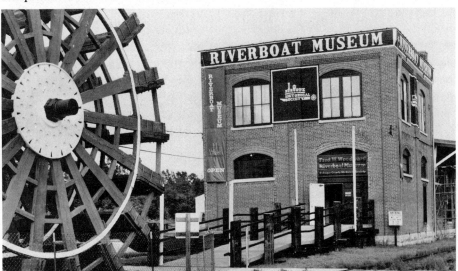

seums, two in separate historic buildings. Above the Welcome Center are the **Dubuque Heritage Center** (a local history museum and archive with interesting changing exhibits and an "urban biography" of Dubuque in the works) and the **National River Hall of Fame,** where not-very-interesting picture-profiles honor river people, past and present. You may find something good on the video screen, like John Hartford singing songs about the Mississippi. Well-done new exhibits at the Heritage Center include **"Showboat Round the Bend"** and **"Gambling on the Mississippi:** An Historical Perspective."

Here are the various parts of the museum:

William M. Black

Closed Nov.-April. Toward the end of the Ice Harbor away from the river. This big sidewheel steamer is a giant suction dredge. It deepened the main channel by sucking up sand and gravel with a dredgehead or dustpan, much like a huge vacuum cleaner, then expelling it out the stern or through a pipe up to a quarter mile away. One of the most powerful vessels ever on the river, it could move 80,000 cubic yards of river bottom in a day.

The Black was built in Point Pleasant, West Virginia, as a Depression make-work project in 1934, during the last decade of steam power. It created steam by burning bunker C oil. Steam power involves far more labor than the diesel engines that replaced it in the 1940s. It took a crew of 40 to run the Black — but that didn't matter, because the

Take a bag lunch —
you could easily spend 3 to 6 hours at the River Adventure. Picnic tables overlook the harbor's edge. Or you can have soup and a sandwich at the fudge shop inside Harbor Place Mall.

Steam power required enormously greater labor than the diesel engines which replaced it. The William M. Black, a giant steam dredge at the River Adventure museum complex, had a crew of over 40. Visitors can tour their quarters, ring the bell, and learn to take a sounding. ▼

boat was supposed to provide jobs.

You can tour the living quarters and mess hall and climb up to the pilot house (where you can turn the wheel and ring the bell). The oiler, a living history interpreter stationed near the entrance, explains the principles of steam power. They were basically the same for the Black's great 1300 horsepower engine as for the earliest steamboats. He'll show you how to take a sounding to measure river depth.

Woodward Riverboat Museum

In the long brick building away from the river.

Memorable life-size recreations of scenes, combined with some striking artifacts and models, cover all the major episodes in the long history of the Upper Mississippi, from Jesuits and the fur trade to lead-mining and steamboating, the lumber boom, early pleasure boating, and local boatbuilding. The dramatic settings give you a sense of being on the scene, right on the river, at different times in its past.

Highlights include:

◆ massive Victorian curio cabinets displaying Richard Herrmann's collections. A cabinetmaker by trade, Hermann had become fascinated with the Indian mounds and artifacts he encountered when he had worked on a railroad construction crew. His Indian artifacts and minerals are arranged in the typical manner of the Victorian era. On America's developing frontier there were numerous scientific-minded and curious Germans like Herrmann. Many of the important amateur archaeologists and students of Indian culture were German.

◆ life-size tableaus showing, among other things, a **floating log raft** (you can step on it), a family outing on an **1890 gasoline launch**, and a real **clamboat** in a backwater setting. Such johnboats dragged bars with dangling hooks across the river bottom. Clams snapped onto the hooks. Clamshells were made into pearl button in factories that soon were common along the Mississippi.

◆ a **passage in a lead mine** in a realistic walk-

*What to see
if time is limited*
The **Woodward Riverboat Museum** *is a must. The* **Boatyard** *appeals most to handymen and small boatbuilders.*

The **Wm. M. Black** *is focused on heavy machinery, most appealing to mechanical types but awesome in scale and worth a quick look, as is the* **Logsdon**, *a small wood-hulled paddle boat.*
The **Dubuque Heritage Center** *has interesting changing exhibits and an evolving "urban biography" of Dubuque but appeals mainly to locals and real history buffs.*
The **National Rivers Hall of Fame** *consists of plastic, predigested honors to river greats of the past.*
Suggestion: *see the two boats and The Boatyard quickly, save your time for the Riverboat Museum. See Hall of Fame and Heritage Center if you have time and interest.*

through, life-size model.

◆ a 29-foot **cutaway model of the steamboat Dubuque**. Dollhouse and miniature fans will admire the interior vignettes — the pilot in the pilot-house, card games, elegant passengers in state-rooms and salons, a grimy fireman in the boiler room filled with cordwood, and stevedores on the docks.

◆ a large model of a snagboat lifting fallen trees and tangled roots out of the channel.

◆ a **model of the Ice Harbor boatyard** circa 1902, showing how railroad and river shipping affected each other.

◆ a six-foot **fish tank** with catfish, turtles, an unusually large eel (it's often hiding behind a rock), and other river creatures.

The Logsdon

This paddlewheel, diesel-run workboat from the 1940s was part of a sand and gravel operation. Visitors to the simple cabin and kitchen table learn about river life as experienced by small family businesses like this.

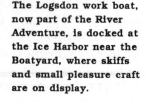

The Logsdon work boat, now part of the River Adventure, is docked at the Ice Harbor near the Boatyard, where skiffs and small pleasure craft are on display.

The Boatyard

A separate building contains a replica of the kind of shop that made the small wood fishing skiffs, clamming boats, and wooden pleasure craft displayed here. Every hour on the hour is a show on the rivers of America.

Dubuque Casino Belle

Open year-round. April-Oct: 3 cruises daily. Brunch or lunch cruises $30, dinner cruises $40. Nov-March: boat stays in port. Boarding fees $12.50-$15 without food; with lunch $20, with dinner $30.

At the Third St. Ice Harbor. Just south of downtown on East 3rd at the river. From Central, take 5th St. entrance. (3rd St. passes over

Central but connects with Locust and the Fenelon Place Elevator.) Winter schedule: boat remains dockside. Lunch, dinner, and mid-afternoon admission. All include entertainment. Admission only, $5; lunch $10, dinner $15. Call for times and reservations: (800) 426-5591. (319) 583-1761.

The $12 million, 2,000-passenger Casino Belle, longer than a football field, is one of the biggest boats on the Mississippi. It's modeled after a 19th-century sidewheeler, but it feels a lot more like Las Vegas, what with crowds of complacent-looking middle Americans (mostly over 55), the constant whir and muted ring of 500 slot machines, and vistas of drop-ceiling grids and marbelized plastic columns. Craps, blackjack, roulette, and big six are among the games played at 26 gaming tables.

Like Las Vegas, the food and entertainment are quite a deal. The cruise package ($30 at lunch, $40 for a prime rib dinner) includes several song-and-dance shows put on by an upbeat, fresh-faced young troupe of six; a four-piece combo in the dining room; a daytime style show; and a banjo player. There's a supervised children's activity center, tours of the pilot house, and great views from the deck of some 15 miles of river bluff and farmland, almost down to Bellevue. By Iowa law no more than 30% of a casino boat can be used for gambling; the Casino Belle uses even less.

The Casino Belle holds 2,000 passengers and a crew of hundreds, including entertainers, dealers, and floorwalkers. It was built specifically as a floating casino for Bob and Ruth Kehl, already successful operators and marketers of dinner cruises from Dubuque.

A good reference on casino gambling Kiplinger's Personal Finance Magazine (August, 1991) suggests **Darwin Ortiz on Casino Gambling** (by Darwin Ortiz; Carol Publishing Group, $12.95).

An even bigger floating casino is being constructed for the Kehls, to be ready for spring 1993. Home port: undecided.

But the gaming tables and slot machines are clearly the main draws. Just after boarding on the lovely October day of my visit, the decks were deserted while the casinos were full. During the 1970s and 1980s, when Dubuque's economic mainstays were withering, Bob and Ruth Kehl, longtime local restaurateurs and owner-operators of Roberts River Rides and now the Casino Belle, have emerged as local heroes. In 1973, after train service and train tours to Dubuque were stopped, they acquired a 150-passenger excursion boat and went about marketing Dubuque as a tour bus destination. They bought a riverfront freight house opposite their dock to house Dubuque's fledgling river museum, and soon built a larger boat for prime rib dinner cruises. Another profitable new sideline was providing food service to movie production crews. As "mass feeders" — a term in the food service industry — Roberts River Rides likes to quote tonnage statistics on food service: 10 tons of chicken in 1990, 7 tons of cabbage for slaw, 1.5 tons of breakfast sausage links.

By the late 1980s, the Kehls, joined by several children and children-in-laws, had built two 800-passenger excursion boats (in Dubuque and the Quad Cities) and a 1,200-passenger boat for Charleston, West Virginia. So they were well positioned to take advantage of the move to pioneer legal riverboat gambling in Iowa.

What's the deal about Iowa gambling?

◆ *There's a $200 limit on any person's losses. Dealers and floor managers are encouraged to offer advice to poor betters and even stop games.*

◆ *Slot machines are mandated to pay back at least 80%, but 90% is typical. That compares with actual returns of 86% in Atlantic City and 95% in Las Vegas.*

◆ *Odds (the percentage of the total bet kept by the house) vary from game to game. They may be as low as 1% at blackjack to 5% for roulette. Ask.*

◆ *Week nights are the best times for inexperienced gamblers. Crowds are less experienced and smaller, so dealers have more time to explain.*

Spirit of Dubuque

Cruises from May through Oct.

Boards at the Ice Harbor, back in from the Casino Belle, towards the River Museum. (800) 426-5591. (319) 583-1761. Reservations required for all dinner and brunch cruises.

This 377-passenger paddlewheeler continues the non-gambling sightseeing cruises and dinner cruises that launched Bob and Ruth Kehl in the tourism business. No reservations are necessary for the narrated, 1 1/2-hour sightseeing cruise leaving at 2 and 4 daily. It costs $8, or $5 for ages 3-12.

The 2 1/2 hour prime rib dinner cruise leaves at 6:30 Sunday through Friday (at 6 in Sept. and Oct.); the cost is $25. Saturday's dinner cruise (same time) goes through the lock at Lock & Dam No. 11, takes 3 1/2 hours, and costs $5 more. The two-hour Sunday brunch cruise costs $21 and leaves at 10:30.

Fenelon Place Elevator

Open daily April-Nov. 8 a.m.-10 p.m. Each way: adults 50¢, children 15¢, under 5 free. Bicycle & rider 60¢.

Downtown terminus: 4th St. & Bluff. Blufftop terminus: end of Fenelon Place off Summit.

If you only have time for one thing in Dubuque, take a ride on this wonderful old funicular cable railway. The ride itself is a thrill, and it begins and ends in two of the most charming neighborhoods in this architecturally rich city. The view of downtown and the river from the top is spectacular.

If heights give you the jitters, the ride's all the more exciting. You climb into the eight-person wood car waiting at the bottom, and pull a cord to have the operator atop the hill start things in motion. (You pay at the top.) A wrist-size metal cable beneath and in front of you starts moving; things creak and wheeze a little as the car moves up above the nearby rooftops. A panorama of industrial and commercial Dubuque unfolds gradually in front of you; look directly down, and you see treetops and plants on the overgrown slope. You don't go straight up — the grade is 65% — but it feels like it.

At the top, take the time to enjoy the view and walk to your left along **Fenelon Place**, with its interesting mix of

Dubuque's funicular cable railway, depicted in the 1890s. The jerky, creaky ride is fun, and the view from the bluff top is terrific. ▼

large houses from the 1850s and the turn of the century. Go all the way past Summit to 732 Fenelon Place, a handsome old house with a cupola and cast iron fence.

A banker who lived on the bluff built the original elevator here in 1882, so he could avoid the long buggy ride around the bluff and have time for a lunchtime nap over the noon hour. Inspired by cable cars he'd seen in the Alps, he built his own rope-drawn private cable car, operated by his gardener. Soon neighbors got rides, too, and he opened the elevator to the public.

After a fire destroyed the elevator during the Panic of 1893, the banker couldn't afford to rebuild alone, so 10 neighbors banded together to form a new, improved Fenelon Place Elevator Company. The fire had not only incinerated the elevator house where the steam boiler was, but it burned the rope, sending the car crashing down into the entry gatehouse. A steel cable and electric motor would be preferable, the neighbors decided; they installed a funicular system which uses two cars to counterbalance each other.

Despite its quaint appearance, the current railway is not old. Its cars and motor were replaced in 1977. But the hilltop operator's house was built in 1916, with a special room on the second floor where neighborhood men could meet to smoke and play cards.

A great view from the top

The gold dome is on Dubuque Co.'s courthouse; next door is the unusual Egyptian Revival jail, now the art museum. On the river by the railroad bridge is the Shot Tower, where molten lead was dropped to form balls used for lead shot. Next to it is the Dubuque Star Brewery.

Cable Car Square

Shops open daily including Sunday, from 10 or 11 to 5 or 6.

At the end of Fourth St., at the foot of the Fenelon Place Elevator, & along Bluff from Fifth to Third.

In the attractive old row houses at the foot of the funicular railway are Dubuque's main concentration of specialty shops and boutiques, geared to both visitors and locals. The place to stop for a quick soup-and-sandwich meal is **Yogurt D'lite** on Bluff at Fifth.

The retailing mix is familiar: fudge, cookies, and

Carriage tours of Old Dubuque

leave from Cable Car Square from April through October, weather depending. Call (319) 556-6341 or make arrangements on the scene. $7 for adults, $3 for ages 12 and under.

ice cream; loads of gifts and crafts, miniatures and collectible antiques (not much furniture); Irish and English imports; a kitchen and gourmet shop; some sportswear and interior accessories. A recent quick visit revealed a lot of country things in mauve and blue. It's worth a quick sashay around Fourth and Bluff to find shops like **Audrey Wallace Interiors** (next to Yogurt D'lite at Fifth), **First Glance** (fashion-forward women's clothing), and **Ex Libris**, a pleasant bookshop, big on metaphysical and self-help and also on literary classics, with tapes and CDs in the basement. Its regional section has books about Dubuque and Iowa, including Dubuque history by John Tigges, a popular author of Westerns and horror stories who lives here, and the *Wapsipinicon Almanac*, a provocative and beaubeautifully printed chronicle of rural life and issues in Iowa.

▲ The Redstone Inn at 5th and Bluff, a block from Cable Car Square, is an elegant small hotel. It's one of four Victorian mansions on Dubuque's popular weekend progressive dinners.

Washington Park

Between Locust and Bluff from 6th to 7th. (319) 588-1478.

This civilized little urban square, accented by an unusual Victorian gazebo with a Chinese-inspired roof, is the scene of many arts and music festivals and regular **Friday noon concerts** by local musical groups. **Benches** and a few **picnic tables** make this a good rest and lunch stop on a walking tour of the surrounding historic areas around Cable Car Square and Mansion Row on upper Locust Street.

A walk from the Ice Harbor to the Fenelon Place Elevator

Described in walking tour booklet "Three Historic Districts: Lower Main, Cathedral Square, Fenelon Place," published by the Dubuque Historical Society ($1.25). Find it at the Woodward Riverboat Museum (p. 185), the Ham House, or Ex Libris (p. 93); or *see below for street directions. Time: 30 minutes.*

Dubuque's paired, one-way streets whoosh motorists by so fast that in order to take in the city's unusually well-preserved architectural fabric, you really have to get out and walk. Seeing Dubuque is especially interesting if you're from St. Louis or some similar old industrial river city that has been chewed up by parking lots and urban renewal. Dubuque offers a window on a vanished past from sometime in the 1940s or 1950s.

This walk isn't all lovely — a lot of Dubuque is down-at-the-heels or remodeled to the point of remuddling. But it *is* interesting. It passes:

◆ the oldest part of downtown, from the decades around the Civil War.

◆ the unusual and ornate Five Flags Theater, built as the Majestic in 1910.

◆ the Fenelon Place Elevator and Cable Car Square, Dubuque's specialty shopping hub.

◆ the Gothic Catholic St. Raphael's Cathedral from 1857-9. Not generally open to the public, but free tours may be arranged in advance with Sister Mary (319-582-7646).

◆ large and beautifully detailed houses in many styles from the 1850s into the 1890s.

Try to buy the booklet. If you can't, the route to follow is this:

Take the 3rd Street Overpass across Central. Turn north (right) onto Main, then left onto Fourth, right onto Locust, left onto Fifth, left onto Bluff. The Elevator is at the end of Fourth just off Bluff. Three blocks south on Bluff at Second, you'll be at Cathedral Square. Go east (left) two blocks on Second, then left on Main to Third. Take the overpass back to the Ice Harbor.

Dubuque architectural walking tours
$1.25 booklets to the Cathedral Square/ Fenelon Place walk and other interesting walks along Mansion Row and around Jackson Park are available at the shop inside the Woodward Riverboat Museum, at the Ham House, and at Ex Libris books, 371 Bluff at Fourth.

"Mansion Row" along Locust Street

Described in walking tour booklet "Dubuque's Mansion Row," published by the Dubuque Historical Society ($1.25). Find it at the Woodward Riverboat Museum (p. 85-87), the Ham House, or Ex Libris (p. 93); or see below for street directions. Estimated time: 30 minutes. Look for on-street parking.

"Here in Dubuque, the merely rich lived up on the bluff, while the super-rich lived down below on Locust Street, along with everybody else, the better to display their wealth," explains an innkeeper at one of Dubuque's Victorian bed and breakfast palaces. The three blocks of Locust from 11th Street to Loras Boulevard are a Victorian show street with few equals in the U.S. today. Most such streets in larger cities have become ragged, interrupted by parking lots and newer buildings.

Locust Street features massive urban castles from the 1870s, 1880s, and 1890s, interspersed with some simpler and older mansions and row houses. Two side-by-side Second Empire houses on Locust south of Loras are so large, with mansard towers so tall and heavy (in the best tradition of Charles Addams' haunted houses) that they could fill in as courthouses of good-sized counties.

Don't be surprised, however, if you finish the tour a little bored by all the show and depressed by the charmless vulgarity of such opulence. It's easy to understand how they could be seen by later generations as lifeless mausoleums to family pride.

Highlights include:

◆ the elaborate Beaux-Arts **Carnegie-Stout Public Library**, a neo-Roman temple of culture. Two paintings by Grant Wood are part of the collection of paintings, sculpture, and furniture on display.

◆ a stop at the **Stout House** B&B, 11th at Locust, to pick up a brochure and see its massive Romanesque entryway. (No informal tours; open to the public on the progressive dinner, p. 100.)

◆ a side trip west on 12th Street to see a delight-

ful **Gothic Revival cottage** on the bluff crest, at
1207 Grove Terrace.

◆ The **Ryan House restaurant** in one of the
courthouse-like mansions, at 1375 Locust. You can
look inside to check out the menu at the front
desk. Lunches run from $5 to $9, dinners $7 to
$17. Good food in elegant surroundings.

◆ The **Mandolin Inn** bed and breakfast on 201
Loras at Main. The innkeeper can't always give
visitors tours, but you're certainly welcome to pick
up a brochure and see the elaborately tiled porch
and entryway stained glass. It is described in the
Jackson Park walking tour north from here to
the bluff.

◆ a detour two blocks east along 13th to **City
Hall** and the **farmers' market** (p. 97).

◆ **St. Luke's Methodist Church** on Main at
12th. This congregation, which built the first
church in Iowa in 1837, seemed determined not
to be outshone by the farmore numerous Catholics
in 1896, when it built this Romanesque fortress of
a church. Its most fabulous feature are a hundred
beautiful windows, all from the Tiffany studio. The
frieze of singing children around the altar
is a copy of the Luca della Robbia Renaissance relief. Visitors are welcome;
come in the front door.

A brochure at
St. Luke's Metho-
dist church tells
about its Tiffany
windows and
other art trea-
sures.

Dubuque Museum of Art in the Old Jail

Open Tues-Fri 10-5, Sat & Sun 1-5. Free.
   *8th St. at Central, behind the big, gold-domed
courthouse. (319) 557-1851.*

This very interesting small art museum is in a
most unusual setting. An unusual Egyptian Revival
style, deemed appropriate for prisons and ceme-
teries, was used for the landmark 1857 jail building. Here renovations haven't destroyed the character of the interior, as they have in the grand
courthouse next door. The jailer's kitchen can still
be seen. The cells remain, too. (One has original
furnishings.) You can even see the basement
dungeons.

A rotating selection from the permanent collection is displayed on the upper level. It consists
mostly of 150 years of works by artists from the
Dubuque area, including many contemporaries and
students of Iowa's famous realist, Grant Wood. His
Stone City art colony was about an hour from here.

Changing exhibits, greatly varied in nature but
mainly by living artists, are on the main level.
These may include one-person shows of interna-
tionally known artists or worthwhile local shows.
The number of fine artists who live in the area, in
Dubuque and Galena, is "almost staggering," according to the museum's director. Their watercolors, oils, and prints are also sold in the small **museum shop**, along with handmade jewelry, cards,
pottery, and a good selection of children's books,
including many by Art Geisert of Galena, illustra-
tor-author of *Pigs A to Z* and other funny pig books.

Farmers' Market

Open May-October, Saturdays 6-12.
   In front of City Hall, 13th and Iowa.

A lively activity center on Saturday mornings for
well over a century. Over 100 vendors of produce,
plants, and crafts set up in front of Dubuque's
stately 1857 City Hall, modeled after Boston's

*For an idea of art
in Dubuque's
lavish homes,*
see the permanent
collection at the Dubuque
Museum of Art, upper
gallery.

Ask for a free tour
of the Old Jail at the
art museum desk.

▲ *Boston's Faneuil Hall*
was the model for Du-
buque's City Hall. A lively
farmers' market takes
place there Saturday
mornings from May
through October.

Faneuil Hall. City Hall was originally built as a combined ground-floor marketplace (like Galena's) with upper-story offices and meeting rooms. Now the vendors are on the pavement outside. Two contend with each other in offering the sweetest Iowa Xtra Sweet corn, picked before dawn. The owner-chef of the outstanding "225" restaurant downtown bases his daily menu on offerings here.

Breitbach's Farmers' Market Food Store

Open Mon-Fri 10-5:30, Sat 8-5.
  1109 Iowa near 11th. (319) 557-1777.

Dubuque's only natural foods and organic grocery is also an important informal social center and political headquarters. Owner Mike Breitbach organizes the summertime folk festival and heads the local chapter of the Mississippi River Revival, which currently has more members than the Minneapolis chapter, thanks to controversies stirred up by the city's plans to expand its incinerator. He's behind a plan for local schoolchildren to send environmental messages to President Bush on cutout leaves. Informal debates over the racial diversity plan were held by its authors over the counter here.

Bulletin boards in places like this are always good sources of local information. As for food, Breitbach has bakers who whip up quick breads, seven-grain bread, and fresh pies from frozen local fruits: apple, peach, blueberry, raspberry. A local grower sells good popcorn (in kernel form) at good prices. Also on hand: organic cheeses and seasonal produce, juices and trail mixes, turkey hot dogs and tempeh burgers for the grill.

Jackson Park Walking Tour

Described in "Jackson Park Walking Tour" booklet published by the Dubuque Historical Society ($1.25). Find it at the Woodward Riverboat Museum (p. 85-87), the Ham House, or Ex Libris (p. 93); or see below for street directions. Estimated time: 30 minutes. Look for metered on-street parking. NOTE:

the book is somewhat out of date; the wonderful stairway and fish pond are gone.

Yet another cluster of Second Empire and Queen Anne mansions is around Jackson Park, toward the north end of the flat part of town below the bluffs. This small, placid park has a gory past. It was first developed as a cemetery for cholera victims in 1833. But runoff from the nearby bluffs kept washing bodies into the street after heavy rains, until the cemetery was moved.

Near Iowa Street, a bronze bas-relief commemorates the Indian Princess Potosa, legendary wife of Julien Dubuque. Walk north on Main a block and you'll come to 17th Street at the base of the bluffs. Look up, and you'll see a number of turreted Queen Anne houses built into the hillside.

If you don't have the tour book but want to follow the interesting walking tour route, here's how:
Start at Loras and Main. Go north (away from downtown) on Main 1 block, turn left onto 15th, then right onto Locust. Follow Locust around the bend. At 17th, turn right (east) and go down 17th for 2 long blocks. Turn right (south) at Iowa. In 3 blocks, go right onto Loras and return to starting point.

Dubuque Greyhound Park

Season from second week in April through first week in November. Races begin at 1:30 and 7:30; admission 1 hour earlier. Schedule changes with day, season. Call for schedule. Grandstand $1, clubhouse $2. There's general admission seating both places, or table reservations taken up to 2 weeks ahead. (319) 582-3647 or (800) 373-3647.

On an island off U.S. 61/151 at the Wisconsin bridge.

"Looking for new ways to have fun? There's nothing quite like the thrill of greyhound racing." So say the operators of the new Dubuque Greyhound Park. Betting at the dog track is part of Dubuque's economic redevelopment plan. TV monitors are at every trackside restaurant table and in all the bars, so diners and drinkers won't miss the action. For novices, the brochure/schedule explains different kinds of wagers, like Doubles, Trifecta, Superfecta.

Mathias Ham House

*Open daily May-Oct. from 10-5:30.
$3 adults, $1.50 children 7-18, $9
family.*

Off Shiras at the foot of Eagle Point on the north
edge of Dubuque. Go northeast out Rhomberg turn
north onto Shiras. Or take Kerper out to Hawthorne,
double back to Shiras. (319)
557-9545.

▲ The grand Ham
House, out by Eagle
Point Park and the dam,
was built by a business-
man who wanted to de-
velop a town there to
rival Dubuque. Today
it's a public showplace
furnished with some of
Dubuque's showiest
antiques.

Having made a lot of money in lead mines and a
smelting furnace at nearby Eagle Point, frontier
speculator Mathias Ham invested it in a ferry and a
railroad, and attempted to develop Eagle Point as a
city to rival Dubuque. In 1856 he built this showy
Italian Villa on a most monumental scale. The large
dining room table, for instance, seems tiny beneath its 13-foot ceilings. Though the household
furnishings were dispersed, the Dubuque Historical Society has carefully researched and restored
the house and furnished it with period antiques
from Dubuque, so it typifies the grandest homes of
the very wealthy in the steamboat era just before
the Civil War. Costumed interpreters show visitors
around the house. Its architect, John Francis
Rague, was widely admired for his work in the
grand manner. He had designed the old state
capitols of Iowa and Illinois.

Victorian House Tour
& Progressive Dinner

*Dinners open to the general public are June through
October, Friday and Saturday evenings. Group tours
offered year-round. $36 for 4-hour tour with five-
course dinner. Starts at 6:15 at the Ham House.
Reservations advised at least 2 weeks ahead. Transportation is not provided.*

"A Christmas Dickens": for the holiday season,
dinner is followed by a reading in the Stout House library. From mid-November through the 1st week of
January. (319) 557-9545.

In this very popular regular event, a four-course

meal is served at four of Dubuque's most impressive Victorian mansions, beginning with hors d'oeuvres at the Ham House, followed by soup at the Redstone Inn, the entree at the Ryan House, and dessert at the Stout House, built by a lumber baron.

The Redstone Inn and Stout House, now bed and breakfast inns, are both merchants' palaces of the 1890s, red sandstone piles trimmed with all the elaborate carved trim and paneling and marble fireplaces that money could buy. The Second Empire Ryan House has a tower so tall, it could be on a courthouse. Between courses, a guide shows diners around the public rooms and tells stories about Dubuque's richest families in the 19th century. The food's good, and there's lots of extravagant ornamental detail for the eyes to feast on.

Eagle Point Park

Open from 1st Saturday in May through last Saturday in Oct. Hours: 7 a.m. to 9:45 p.m., on Fri and Sat to 10:45 p.m. $1/vehicle.

Take Rhomberg north on Shiras, west to park entrance. (319) 589-4263.

Dubuque's 164-acre showplace park offers spectacular scenery and more. It's up on the bluffs, beneath a canopy of big bur oaks, overlooking Lock and Dam No. 11. Its many beautiful structures of natural local limestone — pavilions, terraces, overlooks, rock gardens, and a **fish pond** and **wading pool** — are part of a coordinated Prairie School landscaping plan designed and built as a WPA project. In 1935 Alfred Caldwell came to Dubuque from Chicago with big ideas for the park. Caldwell was a pupil of Jens Jensen, the famous landscape architect who introduced more natural, American landscaping using native plants. He combined Jensen's ideas with the Prairie School style of architectural design developed by Frank Lloyd Wright in the early decades of the 20th

Picnic fixings

◆ *Square Meals gourmet-to-go offers the likes of Seafood Louis (linguine with scallops and shrimp; $4 a half-pound) and a good cold grilled chicken sandwich ($2.65). It's at 744 Town Clock Plaza, the downtown mall between 7th and 8th. Enter off Fifth from the east. (319) 556-1234.*

◆ *The Iron Kettle Deli (13th and Iowa) has takeout deli sandwiches.*

◆ *Breitbach's Farmers' Market, a natural foods store. 1109 Iowa near 11th.* *See p. 98.*

Eagle Point Park's pavilions and terraces are a surviving masterpiece of Prairie School environmental architecture. ▼

century.

Caldwell worked furiously in Dubuque, getting up well before dawn. The early morning hours before dawn he spent designing. Then by day he trained and directed make-work construction crews. People of vision and commitment often fare poorly in bureaucracies. That was Caldwell's fate. After 18 months the city booted him out for paying too much attention to detail and for working too slowly.

Recently, some 55 years later, Caldwell revisited the park for the first time, along with an architectural historian and biographer. To his delight, Dubuque's benign neglect has meant that this park has survived practically intact, while most of his other, later projects, such as Lincoln Park in Chicago, have been completely changed.

True to Eagle Point's name, eagles can be seen here, especially in winter, when there's open water below the dam, and early spring. Unfortunately, the park is closed then, but the viewing area by the locks is open. There are plenty of **grills** and **picnic tables** for visitors, six **tennis courts**, a **playground**, and **horseshoe pits**.

Camping and river access are available at several Dubuque County parks. You can get a brochure from the Dubuque County Conservation Board, 13768 Swiss Valley Rd., Peosta, IA 52068. (319) 556-6745. But you'll need a good map to figure things out.

Sutton Pool & Water Park

Open June-August. Mon-Fri 1-5 and 6-9, Sat & Sun 1-5 only. $2 youths, $3 adults. (319) 588-1478.

On Hawthorne at the end of Kerper, just below Eagle Point Park and not far from the dam.

Nice water park with 135-foot water slide, zero-depth wading area, playground, and concession.

Lock and Dam No. 11

At the north end of Rhomberg Avenue.

It's always interesting, in a very slow way, to see how huge barge tows are broken in two to be locked through. For details on barge shipping, see p. 17-18. For the story of the Upper Mississippi's navigation locks, see p. 17. The Army Corps of Engineers gives **tours of the locks** between Memorial Day and Labor Day at 2 p.m. Sundays.

Dubuque Arboretum & Botanical Gardens

*Open from late April up to hard freeze. Mon-Sat 9-
dusk, Sun 10-dusk. No charge except to tour groups.*

*On W. 32nd at Arboretum Dr. on Dubuque's
northwest side. Take Central/U.S. 52 up and out to
32nd, turn left and look for signs. (319) 556-2100.*

The trees in the newish arboretum section
aren't much yet, but the rose garden is outstanding, and many other sections are constantly growing, thanks to a very large, very active all-volunteer
staff. Over 600 hybrid tea roses are here. **All-
American Selections of roses and annual flowers and vegetables** are tested here. Other special
floral collections include lilacs, peonies, iris, glad-
iouses, mums, and annuals. Perennial plants include hostas, prairie flowers and grasses, dwarf
and full-size conifers, weeping trees, and a shade
garden under a grove of big trees. There's also a
lot for fruit and vegetable gardeners to learn, in
outdoor demonstration areas with fruit and nut
trees, grape vines, and vegetables, and inside in
the **McAleece Gardeners' Learning Center**. In
the nearby Visitor Center is a **gift shop** and
botanical library.

Free concerts are held here every Sunday in
summer, usually at 6 p.m., but sometimes earlier
or later. (Call for schedule.) Performers may be en-
sembles from the well-regarded Dubuque
Symphony, pop vocalists, or folk musicians.

Mines of Spain State Recreation Area & Lyons Nature Center

*Nature Center Building open year-round Mon-Fri 8-
4, plus weekends 8-4 from May through early
October, depending on funding. To confirm, call
(319) 556-0620. Trails open any time, year-round.
Free admission.*

*Just south of Dubuque. Two separate access points.
To reach **nature center** and get a **map**, go south on
U.S. 61/151, cross Catfish Creek, turn left (south)
onto Hwy. 52/Bellevue Rd., turn left immediately*

▲ **Roses are the star
attraction at Dubuque's
busy botanical gardens.**

*again. Center is at 8999 Bellevue Hts. To reach
Julien Dubuque Monument overlooking Mississippi,
go south on U.S. 61/151, but turn left (east)
onto Mar Jo Hills Rd. before Catfish Creek.
Continue straight, at Y go left onto Monument Dr.*

This includes the very site of the Indian
village where Julien Dubuque lived and
worked with the Fox Indian lead
miners whose lead he traded
The beautiful, mostly undeveloped Mines of Spain State Recreation Area has 1,380 acres extending 3 1/2 miles along the
Mississippi.

When Dubuque died in 1810,
his Indian followers marked his grave with a lead-
covered monument. Its romantic replacement
from the 1890s, the medieval-looking stone tower
of the **Julien Dubuque Monument**, is the centerpiece of a dramatic overlook with a view across the
Mississippi to Sinsinawa Mound in Wisconsin. Eagle-watching in winter is good here.

Though budget cutbacks have postponed development, the area today is wonderful "for those
who like to hike through the woods, along
streams, through fields, valleys, and hills," says enthusiastic staff naturalist Betty Hauptli. "There are
hill or goat prairies (see p. 12) with some endan-
gered species, and the woods contain old oak
stands, old lead mine pits, and Indian mounds.
River views are great from Monument Hill and the
old quarry off Mar Jo Hills Road. Canoeists and
fishermen use Catfish Creek." Much of the land
was farmed until recent decades.

"In the springtime," Hauptli continues, "the
woods are full of flowers and migrating birds. In
the summer, the prairies are in bloom and the native grasses wave in the breezes. In the fall, the
trees are golds, reds, and oranges. In the winter,
there's cross-country skiing and animal tracks for
hikers to see in the snow."

Trail maps are available at the nature center,

▲ Woods have grown up on the farm that's now part of the Lyons Nature center, but the pictur-esque chapel built as a study and den by the farm's owner remains, for hikers to come upon in the woods.

which has a short, self-guided **interpretive trail**, **wildflower garden**, and nifty little demonstration **butterfly garden**.

Sundown Ski Area

Anticipated season: late Nov. to mid-March.

About 5 miles west of Dubuque. Take U.S. 20 (Dodge St.) west almost to Epworth. At Y21, turn north. Where Y21 joins Asbury Rd., turn right. (800) 397-6676 or (319) 556-6676. Snow report: (800) 634-5911.

Once you're familiar with the Driftless Region's surprising topography, it doesn't seem odd to find a downhill ski area in Iowa. Sundown has trails through evergreen forests and broad slopes, 19 runs up to 4,000 feet long, and 475' vertical drop. Night lighting. Snowmaking equipment. One quad chair, two triple chairs, one double chair, and three rope tows. Reduced rates for groups. Ski Wee for kids 4-12.

Swiss Valley Park and Nature Center

Park and trails open year-round, sunrise to sunset. Nature center open year-round, Mon-Fri 7-3:30, weekends 9-5. No fee.

About 8 miles southwest of Dubuque. Take U.S. 20 west, turn just west of Country View Motel onto Swiss Valley Rd., continue 3 1/2 miles. (319) 556-6745.

The 475' slopes of the Sundown Ski Area overlook the beautiful, rocky valley of the Little Maquoketa River and the Heritage Trail for bicycles, snowmobiles, and cross-country skiing. ▼

Picnic groves along a rocky trout stream in a deep V valley make this a nice place to stop between Dubuque and Dyersville. Over 10 miles of hiking trails radiate out from the visitor center through forests, prairies, and wetlands. Hurt game birds and wild animals are kept here on display as part of a rehabilitation program, and soil conservation practices are demonstrated. Call for times of **Sunday-afternoon nature hikes** in fall, winter, and spring.

The **campground** is grassy and open, with small trees. It has 20 tent sites and 27 electric sites. Fees are $5, plus $2-3 for electricity. Showers, water, and dump stations are available. No reservations except for large groups. Sites with electricity fill in spring, fall, and holiday weekends.

Heritage Trail and Dyersville

Open year-round for bicycling, hiking, cross-country skiing, and snowmobiling. Trail fee: $1.10/day, $5.25/year; half price for seniors, under 12 free.

***Eastern trailhead:** on U.S. 52, 2 miles north of Dubuque. **Western trailhead:** east of downtown Dyersville on Hwy. 135, north of U.S. 20. Trailside **parking areas** on U.S. 52 in Durango, on D17, on D17 east of Graf, on Gun Club Rd. north of Epworth, on Y13 north of Farley. (319) 556-6745. For a 48-page **trail guide**, send $2 to Dubuque County Conservation Board, 13768 Swiss Valley Rd., Peosta, IA 52068.*

Some of the pleasantest vacation bicycling imaginable is along bike trails just like this. Here a rail line from Chicago to St. Paul followed a winding, narrow valley of the Little Maquoketa River through the beautiful limestone bluff country of the Driftless Region (p. 16). The eastern two-thirds of the trail, almost to Epworth, follows the river so closely that you can fish from it in many places. Most of this part is shady, while the stretch away from the river going into Dyersville is open.

The grade of bike trails on old rail beds is so gentle — here it's a maximum of a foot per hun-

"A journal of rural life" is what publisher-printer Tim Fay calls his **Wapsipinicon Almanac,** an annual book about the nature and direction of agriculture and everyday rural living in Iowa today. "WAP-si-PI-ni-con" is the name of a beautiful river and rolling valley in eastern Iowa.

The book is a fine introduction to a subtly rich way of life that's hard for outsiders to enter. Get it for $5 at Ex Libris or Breitbach's in Dubuque, at Galena bookstores, at southwest Wisconsin co-ops, or write Route 3 Press, Anamosa, IA 52205.

The <u>Utne Reader</u> says its "environmental reportage, arguments for sustainable agriculture, gardening advice, memoirs, fiction, and poetry . . . stay pretty darn close to home. Fay and his writers are serious about wanting to help their little corner of the world regain confidence in its destiny. . . . [It] aims to reflect the genuine communion that exists between the contributors — many are professionals, activists, or craftspeople who have spent time in big cities -- and their less-traveled neighbors."

dred feet — that bicycling is almost effortless, ideal for the very young and the totally out of shape. The surface is smooth, compacted screened stone, and road intersections are few. Unfortunately there are no bike rental facilities along the trail.

The 26-mile trail from Dubuque to Dyersville is not only especially scenic, it connects numerous interesting destinations and passes by old lead mines and limestone bluffs where fossils can be collected. The interpretive displays at the east trailhead highlight the trail's historic and natural features. A half mile off the trail near the eastern trailhead (and clearly signed from the trail) is the **Little Maquoketa River Mounds Preserve**, with 32 ancient burial mounds, a native blufftop prairie remnant, a mature forest with wildflowers, and an interpretive station. The trail also goes past the base of the **Sundown Ski Area** (p. 105).

In Graf (population 100) there's an old general store now geared to the trail. Its commercial **campground** with showers and hookups is right on the trail. Epworth, a mile and a half south of the trail, is the home of the **Divine Word College Seminary** and the Divine Word Catholic missionaries in 59 countries. Of its 80 seminarians, 90% are from missionary countries, and half are Vietnamese refugees. Brother Leonard gives impromptu tours to small groups. (Bicycle attire is welcome.) Just stop at the office by the front door. Larger

▲ **"The mountain trail in prairie country."** Limestone bluffs rise up to 450 feet above the Little Maquoketa River along the route of the 26-mile Heritage Trail between Dubuque and Dyersville, home of the Field of Dreams.

groups, call ahead: (319) 876-3354. Tour highlights include the beautiful chapel and a most
interesting collection of ethnic wood carvings from
New Guinea, Africa, India, China, and elsewhere.

West of Epworth the trail leaves the river. Remnants of tallgrass prairie blooming in late summer
and fall are a highlight of this part of the trail. (See
p. 106.) **Dyersville**, the **Farm Toy Capital of the
World**, is now even better known as the location
for *Field of Dreams.*

Dyersville, Farm Toy Museum
& Field of Dreams

*Dyersville is on U.S. 20 25 miles west of Dubuque.
For more information, call the chamber of commerce, (319) 875-2311. They can tell you about a
public campground.*

Dyersville is the **Farm Toy Capital of the
World** and home of Ertl, Scale Models, and Spec-
Cast Toys. It's a busy farm town of 3,500 — big
enough to have a mall and commercial strip, but
visually dominated, along with the surrounding
countryside, by the soaring Gothic towers of the
Basilica of St. Francis Xavier (open daily; free).

Today Dyersville is even better known as the location for *Field of Dreams.* You can play catch or
hit flies where Kevin Costner heard voices and
Shoeless Joe Jackson (Ray Liotta) walked out of
the cornfield. There's no charge, and don't worry
about trespassing; the man who lives in the movie
farmhouse runs the adjoining souvenir shop, open
daily from April through October. (To get there
from U.S. 20, take Hwy. 136 north out of town and
look for the sign when you cross the tracks.)

The **National Farm Toy Museum**, a long, new
building, has shelf after shelf of die-cast tractors
and agricultural equipment, along with dioramas of
rural Christmas decorations and farm scenes from
different eras and an original toy production line
from the 1950s. *Open 362 days, 8 a.m.-7 p.m. $2
admission, under 12 free. At U.S. 20 and Hwy. 136.
(319) 875-2727.* The **Ertl Toy factory** itself is

open for free tours weekdays at 10 a.m. and 1 p.m.
On Hwy. 136 south of U.S. 20; (319) 875-2000.

Women bored with toy tractors may be more interested in the 800+ dolls in the **Dyer/Botsford Doll Museum**, run by the local historical society in a Victorian house built by Dyersville's founder. *331 First Avenue; open daily from 1-4, possibly longer. $2. (319) 875-2414.*

RESTAURANTS & LODGINGS

All lodgings in Iowa charge a 4% sales tax. The city of Dubuque adds a 7% room tax.

BALLTOWN (population 100) A village about 15 miles up the Great River Road from Dubuque, half way to Guttenberg (see p. 142). Just north of Breitbach's is an overlook with a splendid view.

Breitbach's County Dining. *On the Great River Road in Balltown, about 15 miles northwest of Dubuque. Take U.S. 52 northwest. At Sageville, 2 miles out of Dubuque, take C9Y (The Great River Road) to Balltown. Breitbach's is in the middle of town. (319) 552-2220. April-Oct: open daily 7 a.m.-9 p.m. Nov-March: closed Monday. Visa, MC. Full bar.*

Much-expanded sixth-generation family-owned tavern goes back to 1852, claims to be oldest operating bar in Iowa and the only place visited by the James brothers and Brooke Shield. Dining room has view of flood plain and Mississippi — the same view in a mural painted by a gypsy in the 1930s. Unpretentious home cooking. Buckwheat pancakes, meat side for breakfast ($3.50). Burger and Cindy's special spaghetti soup for lunch ($4). Dinners ($4.50-$7) include corn rolls, salad bar, soup, cinnamon rolls, and the likes of meat loaf, sugar-cured ham steak, broiled chicken and fish. Of homemade pies, banana creme ($1.50) is a specialty.

BELLEVUE (population 2,500) 30 miles south of Dubuque on the Great River Road. One of the prettiest towns on the Mississippi. The town is between two bluffs; quaint businesses like a 150-year-old shoe store and an old hotel/café make downtown fun to explore. Lock & dam is right in town; eagles gather below it in winter. Bellevue State Park on south bluff has groomed x-c trails, big butterfly garden, natural prairie, extensive bike trails. Indian mounds. Contact Bellevue Chamber of Commerce, Bellevue, Iowa 52031. (319) 872-5830.

Potter's Mill. *(800) 397-0248. Off Hwy. 52 at the south edge of Bellevue, 30 miles south of Dubuque. Summer hours (April-Oct): open daily. Mon-Sat lunch 11-2, dinner 5-9, to 9:30 Fri & Sat. Sun brunch 10-2, dinner 4-8. Nov, Dec, Feb, March: open Wed-Sun only. Jan: open Fri-Sun only. Visa, MC. Full bar.*

Carefully restored gristmill built in 1843 nestles into bluff beneath Bellevue State Park, by a creek. When a lumber company almost bought the historic mill to disassemble it, people who'd grown up in Bellevue bought it and created the restaurant. Country favorites are prepared with care and flair. Dinner favorites: roast pork loin with horseradish jelly ($10), prime rib ($13), char-grilled trout with spiced rice pilaf. Dinners come with relish tray or soup, bread loaf, salad. Recommended for lunch: mandarin chicken salad ($6.50), prime rib sandwich ($6.50), lunch-size roast pork loin ($8). Almost everything is housemade, including salad dressings (honey mustard is a specialty), coleslaw. Bread pudding with caramel sauce, fruit crisps (all $2.50) are standouts. Gifts and antiques in **Millstream Emporium**, lower level.

Mont Rest Victorian House. *(319) 872-4220. In Bellevue, just north of downtown. From U.S. 52, turn up at Spring. House is on Spring at 3rd, with entrance in rear.* 5 rooms share 2 1/2 baths. $55-$84. 4 rooms have river view. Air-conditioned. Big breakfast. Most unusual 1893 house on 9 acres, part-way up the north bluff overlooking the pretty town of Bellevue and the Mississippi. Big wrap-around porch with amazing river view. Back wooded bluff full of wildlife. Butterfly garden. Rooms furnished with antiques. Bicycles for guests include one tandem. 1949 Lincoln picks up guests who come by boat.

Fabulous house and site, bikes for guests.

DYERSVILLE (population 3,800) Farm town with many attractions (see p. 106-109) at

west end of the beautiful Heritage Trail. 26 miles west of Dubuque.

Colonial Inn. *(319) 875-7194. On commercial strip along Hwy. 136 at south edge of Dyersville, 1/4 mile north of U.S. 20.* 31 rooms on 2 floors. $33 (1 bed) to $50 (2 beds). Cable TV, Cinemax. Nearby chain restaurants. Free passes to rec center with saunas, jogging track, exercise machines. Coffee in lobby.

Easy biking to downtown, moderate rates.

DUBUQUE (population 57,000)

Mario's Italian Restaurant. *1298 Main at 13th just north of downtown, 1 block south of Loras. Park on street. (319) 556-9424. Mon-Sat 11-11 (bar open to 2 a.m.), Sun 4-10:30 (bar to 12). Visa, AmEx, MC, Diners. Full bar.*

Locals' favorite gathering place is somewhere back a few decades in time: pine paneling, lots of sports trophies, vinyl booths around long central bar, friendly, direct waitresses. Panzerotti a specialty — a huge, tasty fried turnover stuffed with meat and cheese, with Mario's excellent, light tomato sauce. $4.75 at lunch, $7.45 at dinner, each with salad and bread. Minestrone ($1 a cup, $1.25 a bowl) is good, so is quality of Italian sausage used. One well-traveled local marvels at how good the simple pizza cheese bread is: bite-size squares of pizza dough, baked with olive oil, garlic, salt and pepper. ($2-$4 portions.) A large Mario's Pizza (with everything) feeds four or five for $14. Daily $4.25 lunch specials are non-Italian things like beef stew. With 48 hours' notice, Mario will fix "gourmet dinners" with veal, rabbit, duck, several courses.

Paul's Tavern. *126 Locust between 1st and 2nd, south of downtown. (319) 556-9944. Mon-Sat 6 a.m.-2 a.m. Sun 10 a.m.-midnight. No credit cards. Full bar.*

Simple neighborhood tavern, unchanged inside since 1949, serves an unusual hamburger — broiled on top, fried on the bottom. Many consider it the best in town. The price — $1.25 for a 3-oz. patty — beats the chains. Other sandwiches are combinations of beef, ham, and cheese. Kids are welcome until 9 p.m. Two cases of mounted animals include beaver, deer, pheasant, and a jackalope! Darts, pinball. Next to Schoen's Antiques, also crammed with interesting stuff.

Ryan House. *1375 Locust just south of Loras and north of downtown. Parking lot in rear off Bluff. (319) 556-2733. Reservations advised but may not be necessary. Reserve well ahead for weekends in summer and fall. Open year-round. April-Dec: Mon-Sat 11-2, 5-10. Sun: brunch 10-2, dinner 5-10. Jan-March: no Sat lunch, Sun or Mon dinner. MC, Visa, AmEx, Diners. Full bar.*

Massive Second Empire mansion from 1873 is little altered. Diners eat in original dining room, parlor, enclosed porch, bedrooms. Staff knows the house's history and furnishings; guests are welcome to look around and ask questions. Elegant setting, but blue jeans are OK, and prices quite reasonable. Lunch entrees like stuffed beef tenderloin ($8) include starch, vegetable, salad. Meal-size salads ($5-$6) include house salads with citrus-marinated chicken on spinach. Dinners, which start at $9, include soup or salad, starch, vegetable of the day. Recommended for dinner: sole and salmon roulade poached in mousseline sauce (like hollandaise), $15; three beef tournedos Ryan with asparagus and bernaise sauce, $18. Four-course Sunday brunch ($13) includes lobster bisque, salad, entree, dessert. All chicken is skinless. Broiled fish available. **Hog Ryan's Wine Bar** in cellar opens at 5 Tues-Sat. **Gift shop** with collectibles. Ryan House is a stop on **Victorian Progressive Dinner**, p. 100.

Tollbridge Inn. *At the very end of Rhomberg, beneath Eagle Point Park and above Lock & Dam #11. (319) 556-5566. Tues-Sat 11-2, 5-10. Sun 9-1, 5-10. Major credit cards. Full bar.*

90-seat contemporary restaurant with lots of glass is perched on stone abutment of the toll bridge that was dismantled in 1982. The view of the Mississippi, seen from all tables, is among the very best anywhere. One way overlooks the dam across to the Wisconsin bluffs. The lock and dam is lighted at night in summer. In January and February, eagles can sometimes be seen diving for fish in the open water below the dam. In the other direction are the spires and roofs of old Dubuque on the flats. Menu entrees include 10 seafood, 7 beef, 4 pork, and 3 poultry; nothing is fried. Popular at lunch: tomato stuffed with crab and lobster ($6.25); prime rib sandwich with relish and soup or potato, (also $6.25). Prime rib is cooked fresh daily. Dinner favorites (all include relish tray, soup, salad, starch): prime rib and shrimp scampi ($16), breast of chicken cordon bleu ($11). **Piano bar** or guitarist and vocalist 6 nights/week.

225. *225 West Sixth, a block north of Five Flags Civic Center. Sixth dead-ends at Clock Tower Plaza; enter off Locust, park between 5th and 6th. (319) 556-2725. Reservations requested. Mon-Sat 11-9, Fri & Sat to 10. Visa, MC, Diners, AmEx. Full bar.*

Inventive, French-trained American owner-chef features locally raised food (rabbits, trout, capons, herbs, Iowa beef, terrific Iowa corn & other produce from farmers' market) on eclectic menu whenever possible. Menu changes daily with seasons and produce. Some dinner examples: fresh rabbit with wild mushroom risotto, sweet-sour red onion relish ($14); filet of beef with red Zinfandel sauce, toasted hazelnut butter ($16); spinach pasta with cream sauce of fresh spinach, Gorgonzola cheese, local black walnuts, country bacon ($10). Dinners include bite-size appetizer like rabbit saté, grilled scallops with caviar; salad; sorbet; vegetable; starch; bite-size dessert. Generous lunch portions include bread. Lunch menu changes, too. Some samples: pecan pasta with chicken, red onions, raisins, pasta shells, bourbon-honey mustard ($6); Caesar salad with grilled flank steak ($5.50); smoked cheddar sandwich with charred onion, broiled tomato on cracked wheat bread ($4.25). Vegetarians can eat well here. Contemporary, glass-walled space looks out onto promenade.

Yen Ching. *926 Main between 9th and 10th, at north end of downtown. On-street parking. No problem in evening. (319) 556-2574. Mon-Sat 11-2, 5-9:30. Visa, MC, Disc, AmEx. Full bar.*

Good Chinese food. That's often hard to find in smaller cities and towns. Mostly Mandarin, with some spicy Hunan and Szechuan specialties. Half the menu is seafood. Lunches average $4, dinners family-style are $8.50 (including soup, appetizer, main course). Popular dishes include Princess prawns, seafood delux with Hunan sauce, Three Delights (shrimp, beef, chicken).

Clarion Hotel. *(319) 556-2000. 450 South Main between 4th and 5th, downtown, close to Five Flags Center and Ice Harbor. Adjoining parking garage.* 193 rooms on 5 floors. $69-$135 for king suite with whirlpool, microwave. Cable TV includes pay channel. Restaurant and bar on premises. Small indoor pool with hot tub, sauna, game room, exercise room. Walk to several historic areas.

Large new hotel with excellent downtown location

Hancock House Bed and Breakfast. *(319) 557-8989. 1105 Grove Terrace, just off 12th St. at the top of the bluffs.* 9 rooms with private baths, on 2nd and 3rd floors. $75 (for smaller 3rd-floor rooms) and $95. Whirlpool suites $125 & $150. $10 less in winter. Midweek corporate rates: $50 & $60. 1891 painted Queen Anne house has two turrets, large wraparound porch with spectacular view of the city's roofs and factories and the river beyond. Walking distance to Mansion Row, downtown & Ice Harbor if you like to hike. Contemporary Victorian decor with interesting antiques (owner-innkeepers are dealers). Cheerful, not oppressive. House has 8 fanciful fireplaces, 6 original bathrooms, wonderful dining room murals of an imaginary city and park. Player piano. Full breakfast. Guests have use of several sitting rooms (there's sherry to sip), library, dining room. Complimentary beverages in fridge.

Best view of any lodgings in Dubuque, fabulous late Victorian details

Juniper Hill Farm. *(319) 582-4405. 15325 Budd Road, near Sundown Ski Area.* Bed and breakfast with 3 rooms with private baths. $65 (small room), $85, $125 for suite with Jacuzzi. Full breakfast, afternoon snacks. 2 gathering rooms, TV & smoking in one with fireplace. Outside hot tub. Spectacular views east as far as Platteville. 40-acre nonworking farm on hilltop. Bird-watching, pond fishing, ice skating, hiking, cross-country skiing on premises. Owners live in separate part of large, sunny house.

Country living close to Dubuque, downhill skiing

Mandolin Inn. *(319) 556-0069. 199 Loras at Main in prime area of historic homes.* 4 rooms with private baths $75-$95. 4 rooms share 2 baths, $65. Off-season corporate rates $55. Comfortably elegant, super-solid 1908 brick house with glowing oak woodwork, stair hall with stained-glass window of arts patron St. Cecilia with a mandolin. Furnished mostly with period antiques that suit the house. Guests have use of parlors, dining room with unusual fantasy forest murals, big wrap-around porch. No outside events interfere with guests. Elaborate multi-course breakfasts a trademark. Innkeeper loves to walk, knows city well.

Comfortable elegance, great breakfasts, good for walks

Best Western Midway Hotel. *(319) 557-8000. On U.S. 20 on Dubuque's west (suburban) side, 4 blocks east of regional mall.* 151 rooms, 90 in 4-story section, 60 in 2-story portion around pool. April-Oct: regular rooms $74, otherwise $69. Packages for skiing, gambling, getaways, more. Cable TV, Showtime, in-room VCR with a hundred free movies. Hoffman House restaurant, bar on premises. Coffee in lobby. Picnic tables on 7-acre property. Fax machine, copier. 10,000-square-foot bright, domed recreation area with largest

hotel pool in town, whirlpool, 2 saunas, hot tub, ping pong, billiards.
Big indoor pool, lots of activities, in-room VCR

Redstone Inn. *(319) 582-1894. 504 Bluff at Fifth between downtown Dubuque and Cable Car Square.* A small hotel on 3 floors. 9 rooms are $70-$98/night. 6 whirlpool suites are $120-$175. One of Dubuque's largest and most impressive mansions of the 1890s, full of elaborate woodwork and stained glass. Guests may use parlor. Bar service in dining room. Continental breakfast, afternoon tea. Cable TV, phones in rooms. Inn also used for group meetings, social events, Victorian Progressive Dinner (p. 000).
Small hotel in elaborate mansion, close to downtown and Cable Car Square.

Stout House. *(319) 582-1894. 11th at Locust.* 2 rooms with private baths ($100 weekends), 2 share a bath ($59 and $69), one two-room suite with bath ($148). Midweek rates $10 a room less. Live like the lumber baron who built this house (or the archbishop who followed him) for a day or two in this opulently detailed red sandstone mansion from 1890. Period antiques and some original furnishings play up the grandeur of the carved rosewood reception hall with stained-glass windows. Richly cozy library with green onyx mosaic mantle is available to guests, as is a second-floor lounge with TV and phone. (House may be used for meetings, receptions, too.) Across from public library on Mansion Row. Good location for walks. Full breakfast. Professional innkeepers instead of an owner-innkeeper.
Late Victorian opulence, inside and out

Prairie du Chien and McGregor

Wildlife and ancient Indian cultures, steamboat architecture and Rhine-like scenery come together at these relaxing river towns.

THE MISSISSIPPI RIVER at Prairie du Chien, Wisconsin, and McGregor, Iowa, makes for a wonderfully relaxing, inexpensive weekend getaway. Prairie du Chien is the unpretentious fur-trading center that goes back to Nicholas Perrot's trading post of about 1685. It was strategically located just above the point where the Wisconsin River joins the Mississippi — strategic, that is, as long as water transportation was dominant, up into the time of the Civil War.

Today it is appealingly slow-paced, removed from the vacation crowds around Dodgeville. That makes it quite a find, because Prairie du Chien and McGregor feature the best all-around combination of natural and historic attractions on the Upper Mississippi. The only thing the area lacks is any kind of night life beyond a bowling alley and an active tavern scene with occasional live music. It does have:

◆ spectacular scenery.

◆ two accessible and interestingly different river

Distance from Prairie du Chien

Chicago	230
Minneapolis	211
Madison	105
Milwaukee	182
La Crosse	59
Dubuque	62
Lansing, IA	30
Guttenberg, IA	32
Cassville ferry	42
(closed winters)	
Ferryville, WI	23
Gays Mills, WI	32
Boscobel, WI	29

fronts, on the Mississippi and Wisconsin rivers, with many opportunities for canoeing and boating, fishing and bird-watching.

◆ two thousand years of colorful human history (from Indian burial and effigy mounds to French fur traders, a military fort, and Victorian villa). superbly interpreted at **Effigy Mounds National Monument** and **Villa Louis**.

◆ interesting historic architecture and antiquing in McGregor, Iowa, just across the river from Prairie du Chien.

Extra advantages are the area's low cost, small size, and relative lack of crowds. This is not a densely populated area. Prairie, as it's called, is the region's metropolis, with all of 6,000 people. (It's sometimes pronounced "PRAR-duh-sheen," but never said the French way.)

Marquette and McGregor, picturesque towns just across the river in Iowa, both have under 1,000. It's easy to get around here, unlike many larger river towns, clogged with traffic, whose streets are jammed on the narrow land between bluffs and river. Prairie's own commercial and motel strip beneath the river bluffs is ugly but not numbing. You'll enjoy the area more, however, if you stay away from it.

Tourism is an important industry here, second only to two 3-M plants employing some 600 people. But Prairie also serves as a year-round commercial and service center for an extensive trading area back in the isolated coulees (the regional name for small valleys or hollows) leading into the valleys of the Wisconsin, Kickapoo, and Mississippi rivers. This makes for some better restaurants, with lower prices, than in areas like Spring Green, where restaurants only have the tourist season to earn their money in.

Here there aren't enough commercial blandishments to divert visitors from the powerful and pervasive sense of the beauty of the nearby landscape and wildlife — and a gently remote past. Most everybody fishes; the Upper Mississippi

"Prairie of the Dog"
The name Prairie du Chien is a French translation from its Fox Indian name.

The Wisconsin and Fox rivers
formed the historic water route between the Great Lakes and Upper Mississippi, much used by Indians and voyageurs. Up through the fur-trading era, the confluence of the Wisconsin and Mississippi at Prairie du Chien was akin to a key expressway interchange on today's interstate highway system.

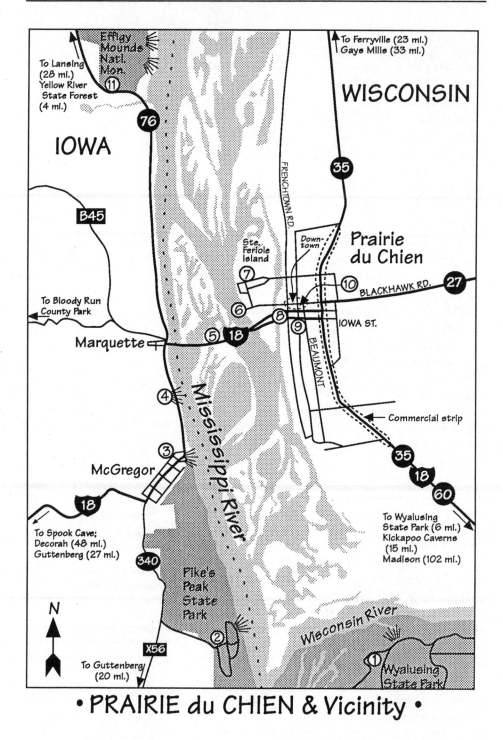

• PRAIRIE du CHIEN & Vicinity •

PRAIRIE du CHIEN MAP NOTES

① **Wyalusing State Park.** One of Wisconsin's top parks. Spectacular blufftop views, great bird-watching, a Mississippi canoe trail, 15 miles of hiking and cross-country ski trails, caves and ravines to explore. Yet it's not crowded. P. 127.

② **Pike's Peak State Park.** Fabulous view of the confluence of the Mississippi and Wisconsin rivers from blufftop picnic area. 12 miles of trails pass Indian mounds, fossils. P. 136.

③ **Downtown McGregor.** Quaint Victorian river town tucked between steep hills. Don't miss 1880s-style outfitter's store, storefront museum with local artist's sand paintings. Several antique shops. Pp. 131-135.

④ **Upper Mississippi National Wildlife & Fish Refuge Visitor Center.** Excellent info source on the river's natural habitats, bird-watching, fishing, boating & more. Only open weekdays. P. 136.

⑤ **Pullover on mid-river island.** Non-boaters seldom have a chance to see islands and backwaters on foot. This pullover lets you do that.

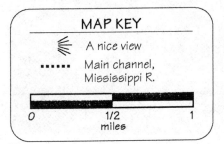

MAP KEY

≋ A nice view

•••••• Main channel, Mississippi R.

0   1/2   1
miles

⑥ **Lawler Park.** Pleasant riverfront picnic spot. Backwater tour on excursion steamer Addie May narrated by former sheriff is a treat. Canoe rental is by bridge to downtown Prairie du Chien.

⑦ **Villa Louis.** Outstanding Victorian estate goes well beyond fancy furniture to act as a window on a lavish way of life and the austere fur-trading era it grew from. Don't miss vivid French fur-trading stories, elaborate billiard room.

⑧ **Wisconsin Welcome Center.** Maps & info on statewide sights. 150 pp. The "Wisc. Auto Tours" book & the state recreation guide are useful free references. Open April through October, 9-5 at least. From June to mid-August, open 8-6 except Sun.

⑨ **Valley Fish.** Get fresh or smoked fish from Mike Valley, a true descendant of the old French-Canadian voyageurs. Recommended: smoked carp. One of the Upper Mississippi's last commercial fishermen. Located at Iowa Street and Prairie.

⑩ **Zach's.** Excellent fresh food, prepared with care. Vegetables stir-fry have crunch. Caesar salad is tops! Outdoor terrace, occasional live music. Downtown on Blackhawk.

⑪ **Effigy Mounds National Monument.** Mysterious, ancient mounds shaped like bears & birds are reached by interpretive trail up to the bluffs. Splendid film exhibits. P. 138.

south of Lake Pepin is quite clean.

All that time spent down by the river seems to slow people down and mellow them out. For generations many people here lived off the river. Amid all this natural bounty, solid Prairie du Chien is the kind of plain, tidy kind of place that favors aluminum siding over meticulous restoration of its old houses. Its people are a blend descended from Bohemian and German farmers, Irish railroad workers, and French-Indian fur traders. The town is 60% Catholic, but far more of an amiable melting pot than the polarized Irish and German Catholics in nearby Dubuque. It's "exceedingly unselfconscious," points out a history-minded transplant. He values Prairie's down-to-earth quality far more than the classier aura of picture-book towns like nearby Galena and Spring Green.

"Rendezvous in Prairie du Chien — a center of trade for 300 years!"

Prairie du Chien's slogan and its big annual event, the Rendezvous, play on its long history as the most important fur-trading center on the

At Villa Louis, layers and layers of early Wisconsin history come together: Mound Builders, fur-traders, the first Fort Crawford, and fortunes made from the developing frontier. Villa Louis's multifaceted tour is outstanding. The grounds and duck pond serve as a local park especially popular with parents and young children. ▼

Upper Mississippi. Here, where two important river highways joined, was a natural place for Indian tribes to meet. The Wisconsin River, though shallow and shoaly, was navigable by canoe. Via the Wisconsin and a short portage at Portage, Wisconsin, 30 miles north of Madison, canoes could reach the Fox River, Lake Michigan, the trading post at Mackinac Island, and, eventually, Montreal — the center of the French fur-trading world and later the British fur-traders' capital as well. The Mississippi led to St. Louis, another important fur-trading market, long in Spanish territory.

Many tribes from a wide area gathered here each spring to trade, to celebrate the end of winter, and to get wives from other tribes. It was natural for later French fur traders to set up permanent trading posts here, too, beginning in the late 17th century. Fur traders continued the spring rendezvous. At the rendezvous, furs were traded and reassembled into new packs for distant markets. Traders emerged from winter outposts, sometimes bringing their metis (mixed-blood) families along, and unwound for a big, rowdy party with lots of drinking.

By 1805, some 20 independent traders were permanently stationed at Prairie du Chien. Gradual consolidation of the fur trade would result in the preeminence of John Jacob Astor's American Fur Company. As lands to the east became over-hunted, Prairie remained an advantageous spot because it was close to still-productive hunting grounds in Iowa and Minnesota, and because it was linked to bigger markets in *two* directions, toward St. Louis as well as Montreal.

The important role of frontier forts in the frontier economy
◆ *Settlers used military roads built to move troops in war. U.S. 18 follows the Military Ridge Road from Prairie du Chien to Milwaukee*
◆ *Supplying forts was the first cash market for early farmers.*
◆ *Military officers were the pre-territorial frontier's only government and law.*
◆ *Supplying Mississippi River forts led to improved river transportation.*

Fort Crawford was one of 5 forts in the Northwest Territory established after the War of 1812 to control frontier trade routes and thereby control Indians. These forts filled the power vacuum left by the departure of British fur traders and military units.

WHEN TO VISIT

Spring: morels, common & uncommon wildflowers in big state parks/forests. Spring bird migrations peak last weekend in April & early May.

Summer: hot, humid continental weather, cooler on river. Swim in Mississippi, swim & tube in Wisconsin River. Great backwater canoeing. Historic sites open May into fall.

Fall: hardwood forests on rugged bluffs and steep valleys make for very good color in this mostly cultivated part of Midwest. Some wetlands add extra verve at color time. Best color is on first two Oct. weekends (reserve rooms early). Late Sept. is also nice. Water-fowl migration peaks early Nov. Most historic sites open through Oct.

Winter: cold, sunny continental weather. Late Jan. & Feb. is the best time to see eagles in open water by dams, power plants. Beautiful hiking, best wildlife viewing. In winter without snow cover is the best time to see Indian mounds. Some cross-country skiing at state parks & forests; snowmobile trail at Yellow River State Forest.

ANNUAL EVENTS

Spring/Fall Arts & Crafts Show. *2-day event, Mem. Day weekend/1st weekend in Oct. Triangle Park in downtown McGregor.* **Prairie Villa Rendezvous.** *Father's Day Weekend (3 days, 2nd weekend in June). At Lawler Park across from Villa Louis. Free. 1-800-732-1673.* Loose reenactment of early 19th-century fur-trading Rendezvous. 2,000 set up tipis & tents, and play traders, frontiersmen, Indians — all doing their thing (Indian fry bread, black-smithing, selling trinkets, weaving, fiddle-playing, etc.). Some 10-20,000 visitors watch. Contests in black powder marksmanship, knife- or tomahawk-throwing, fire-building, etc. Family fun in Prairie. Reserve rooms 6-8 weeks ahead.

McGregor Antique Show. *2nd Sat. July, downtown.* **Victorian Picnic, Villa Louis.** *2nd Sat. in August. All evening. $25; reservation required, limited space. (608) 326-2721.* Festive gastronomic tour of 1890s society: samplings from 60+ desserts, beers, drinks, plus fried catfish, roasts, etc. Carriage rides, lamplight tours. **Echoes of Pocket City.** *2 days, Labor Day weekend.* Old-time melodramas, music in downtown McGregor's Triangle Park. **Carriage Classic, Villa Louis.** *Weekend after Labor Day. 2-day pass: $5/adult, $2 kids 5-12.* Among the largest North American competitive driving events. Stylish carriages (drawn by singles, pairs, 4-in-hands) perform maneuvers, obstacle course.

For complete events info, call the Prairie chamber, (608) 326-8555.

ENTERTAINMENT

Movies: Metro Theater, 203 E. Blackhawk, downtown Prairie du Chien. (608) 326-4541. Showboat Cinema, 710 E. Blackhawk (east of Hwy. 35) in Commerce Mall. (608) 326-4541.
Live music: Thursdays at Zach's, p. 144. **Bingo:** Sundays in McGregor, Thursdays in Prairie du Chien. Inquire locally.

POINTS OF INTEREST

Villa Louis

May-Oct. 9-5 daily. Last tour starts at 3:45. Video introduction starts every half hour. $5/adult, $2 kids 5-12.

On St. Feriole Island west of downtown Prairie du Chien. Take Black Hawk St. (the main retail street, parallel to U.S. 18 but one block north) west across bridge to island. (608) 326-2721.

Layers and layers of history, going back to Indian mounds and early fur-trading days, are piled up on the site of this Victorian country estate, restored to the 1890s. Villa Louis (pronounced "Lou-ee," in the French way) is lavish indeed. But it is not just another Victorian house museum that never gets beyond decorating razzle-dazzle and unreflecting worship of the Victorian era's famously excessive material culture.

A superbly intelligent tour gives visitors a window onto the luxurious lifestyle of a wealthy family which was quite influential in the mid-19th-century development of the Upper Mississippi frontier. The adjacent museum illustrates Prairie du Chien's important role in the long and full history of the Upper Mississippi.

The tour also includes visits to a fine **museum of Prairie du Chien history** and to a recreated **fur-trading post**, where Ginette Teter tells tales of French and Indian fur-trading days, with robust French flair and a genuine Breton accent.

What makes this such a special attraction is a happy combination of things:

◆ a lovely setting on the river. The villa's lawn, with a willow tree and Victorian flower beds, a duck pond and artesian fountain, are a locally popular family park.

◆ the impressive house and outbuildings.

◆ the lucky circumstance that 90% of the furnishings are original household items.

Tips
Villa Louis is best enjoyed in a leisurely fashion. We recommend allowing at least 2 1/2 hours, with a break for a picnic at nearby Lawler Park on the river (see suggestons, p. 133). Come before 1:30 or 2 to see the cook at work in a state-of-the-art Victorian kitchen.

Everyday meals and Victorian holiday celebrations such as this Christmas banquet are replicated with unusual accuracy at Villa Louis, thanks to much surviving documentation. If you take the tour before 2 or 3 p.m., you can see and smell cooking in the kitchen, state-of-the-art for the 1870s.

◆ the wealth of documentation. Letters, records, diaries, even recipes, and 200 photographs provide accurate details and anecdotes.

◆ the site interpreters' emphasis on social history, giving perspective on the lifestyle associated with wealthy capitalists of the late 19th century.

Villa Louis was built by the wealthy Dousman family at the first site of Fort Crawford, the U.S. army fort intended to secure the United States' western frontier. It was relocated to higher, less flood-prone ground in 1829. Hercules Dousman, who had started as a clerk for John Jacob Astor's fur company, grew rich from astute investments. He had built an earlier house on the site, even larger but less grand. To escape floodwaters, both houses were sited on a Hopewell Indian ceremon-

Other outstanding Victorian showplaces interpreted with intelligent perspective:
◆ *the magnificent **Ramsey House** in St. Paul (612-296-0100). Good info on upstairs/downstairs contrasts between lives of the wealthy and their servants.*
◆ *the **David Davis Mansion** in Bloomington, Illinois (309-828-1084; opens late 1992). Unusual focus on servants, their interactions within the house, and elaborate indoor plumbing and central heating systems made possible by the new industrial technology.*

ial mound. In 1870 his widow and son built this house, then very modern — complete with early indoor plumbing and a hot water system.

Dousman had come to run Astor's Prairie du Chien post in 1826. The fur trade was then in its declining years, but Indians from across the Mississippi still brought in enough fur to earn Dousman the beginnings of a large fortune. The old French traders were generally too easygoing and too ignorant of the fast-developing world of steamboats and railroads to amass great fortunes on the fast-changing frontier. Dousman's family, of Pennsylvania German descent, had long been involved in the Mackinac fur trade. Hercules made the most of new business opportunities presented by permanent settlement of the frontier.

His **office**, built in 1855 as a separate building, is furnished austerely, as the hard-working frontier businessman might have had it. Here visitors see how Dousman's fortune grew from $6,000 in 1850 to $75,000 in 1860, thanks to land investments (he bought lots in the original plats of St. Paul, Madison, and Prairie du Chien), lumber mills in Eau Claire, sales of his land to the Milwaukee Railroad, and an interest in a steamboat company.

Visitors encounter a very different lifestyle as they walk into the adjoining 1890s **billiard room**, outfitted by Dousman's son, known to all as Louis (pronounced "Louie," just like the villa). To maintain his position as a gentleman among the newly rich capitalists of Victorian society, Louis was expected not to work but to travel and "to flaunt his wealth and entertain lavishly," we are told. For awhile Louis collected art, when he lived in St. Louis, a better place from which to manage his father's investments. (In 1870, St. Louis was the third-largest American city and the cultural center of the West.) After his mother's death, he returned to Prairie du Chien to develop the family estate into an standardbred horse farm for breeding trotting horses. Drinking from the property's artesian wells would improve race horses, it was assumed.

Exercise clubs,
kept in the billiard room at
Villa Louis, were much
used by active, modern
American girls of the 1890s
to develop upper-arm
strength for newly popular
racquet sports.

The billiard room, with its dark, richly complex decorating scheme of the 1890s, is a real high-light. Its ornate Brunswick three-cushion billiard table is merely the largest of many fascinating original furnishings, including paintings of favorite dogs and horses; mounted hunting trophies; and sports equipment.

The **main house** will not disappoint lovers of Victoriana. It is done up in a slightly more re-laxed, country version of sophisticated St. Louis style in the opulent post-Civil War era. It has 12-foot ceilings, statuary, exotic objets d'art, and a pretty devotional altar for Hercules' widow, Jane, who was a devout Catholic of French and Indian extraction.

In the **kitchen**, an interpreter-cook can be seen preparing meals until 3 o'clock or so. She uses original recipes and vegetables grown from her-itage seeds in the Villa's garden. Outbuildings re-tained from the Dousmans' earlier estate included a **preserve house** that includes the summer kitchen, storage rooms, and outhouse; a laundry and servant's room; and an **ice house** where food and ice were stored.

At this point in the tour, visitors see the site of the original Fort Crawford and go to the interest-ing museum in the Villa's carriage house. This would be a good time to take a **break**, bring out a snack or bag lunch, and eat on a bench by the duck pond — a fine spot to linger and enjoy the quintessentially romantic grounds. (Cold pop is available in the museum.) Then, refreshed, you can return to the interesting **Museum of Prairie du Chien**, able to enjoy the museum's diorama/ vignettes covering 2,000 years of native cultures and several phases of fur-trading and military his-tory under the French, British, and Americans. The **gift shop** here has a fine array of regional books and gifts relating to periods included in the Villa.

Be sure to leave time to enjoy the stories told over the counter in the **fur-trading post**, installed in an old store building from the 1850s. Ginette

The truth behind the Mad Hatter
At the fur-trading post, you'll learn how beaver fur was turned into felt for fashionable high hats like the one the Mad Hatter wore in Alice in Wonder-land, and how the steam and mercury vapors used to release the beaver hairs attacked the central ner-vous systems, causing many hatters' apprentices to go mad in the process.

Frenchwoman Ginette Teter's entertaining and revealing stories about the fur trade and the perils of hatmaking are told in the reconstructed trading post that's part of the Villa Louis complex.

Teter, an earthily vivacious French woman, encourages visitors to feel pelts from animals traded. One obscure but ferocious prey was the fisher — "meaner than a wolverine," Teter says darkly. "So mean . . . he will kill and eat a *porcupine.*"

Best of all, you'll begin to see afresh those poignant, far-away days when Indians first came into contact with French fur-traders and their wondrous goods.

Displays illuminate the rigidly hierarchical fur trade. Merchants in Montreal, Mackinac, and St. Louis were at the top. In the middle were their middle-class representatives like Dousman, who conducted their affairs at distant outposts. At the bottom were the colorful voyageurs reaching out along interior waterways throughout northern North America. The museum indicates the fascinating political complexities introduced by the fur trade — the network of trade extended from Hudson's Bay to the capitals of Europe — and the disastrous long-range social impact of the fur trade on North America's native peoples.

Addie May, Belle of Prairie du Chien

*Season: Mem. Day to mid-Oct., daily except Thurs. Visa, MC. **Sightseeing cruises** (1 1/2 hours): $7 , $4 ages 3-12, senior discounts. June-Aug: Mon-Wed*

"What was the first thing Indians traded for?,"

storyteller Ginette Teter asks. "Blankets! They were warm and they were colorful. Deerskin and fur were boring colors, let's face it. The first time the Indian laid eyes on a beautiful blanket like this, he fell in love with it."

*11, 2, 6:30, Fri & Sat 11 & 2,
Sun 2.* **Dinner buffet** *or*
champagne brunch *(narration
included) Sundays at 10:30 (2
1/2 hours): $21, $12 ages 3-12.
June-Aug: Fri & Sat 6:30, except
at 6 after Aug. 15. Call for fall
schedule.*

On St. Feriole Island at the foot
of Blackhawk (the street the bridge to the island is
on). (608) 326-6065.

A 100-passenger paddlewheeler from 1923
takes you on an interesting narrated tour of the
Mississippi's east and west channels. The Addie
May is thought to be the oldest operating stern-
wheel excursion boat on the Upper Mississippi.
The captain is an experienced native (a retired
Crawford County sheriff, in fact) who loves investi-
gating river history and lore.

Lawler Park

*On the west shore of St. Feriole Island, along the
Mississippi's East Channel. Go west on Black Hawk
to the island. Free.*

This riverfront park, a popular picnic spot, is
located on a levee built as a WPA project in the
1930s. The Delta Queen and Mississippi Queen
dock here on their summer cruises.

The original fur-trading village of Prairie du
Chien and the first Fort Crawford were located
right here along the river on St. Feriole Island.
But because of frequent floods, the town developed away from the river, on higher ground. After
a 1965 flood inundated the entire first floors of
buildings in the area, a relocation program removed all but the most historic buildings. Except
for the buildings of the Villa Louis complex, they
stand empty and boarded up, like historic ghosts.
The city hopes to find a developer to renovate the
stately old hotel, whose main floors sit above the
historic high-water mark.

During Prairie du Chien's brief Civil War boom,

Tips for the Addie May
*Reservations are required
for dinner and brunch.
Casual dress, comfortable
shoes are suggested. Call
ahead; charter bookings
prevail over scheduled
cruises.*

*A lovely day
on St. Feriole Island
and the Missisippi
combines a leisurely visit to
the* **Villa Louis** *complex (p.
121), a snack or* **picnic** *on
the lawn or riverfront park,
and a* **river trip** *on the
Belle of Prairie du Chien
(p. 125). The captain-nar-
rator is the retired sheriff
and a real history buff. His
commentary is a wonderful
introduction to the river.*

*Visit the Villa at 9 a.m.,
in time for the 2 p.m.
sightseeing cruise. Or visit
it after lunch, followed by a
picnic supper and 6:30
cruise.*

A canoe livery
*is on the backwater chan-
nel between St. Feriole
Island and the east bank,
just off Blackhawk.*

St. Feriole Island had been a bustling center of commerce. It had a new warehouse built by the Diamond Jo packet line and a large grain elevator.

The island was a community of its own, with school, firehouse, and stores. By the 20th century, St. Feriole, known as the Fourth Ward or simply "the ward," had become the wrong side of the tracks. It was a colorful place mainly inhabited by commercial fishermen, trappers, and other "river rats." Fishing boats and nets were all around. Shacks were intermingled with old log and timber-frame buildings from fur-trading days and some grand homes of the steamboat era. The long-abandoned hotel was used as a meat-packing house. Taverns flourished here, and elsewhere in Prairie du Chien, in the days of the Iowa blue laws.

Fort Crawford Medical Museum

Open daily, May 1-Oct. 31, 10 a.m.-5 p.m. $2.50/adult, $1 children, $6 family. Ask about combined tickets with Villa Louis.

717 Beaumont Rd. at the foot of Taylor, 6 blocks south of downtown Prairie du Chien and 4-5 blocks south of U.S. 18. (698) 326-6960.

The museum, owned and operated by the State Medical Society of Wisconsin, is in a reconstructed version of the one-story stone Fort Crawford military hospital where military surgeon William Beaumont conducted some of his famous studies on digestion. Displays include some memorabilia of the old fort; a reconstructed pharmacy from the 1890s; "The Transparent Twins," female models showing internal organs and bones; and dioramas from the 1933 World's Fair showing the development of surgery in the 19th and early 20th centuries.

Wyalusing State Park

Open year-round. Wisc. State Park vehicle sticker required. 1-hour sticker: $2. Daily: $4/resident, $6/non-resident. Yearly: $15/$24.

About 6 miles southeast of Prairie du Chien, turn

Fort Crawford, the frontier outpost at Prairie du Chein, was commanded by Zachary Taylor during the Black Hawk War in 1832. The young lieutenant Jefferson Davis met Taylor's daughter here and later married her.

The fort surgeon, Dr. William Beaumont, pioneered understanding the digestive system. Here he continued his famous observations on Alexis St. Martin, whom he had treated at Mackinac Island. A shotgun wound had left a permanent hole in the voyageur's stomach, giving Beaumont a window on how digestion works.

▲ Spectacular views across the twisting backwaters of the Mississippi and Wisconsin rivers are enjoyed from stone overlooks like Point Lookout, WPA projects from the Depression. This vacation photo is from 1940.

west off U.S. 18 onto Co. Rd. C. Entrance is in about 5 miles. (608) 996-2261. For advance camping registration forms or an interesting guide & map, write: 13342 Co. Hwy. C., Bagley, WI 53801.

This big (2,600-acre) blufftop park overlooks the place where the Wisconsin River flows into the Mississippi — the very place where Joliet and Marquette, canoeing from Lake Michigan, first saw the great river. **Point Lookout**, by the **Green Cloud Picnic Area**, offers the best view of the two rivers joining together.

Wyalusing — the name means "home of the warrior" — is one of the gems of Wisconsin's state parks system, yet not that heavily used because Prairie du Chien is farther than others from major population centers.

Hiking and canoeing are outstanding. Varied elevations and terrain make for an exceptional variety of plant and animal life and fine fall color. Fifteen miles of scenic **hiking trails** pass spectacular river views from bluffs 500 feet above the water, secluded ravines and hollows, caves and rock faces of multi-colored sandstone, and veins of chert (flint) used for Indian projectiles.

An excellent interpretive guide and map is available for a marked **canoe trail** on the Mississippi, starting at the boat landing. It involves 3-4 hours of leisurely paddling while making a 6-mile circle, through islands and backwaters and along the main channel a ways. (See p. 6 for more on the rich wildlife of such backwaters.) Ask about summertime midweek **guided canoe tours**, with stops for exploring on land. Canoeists can use sandbars on the Wisconsin and Mississippi for swimming and camping. The **concession stand** at the Wisconsin Ridge Campground handles **canoe rentals** ($3/hour, $15/day).

Wyalusing was established in 1917. Trees planted in its oldest parts are now big and beautiful; in fact, the hardwood forest at Wyalusing is a registered natural landmark. The stone and log park shelters, concession stand, and other buildings built by the Civilian Conservation Corps in the 1930s create that rustic, traditional park atmosphere people like a lot.

Displays at the **nature center** at the Wisconsin Ridge Campground show the area's plants, animals, and geology — how the bluffs and uplands in this unglaciated area were formed by a succession of shallow seas depositing layers of limestone, sandstone, and shale on the of each other. The nature center is open from 9 a.m. to 11 p.m. in summer, and on spring and fall weekends. It overlooks the sandbars and marshes of the Wisconsin River delta. Summer **nature hikes** start here on weekend mornings or afternoons. There's always an early-morning **bird walk**. Call for complete schedule.

Two marked **nature trails**

A swimming beach on the Mississippi is at the Wyalusing Recreation Area, 2 miles south of the park on Highway X. Picnic area, boat landing. Free admission.

Wild turkeys, long extinct in Wisconsin, are making a big comeback with state help. They are increasingly seen in old alfalfa fields and oak ridges, looking for acorns. Corn is grown near the office and cross-country ski trail, and some is left for turkeys.

stand out as excellent introductions to the park's scenic and historic features. The **Sentinel Ridge Nature Trail** (1.6 miles, 3.2 miles round trip) starts at Point Lookout, used by Indian sentries, and goes along a high ridge past effigy and compound mounds. Then it descends to the Mississippi boat landing, where it joins the **Sugar Maple Nature Trail** (a 1.5-mile loop), which also can be started at the Glen Homestead Picnic Area. It passes by the beautiful **Pictured Rock Cave** of colorful striped sandstone, with a small waterfall in front. (This is especially nice in winter.)

Eight other **trails** take hikers through other areas of much natural and historic interest. Hikers can go past the rugged rock faces of bluffs above the Wisconsin, or along a brook in a deep ravine, or along an old trail to the site of a one-time ferry across the Wisconsin to Prairie du Chien.

There are two **groomed cross-country ski trails**: Mississippi Ridge, a 3.5-mile double loop, and Whitetail Meadows, a 3.2-mile double loop.

CAMPING: The **Wisconsin Ridge Campground** has good-sized 74 sites, all under a canopy of mature trees, but with little shrubby buffer between sites; 27 of the sites enjoy spectacular Wisconsin River view, and 32 have electricity. No showers; pit and flush toilets. The 15-year-old **Homestead Campground** has 58 large, grassy sites with more landscape buffering and with showers; trees are still small. Showers, no electricity, pit toilets.

Campgrounds fill up on weekends in summer and color season. It's good to make a reservation a few weeks ahead, but some sites are usually available on Friday afternoons. Half of all sites are reservable, after January 1, by mailing in a form. In winter, some sites are kept open, and water is available at the office.

SPRING WILDFLOWERS abound in ravines on many trails and in wetlands along the canoe trail. The uncommon shooting star covers the Sentinel Ridge Trail and hillside in late April.

FALL COLOR is best in the hardwood forests on the bluffs and ravines, including the two nature trails.

WINTER ACTIVITIES include cross-country skiing and **ice fishing** on Mississippi backwaters for pike, bluegills, and crappies. The **Mississippi Ridge cross-country ski trail** is a 3.5 mile loop to a shelter overlooking the river; skiers are

A paradise for canoeists

The shallow, shoaly Wisconsin River by Wyalusing has the same intriguing backwaters and wonderful sandbars as does the more popular stretch by Spring Green and Sauk City, but without the summer crowds. It's a little wider here, and the current is a little slower. Caution is advised because of dropoffs and undercurrents.

The Mississippi along the canoe trail (p. 129) is maintained with canoeists, not power boaters, in mind. Snags are left wherever they won't interfere with canoeing, to insure a peaceful, slow pace.

Call the area's big canoe livery with shuttle service on the Mississippi, Wisconsin, and Kickapoo: (608) 326-8602.

Sandbars

on both the Mississippi and Wisconsin rivers are much enjoyed for sunning, lounging, and even camping. The scenery is delightful. Both rivers carry heavy sediment loads and can be muddy.

welcome to make fires with fallen wood. Winter hikes are best for seeing wildlife and wild turkeys; tracks can be followed.

Kickapoo Indian Caverns

May 15-Oct. 31. 9 a.m.-last tour at 4:15. $6 adults, $3 kids 5-12.

2 1/2 miles north off Hwy. 60 and the Wisconsin River, 15 miles east of Prairie du Chien and 2 miles west of Wauzeka, Wisc. (608) 875-7723.

The Driftless Region is full of caves; many people mention this one as a favorite. "Carved by an underground river and glistening with onyx," with stalactites and a turquoise room — the brochure makes it sound awfully exotic; in fact, all the caves in the area look pretty much like this. A Native American museum is attached.

McGregor and Marquette, Iowa

Marquette is just across the Mississippi from Prairie du Chien at the west end of the U.S. 18 bridge; McGregor is a mile south along the river on U.S. 18.

Many river towns have ended up turning their backs on the river that created them. An industrial zone separates Dubuque from the Mississippi. Prairie du Chien abandoned its flood-prone riverfront for higher ground. And beautiful Winona lies behind a levee. But at sleepy McGregor and Marquette, just across the U.S.-18 bridge from Prairie du Chien, the river's presence remains visually powerful. Both towns are tucked into coulees (the regional term for narrow valleys, derived from the French word for flow) that run into the Mississippi. "Pocket City" is an old nickname for McGregor, the older and larger town, referring to its narrow site, like a pocket in the hills. It began in 1837 as McGregor's Landing, connected by ferry to Prairie du Chien.

Best picnic spots
- ◆ *Lawler Park on St. Feriole Island.*
- ◆ *Pike's Peak Park in Iowa, overlooking the confluence of the Wisconsin and Mississippi rivers (p. 136).*
- ◆ *benches and picnic tables along the Mississippi's main channel in McGregor and Marquette, especially if a tow with barges is coming.*
- ◆ *Wyalusing State Park (p. 127). The main picnic area by the Wisconsin Ridge Campground enjoys a spectacular view of the Wisconsin and Mississippi.*

Here, right on the Mississippi's main channel, the slow passage of a huge barge train is a visually dramatic event, visible all up and down the main street. At the west end of the river bridge is **Marquette** (population 500). It developed as a rail junction along the Mississippi's west bank. Across from a little park with picnic tables, the barroom of the old railroad hotel attracts workers from all around with its good, incredibly cheap home cooking (see p. 143). Breakfast with excellent home fries and coffee is $2.

McGregor (population 950) is of greater interest to visitors because of its rich mix of mid-19th century architecture and its six or so antique shops. During the Civil War McGregor boomed as a port. Here grain was brought in by riverboat from the new-ly opened wheat-producing regions of Iowa and Minnesota to the west, then ferried across the Mississippi to the rail–head at Prairie du Chien. A mile of warehouses lined McGregor's waterfront; 5,500 people lived here at the war's end. Of its 120 businesses, a fourth were saloons.

In the days of river commerce, showboats and other entertainers stopped here often. Seeing a circus boat here so inspired young Charles and John Ringling, sons of a local harnessmaker, that they and their brothers formed a traveling show headquartered in Baraboo, Wisconsin that eventually grew into Ringling Brothers Barnum & Bailey Circus, "The Greatest Show on Earth."

Grain made the fortune that built McGregor's landmark **Huntting Mansion**, an almost impossibly ornate Queen Anne house. It was built by northeast Iowa grain magnate W. H. Huntting for the princely sum of $49,000 in 1880. To find it, go west on Main to the library, turn right (north), and you'll see it up the hill to your left.

A likeness of McGregor's most elaborate home, the Huntting Mansion, was made in sand by the celebrated Andrew Clemens. He used colored sands from local sandstone bluffs. Several of his works and the tools used in this painstaking craft are at the delightful McGregor Historical Museum (p. 135). ▼

McGregor's grain trade also formed the basis of the famous Diamond Jo steamship lines. Diamond Jo was best known for the passenger steamship cruises developed on the Upper Mississippi to replace grain trade lost when the wheat belt moved way west of McGregor. **Diamond Jo Reynolds' office** was on the ground floor of the elaborately detailed 1880 brick building at the corner of Main and "A," opposite pretty little **Triangle Park**. Terra-cotta tiles with sunflowers flank its big arched windows; a sheaf of wheat embellishes the entrance. The Reynoldses lived in the upper apartment, following a fashion of the era for luxurious in-town living.

With the decline of both river transportation and the railroads that supplanted it, McGregor went to sleep. A lone vestige of its grain-shipping heyday is the big, modern Agri-Grain elevator near the river. The old grain market was held in that area.

Today McGregor, though faded, is probably prettier than in its prime, when warehouses blocked scenic river views. The surrounding steep hillsides, purchased by town founder Alexander McGregor, have become state land managed by Pike's Peak State Park. These extensive public lands have limited any development and preserved the picturesque image of an architecturally rich, old river town wedged between leafy limestone bluffs and the river's complex maze of islands and channels.

In the past two decades, a mall, commercial strip, and Wal-Mart across in Prairie du Chien have pretty much finished off most small-town retailing in McGregor. A half dozen antique and gift shops have helped fill the void. A walk up and down Main Street uncovers numerous interesting small sights, including tiny backyards with limestone outcrops as rear walls, and little rooms with doors chiseled out of the stone. If you park near the library at Fourth Street and walk down Main *toward* the river, you can take a midpoint break in a restaurant downtown or overlooking the river.

For a distinctive picnic, get smoked fish or turtle at **Valley Fish**, *Iowa at Prairie (326-4719) in Prairie du Chien. It's a survivor of the vanishing world of commercial fishing on the Upper Mississippi. Fisherman and master decoy carver Mike Valley is a true descendant of the voyageurs. Smoked carp here is delicious.*

Get rolls and delicious homemade soups and deli sandwiches from the deli case at **Specht's IGA**, *on Beaumont near Black Hawk downtown. Mrs. Koecke fixes simple food from scratch — the roast beef for her sandwiches started the day in the oven, not a portion pack.*

Antique shops are almost all open only from May through October. All are open weekends; most close one day a week, often Tuesday or Wednesday.

◆ the **Huntting Mansion** (see p. 132).

◆ **Aimes and Aitch Ltd.**, *324 Main. Closed Tues. (319) 873-2364.* Unusually nice antique shop, and not overpriced, in a Greek Revival house that's very old for this area. Interesting general line; pen knives, glass bread dishes are two unusual specialties.

◆ **Main Street Mall**, *322 Main. Closed Wed.* Six rooms. Not terribly selective, but interesting.

◆ **River Junction Trade Company.** *312 Main. Call (319) 873-2387 for catalog. Phone orders taken 9-9 Mon-Sat. Retail hours Mon-Sat 9-5, most Sundays in summer.* Step inside the door of this old storefront, and you may feel as if McGregor's backward-looking aura has sucked you into a time warp, circa 1880. Kerosene lamps and utilitarian buckets hang from the ceiling. A varied array of work hats and dressy hats for cowboys, soldiers, railroad workers, and gentlemen dangle from a rope strung across the room. Behind beat-up wood and glass counters, shelves hold neatly folded bib-front shirts and union suits; bolts of calico and solid cotton fabrics; pocket watches and spittoons; Bowie knives and bugles; saddle-bags and high-top shoes. On one wall hang mackinaws and long linen coats, designed to protect the Western businessman's good clothes from the dust of trail and cattle lot.

Nothing is out of character, and yet nothing is old, except for a few posters and display devices. In the back room, women sew dresses and shirts that round out River Junction's inventory.

Reliving the days of the Old West with absolutely authentic accoutrements has been an obsession with owner Jim Boeke ever since he watched Westerns as a kid in Prairie du Chien and took part in its big Rendezvous, a reenactment of Prairie's 300-year-old spring fur-trading event.

▲ **River Junction Trading Company is a startlingly authentic 19th-century dry goods store that sells everything from horsemen's dusters like this to spittoons. petticoats, and period yard goods.**

He started his business in 1973, well ahead of several competitors. "This business is my hobby, my life style, and my only business," he writes in the preface of his handsome catalog. For fun, he and his buddies in the Hole-in-the-Sock Gang ride horses and stage mock gunfights. He encourages new customers to come in and sit down by the Round Oak stove "and jaw about the Old West." But call first; he's often away at trade shows.

◆ **McGregor Historical Museum**, *254 Main. Open Mem. Day-Oct. 15, Tues, Thurs & Sat 2-5 and by appt. during the season. (319) 873-3450. Free; donations appreciated.* This storefront museum has so much interesting stuff, it's like a wonderful community attic and photo album. Three works by McGregor's celebrated **sand artist**, Andrew Clemens, are on display. They are tightly capped bottles of sand which has been arranged in minutely detailed images of natural motifs and local landmarks. Clemens, a deaf mute, made them to earn money. He collected colored sands from bluffs beneath Pike's Peak (p. 137) and used long tools (also on display) to "paint" his pictures. Two more bottles are at the library down the street.

▲ **Riverside bars can be great places to overhear fishing tips and see birds and barges while having a bite to eat. The Riverview Inn is in McGregor. At Sweeney's in Lansing, Iowa, in winter you can watch eagles dive for fish in the unfrozen waters of the nearby power plant outlet.**

Other highlights include a set of miniature furniture made of turkey feathers by a tramp; lots of clothing; 200 interior photos of the spectacular Queen Anne Huntting Mansion (p. 132); and loads of scrapbooks and family albums. Old photos depict the steamboat era, clamming, flood damage, and many aspects of everyday life. When well done, museums like this are a treasure — heartfelt assemblages of that past which people want to remember, run by people who are part of the history themselves. A fine place to spend a rainy afternoon.

Upper Mississippi National Wildlife & Fish Refuge Office/Visitor Center

Open Mon-Fri 8-4:30, year-round. Free.

Highway 18 just north of McGregor, Iowa 52157. Write or call for information and publications: (319) 873-3423.

It's well worth while making your plans to allow for a weekday visit to the small visitor center of the 260-mile refuge. Fine displays cover conservation history and the area's wealth of wildlife. They show how the Corps of Engineers' dam system that creates the Mississippi's nine-foot navigation channel has created three distinct kinds of environments in each pool above each dam.

Many excellent free publications available at the center are listed on p. 15. It's closed on weekends, so here are selected titles, if you need to request them by phone or mail.

Pike's Peak State Park

Free admission. Open year-round; road to overlook is plowed, some campsites are open all winter.

2 miles south of McGregor, Iowa. Take Hwy. 340 south out of McGregor. (319) 873-2341.

The Upper Mississippi has lots of terrific views, but the one from the blufftop **picnic area** here is surely among the very most spectacular. You stand 500 feet above the Mississippi River, which is up to a mile and a half wide at this point. A vast

Antiquing along this part of the Upper Mississippi
is centered in McGregor, Iowa. Pick up a flyer in any of its seven Main Street shops to get listings of nearby shops. But prices are better off the beaten tourist track in places away from the river ike Elkader and Maquoketa, Iowa, not far from Dubuque.

Pike's Peak
gets its name from Lt. Zebulon Pike's 1805 expedition, shortly after the Louisiana Purchase. The next year he ventured up the Arkansas River into the Rockies, whose most famous mountain bears his name. Pike set out up the Mississippi from St. Louis to show the flag; learn about Indians, flora, and fauna; and scout for potential military posts. He marked some trees at this very park, but the fort was eventually built across the river.

panorama stretches out before you: two bridges at Marquette to the left, the great river's main channel below (often accented by a thousand-foot barge train that looks like a toy), and behind it, a map-like tangle of islands, sloughs, and interior lakes, where motorboats and fishermen putter along.

In the distance beneath the bluffs, a silver thread leads to the marshy delta. This is the Wisconsin River. Remarkably little has changed in this river panorama since 1673, except for the boats and some rail lines flanking the river. In that year Louis Joliet was sent by King Louis XIV to explore the extent of the lands where Frenchmen trade for furs, a lucrative business that enriched the French crown. He set out from Lake Michigan along the Fox and Wisconsin rivers. Joliet and his companion, the Jesuit priest Jacques Marquette, picked their way through this convoluted delta and finally emerged at the immense Mississippi, unknown until then by European explorers.

Trails start at the concession stand and parking lot. The boardwalk from the main overlook has railings and easy stairs but is not entirely wheelchair-accessible. **Twelve miles of trails**, relatively easy, follow the contours of hill edges and ridges and pass by four clusters of Indian mounds. Paths are wide enough for **cross-country skiing**, on ungroomed trails. **Pictured Rocks Trail** descends to a steady trickle of a waterfall, past sheer limestone walls rich in fossils. Brachiopods, gastropods, and cephalopods can be seen.

Point Ann (5.5 miles from the concession) offers another splendid view; then the trail winds gradually down to the town of McGregor (6 miles from the concession trailhead). **To climb trails up into the park from McGregor**, take the road along the river and the railroad south behind the grain terminal; the trail starts at the parking lot to the rear of a trailer court.

No logging or settlement ever occurred on some portions of the land that makes up this

Tips for visiting Pike's Peak
Allow at least 15 minutes to take in the view, 1 hour for nearby sights, most of a day to make a round trip of complete trail system between McGregor and park. See p. 133 for picnic ideas.

The colorful layers of sandstone
in the Pictured Rocks at Pike's Peak State Park — mustard, brick red, greens, browns, black, and white — were used by McGregor's celebrated sand painter, Andrew Clemens, to create his remarkably elaborate images in tightly corked bottles. They're on display at the McGregor Museum, p. 135. Today's visitor can enjoy the view with all the amenities: picnic tables and grills, a concession stand, rustic stone shelter and gazebos, a spiffy new playground, and a boardwalk and stairs descending a bit from the main overlook.

park, so it looks much as it did when Indians and fur-traders plied the Mississippi. Some oaks in its oak-hickory forest are probably 200 years old. The park's original acreage was acquired by Andrew McGregor, who founded a town at the site of his ferry in 1837. His heir bequeathed it as a park.

CAMPING: The campground is about 150 yards away from the main overlook; 76 spaces (60 with electricity) are packed into a small area beneath a canopy of oaks and hickories, some very old. There is no landscape buffering between campsites. Rates are $7/night, $9 with electricity; 2-week maximum stay, no reservations. **Showers** from May through October; off-season rates are $2 less.

SEASONAL ATTRACTIONS: Similar to Wyalusing, p. 130. Cross-country skiing: see above.

Spook Cave

Open daily 9-4 May-Oct. to 6 in summer. $5/adults, $2.50 kids 4-12.

Take U.S. 18 west of McGregor, turn at sign. (319) 873-2144.

This limestone cave is toured by boat. No walking is involved! The temperature stays a constant 47 degrees, so jackets are advised on the 40-minute tour. The cave is in a pretty spot on Bloody Run Creek. Cave-goers can use picnic tables. The adjoining **campground** ($6.75-$10.50 a night) offers lake swimming with a sand beach, horseshoes, volleyball, showers and flush toilets, and fishing in a trout stream.

Effigy Mounds National Monument

Trails always open. Visitor Center open year-round except Xmas Day, 8 a.m. to 5 p.m., to 7 p.m. from Mem. to Labor Day. $1 admission, $3 max. per car; 16 and under, 62 and older free. Short film shown every half hour. Ranger-guided tours Mem.-Labor Day.

On Hwy. 76, 3 miles north of Hwy. 18 and the Mississippi River bridge between McGregor and Prairie du Chien. (319) 873-3491. Write: RR1, Box 25A, Harpers Ferry, IA 52146.

Many mysterious, ancient mounds, made by three native American cultures beginning 500 years B.C. or earlier, can still be seen here on bluffs that tower above the Mississippi. The most striking are in the shapes of bears and birds. They give the place a powerful extra dimension, a sense of kinship both with nature and with other unknown peoples beyond our own time and culture.

191 mounds in about two square miles have been protected since 1949 as part of this national monument. The **film** shown in the visitor center provides an outstanding introduction to the mounds, what they may have meant to their builders, and what American settlers in the 19th century thought about them.

Of all the recorded mounds in this section of Iowa, Wisconsin, Illinois, and Minnesota, 80% have been destroyed, mostly during the late 19th century, when the lands along the Upper Mississippi were plowed, logged, and used for towns, ports, and roads. Only the mounds in the most rugged places remain, on steep river bluffs like these or in remote or insect-infested hollows.

Carbon dating has shown that mounds in the National Monument, at the western periphery of the Eastern woodlands, date to around 500 B.C., though many archaeologists think some were built up to 500 years earlier. Little definite is known about any of the three mound-building cultures. Some conical burial mounds are clearly the work

▲ Bears are the most common shape of the effigy mounds built along the Mississippi and Wisconsin rivers about 500 years before Christ, possibly earlier. To be visible in an aerial photograph, these bears were outlined by a 16" band of crushed lime, now invisible. Interesting exhibits at Effigy Mounds National Monument explain what little is known about the moundbuilding cultures.

of the so-called Hopewell culture, centered in the Ohio River valley and celebrated for their finely wrought pottery and decorative copper. Around 650 A.D. that culture for some reason dissolved.

Only along the Upper Mississippi, and in the vicinity of the Wisconsin River extending east through Madison to Lake Michigan, was the Hope–well culture followed by a people who built along-side older mounds. Their new groups of burial mounds were shaped like animals, most often birds and bears.

At the time American farmers and town build-ers were destroying mounds, many inquiring Americans were also fascinated by them. The first project funded by the infant Smithsonian Institu-tion was excavating Hopewell Mounds near Chilli-cothe, Ohio. Many Americans felt that the Indians they knew lacked the discipline required to build such mounds and create the artistic stone pipes and personal ornaments found in them.

They contended there must be a lost race of mound builders responsible for all the glorious achievements of native American cultures, from Peru and Mexico to the mounds of the Mississippi and Ohio valleys. This notion fit in with the wide-spread view that America was a very special land intended by God for some higher purpose. What white Americans couldn't see was that the Indians they observed had already suffered from 200 years of cultural disruption during the fur-trading era, which brought disease and alcoholism, destroyed their self-sufficient economy, made them depen-dent on foreigners for modern trade goods like guns and blankets, and stirred up intertribal wars.

The **exhibits** are well worth a leisurely study. They include:

◆ hands-on nature specimens.

◆ a detailed topographic model showing the mounds in both parts of the national monument.

◆ concise displays on all three mound builder cultures, with parallel artifacts grouped for easy comparison.

Tips for a visit
to Effigy Mounds

◆ *Allow 30-45 minutes for Visitor Center, 1-3 hours for foot trail to mounds. See film, exhibits at Visitor Center one day.*

◆ *Return in early morning to hike to mounds. It's quieter, and you feel more a sense of connectedness to nature and the spirit of the place, free from the dis-tractions of tourism.*

◆ *Mounds are best seen in early spring or in fall after leaves have dropped but be-fore snow cover. The trail to the mounds ascends a steep bluff with four switch-backs.*

◆ how the rhythm of mound builders' lives changed with seasons.

The small **bookstore** sells select books on natural and human history of the area, along with interesting stone pipes and effigy-shaped amulets carved as souvenirs by modern Indian craftsmen. Well-informed **park rangers** can field a huge variety of questions.

Reaching the main mounds themselves up the **blufftop trail** is a steep hike, enough to make you breathe hard unless you're quite fit. But the hike is worth the effort, thanks to interesting interpretive signs about the mounds and plant life along the way. Early morning, when the warm, slanting light casts long shadows on the low forms of the mounds, is the nicest time to come. An extra plus: no noisy sightseers to disturb the peaceful mood. A one-mile round trip to the Great Bear Mound and back would take almost an hour; a side loop would gain a view of the river. Farther spurs (3, 4, and 6 miles round trip) extend to other views and clusters of mounds.

Yellow River State Forest, Paint Creek

Open all year. No charge.

About 7 miles north of Marquette, Iowa, and 5 miles southwest of Harpers Ferry. Watch for signs off Route 76 out of McGregor/Marquette and off Route 364 south of Harpers Ferry. An **info kiosk** *and big color map are at Headquarters/Visitor Center. Most* **trails** *start at the fire tower or headquarters, or along Big Paint Creek east of the bridge. (319) 586-2548. Write: 427 N. First, Harpers Ferry, Iowa 52146.*

The Forestry Division of Iowa's Department of Natural Resources manages 8,000 rugged acres of unglaciated northeast Iowa, primarily for forestry research and timber production, and also for recreation and hunting. Forestry management makes for numerous experimental pine and larch plantations, some logging, and a sawmill on the site. Little and Big Paint Creeks are among Iowa's best **trout streams.**

Recreation is centered in the 4,500-acre Paint Creek Unit. It has **25 miles of hiking trails** and **13 miles of equestrian trails.** Hollows, streams, hillside springs, a fire tower, and fine **scenic overlooks** highlight the trail system. The 45-minute **Evergreen Trail** begins near the fire tower. It passes many conifers planted here on marginal farmland in 1946. Signs identify tree varieties. The more hilly, one-hour **Research Trail** passes experimental plantations of pine and larch from worldwide seed sources. For excellent **fall color,** the **Bluff Trail** (1 leisurely hour, round trip) starts at the Paint Creek bridge and climbs to two scenic overlooks.

About 10 or 12 miles of ungroomed **cross-country ski trails** and 12 miles of **snowmobile trails** are marked in winter. A three-color map, available upon request, shows them and indicates degree of difficulty for skiers.

CAMPING: 176 closely spaced, **primitive campsites** ($5 a day, first-come, first-served) . Pit toilets, fire rings, camper pads, and picnic tables are provided, but water is only at the sawmill and headquarters. Campgrounds typically fill up only on summer holiday weekends. Two **backpackers' camping areas,** reached by foot from designated parking areas, are free and never full. There are also two separate **equestrian campgrounds** (also $5/night).

SEASONAL ATTRACTION. Spring: Woodland wildflowers, hiking, fishing. **Summer:** Fishing, hiking. **Fall:** Excellent fall color, hiking, fishing. **Winter:** Snowmobiling, cross-country skiing.

RESTAURANTS & LODGINGS

GUTTENBERG, Iowa (population 2,400)

Diamond Jo Warehouse. *431 S. River Park Dr. in the center of downtown. (319) 252-2322. Tues-Sat 7 a.m.-2 p.m. and 5-9 (to 9:30 Fri & Sat). Bar open to 2 a.m. Sun brunch 9-2. Winter hours: call to confirm. Visa, MC. Full bar.*

1856 stone warehouse backs on Mississippi, with excellent river views of Dam #10. Eagles diving in Dec. and Jan. are quite a show. (U.S. Grant's father built the warehouse as a leather-purchasing depot; Diamond Jo steamboats used it for decades.) Lots of boaters join local business people, tourists for a casual mood. Decor based on Diamond Jo steamboat history. Breakfasts range from $2 specials to $4.50 steak, potatoes, and eggs. For lunch, salads (chef, seafood, taco, grilled chicken on greens) are $4.50 and under. Sliced ribeye steak sandwich with cheese and mushrooms ($4.25) is popular. Fries come from fresh potatoes. Varied dinner menu features fresh fried catfish and broiled fresh trout ($11), rack of pork ribs ($10), much-praised baby beef liver ($7), beer boiled shrimp. Friday-night fish buffet is $7 or so, Saturday-night prime rib is $9-$13. Dinners include potato, salad bar, soup, roll. Saturday dancing to a DJ or band starts at 9. Video games, darts, pool, golf machine, fussball.

MARQUETTE, Iowa (population 525). Iowa sales tax is 5%.

Marquette Bar & Cafe. *Just north of the bridge across from the park by the tracks in downtown Marquette. (319) 873-9663. Open Mon-Fri 6 a.m.-9 p.m., Sat 7 a.m.-9 p.m., Sun 8 a.m.-9 p.m. bar stays open to 2 a.m. No credit cards. Out-of-town checks OK. Full bar.*

This extremely unpretentious place is in the old railroad hotel of this once-bustling railroad town. Back room looks out onto Mississippi's main channel. Big portions of good, cheap food draw workers from across the river. All potatoes except french fries are prepared from scratch. At breakfast, scrambled eggs, toast, and a big serving of American fries are $1.55. Weekday lunch specials (under $3) may include roast beef dinner, oven-fried chicken, roast pork & dressing. Half-pound burger is $2 with fries. Dinner favorites include pork chops, shrimp, and, at the top of the menu at $6.75, ribeye steak. Pool tables, video games.

Frontier Motel. *(319) 873-3497. Just south of the bridge on U.S. 18, within walking distance of Captain's Reef restaurant, downtown Marquette and its park.* 20 rooms on 2 floors. May-Oct. $52-62. Nov-April: negotiable. Large rooms, all overlooking Mississippi's main channel. Coffee in rooms. Cable, HBO. Many helpful informational publications, other books on local subjects in office/lobby. Owners are longtime local residents who know a lot about the area. Marina across the road. Recommended by AAA. Up-close look at barges.
Very pleasant motel with small outdoor pool across road from river

Mississippi Inn. *(319) 873-3477. On U.S. 18 just south of bridge and the Captain's Reef Restaurant.* 21 rooms on 3 floors. Open April-Oct. only. 2 people $68, 4 people $80. Cable TV. Coffee, continental breakfast in lobby. Motel sits part-way up the bluff for dramatic views up and down the valley. The site is so intriguing, the parking lot bristles with signs warning non-guests to stay away.
Spectacular river views from all rooms, each with balcony

McGREGOR (population 950). Iowa sales tax is 5%.

Red Cedar Inn. *1118 West Main (U.S. 18) on the west edge of McGregor. (319) 873-3844. Tues-Sat 5-10, Sun 11-2. No credit cards; out-of-town checks accepted. Full bar.*

In the area this casual, full-service restaurant is famous for its 15-foot salad bar of mostly housemade dishes and desserts and its bread table with 20 kinds of bread made on the premises. It comes with all dinners or is $4.75 alone ($3.75 for children). Saturdays and Sundays there's also a $10 buffet with prime rib, smoked ham, a chicken and a fish dish, and the salad, bread, and dessert selections. The weekday menu includes steaks, chops, BBQ ribs, and fish (all with salad bar), at prices from $6.75 for half a chicken to $13 for shrimp. Sandwiches are also served. Many heart-healthy selections are offered as specials — for instance, herb-broiled cod and skinless chicken breasts in honey-mustard sauce with oven-roasted potatoes and fresh broccoli. Health-conscious diners may always request broiled fish or chicken breasts with white wine and herbs. Video games and pinball.

Riverview Inn. *On U.S. 18/Main Street at the north end of downtown McGregor. (319) 873-9667. May-Oct: Mon-Thurs 5 a.m.-9 p.m., Fri & Sat to 10 p.m., Sun 7 a.m.-8 p.m. Nov-April: Mon-Thurs 5 a.m.-8 p.m., Fri & Sat 5 a.m.-9 p.m., Sun 7 a.m.-3 p.m. Bar stays open later. No credit cards; out-of-town checks OK. Full bar.*

This simple, locally popular spot on the river is as much of a diner as a bar; it opens early for fishermen. Breakfasts run $2 for eggs and bacon or potatoes. For lunch and dinner, there's spaghetti with meat sauce ($3.25 and $5.25 portions), and deep-fried catfish or cod ($6), plus hamburgers and steaks. Meals include salad, garlic bread, and usually a potato. Good-size windows look out on the main channel. Pool table, video games.

White Springs Supper Club. *On U.S. 18 1 1/2 miles west of McGregor. (319) 873-9642. Mon-Sat 12-12, Sun 4-10. No credit cards; cash or traveler's checks only. Full bar.*

Ethel's old-fashioned barbeque ribs ($7 a dinner), cooked over hickory, are the big drawing card here, along with prices that seem stuck somewhere back in time, like the utterly plain non-decor. Also on the menu: fried chicken ($4.50), "from fresh," Ethel says, the pond-raised catfish ($5), fresh bullhead ($5), chicken gizzards, lobster tail ($19). Prices include coffee, potato, salad, and a relish tray. Sandwiches are available any time; a good-size burger is $1.25. A brewery used to be on this site; the lagering caves are out back.

Holiday Shores Motel. *(319) 873-3449. At the foot of Main St. on the Mississippi in downtown McGregor.* 33 rooms on 3 floors, all with river views. $38 (1 bed), $45 (2 beds), $75 (best views). Cable TV. Riverview Inn restaurant next door. 18' x 36' indoor pool, plus a small hot pool. Modernistic 1960s styling. Trails up bluffs to Pike's Peak State Park begin nearby.

Enjoys river views, handy in-town location, indoor pool

RiverTown Inn. *(319) 873-2385. 424 Main, two blocks from downtown McGregor.* Homestay bed and breakfast. 2 rooms with private baths, $60 & $65; 2 rooms share 1 bath, $50 & $55. Handsome large home with Prairie Style interior details, leaded glass. Guest rooms furnished with wicker and oak, downstairs an attractive mix of antiques and contemporary. Guests can use living room with TV, small upstairs deck, large front porch, back yard with medium-size pool and views of wooded bluffs. Continental breakfast.

Beautiful large home in town with backyard pool

PRAIRIE du CHIEN (population 6,000)

5 1/2% room tax plus 5% Wisconsin sales tax. Book for summer weekends a month in advance, even earlier for fall color season.

Zach's. *106 S. Beaumont at Blackhawk. (608) 326-4848. Mon 11 a.m.-2 p.m. only. Tues-Sat 11-2, 5-10. Sun 10:30-2 and (May-Oct only) 5-10. Visa, MC. Full bar.*

Separate bar area, outdoor patio. Fine but not stuffy dining with attention to details. Superior ingredients make simple chicken or shrimp stir-fries shine: $5 at lunch, at dinner $4.75 (half portion) and $6.75. Dinners include your choice of 2 from 14 items: salad, rice, baked onion, potato, some unusual vegetables. Dinner entrees range from $6 grilled chicken breast to $14 steak au poivre with cognac sauce. Also: Alaskan salmon filet ($10), blackened Cajun catfish ($9.25). For lunch: 1/3 lb. burger on fresh Kaiser roll with fries ($3.50 and up). Caesar salad a specialty. Thursday nights in season: **music** (country, rock) **on the patio.**

Best Western Quiet House. *(608) 326-4777. (800) 528-1234 (Best Western reservations). On U.S. 18/Hwy. 35/60 strip about a mile south of Blackhawk, across from Wal-Mart.* 42 rooms on 2 floors. Regular rooms with 2 queen-size beds, 1 sofa-sleeper, table and chairs, $79. Executive suites with 1 queen-size bed, sofa sleeper $62. Specially decorated theme rooms — riverboat, fur trader, Villa Louis — and whirlpool suites $83-$120. Cable TV, Showtime. Can rent VCR, movies. Indoor pool big enough for laps. Fitness equipment. Video games. Attractive lobby with fireplace, game tables, free coffee, continental breakfast. Some rooms have views of bluffs away from busy commercial strip. Walking routes on residential roads toward bluffs.

Beautifully decorated; indoor pool, many amenities

Bridgeport Inn. *(608) 326-6082. On U.S. 18/Hwy. 35 at south edge of Prairie du Chien strip.* 50 rooms on 2 floors. $58 king single, $62 queen double, $86 king whirlpool. Nov-April discount: 10% for 1 night, $15 for each of 2 nights. Cable TV, HBO. 24-hour coffee in lobby. Continental breakfast with cereal. Indoor pool big enough for laps with adjacent sun deck, patio. Next to Jeffers Black Angus. Newest motel in Prairie.

Indoor pool, continental breakfast

Brisbois Inn. *(608) 326-8404. Reservations: (800) 356-5850. On Hwy. 35 North, about 4 blocks north of Blackhawk. Across from Design House; look for beaver on sign.* 45 rooms on 2 floors. May-Oct: $34 (1 bed), $49 (2 beds), $59 (2 king-size beds). Off-season: $31, $44, $44. Cable TV, HBO. In-room coffee. On commercial strip but walking distance to downtown, neighborhoods. Cafe next door. Outdoor pool big enough for laps. Swing set. AAA recommended.

Outdoor pool, attractive rates

Winona, Minnesota

An old Mississippi River town offers scenic beauty, good food, excellent bird-watching, and great architectural charm.

THIS GRACIOUS OLD CITY is built between dramatic 500-foot limestone bluffs and the Mississippi River, at a point where the river is a ropy maze of channels and islands. Winona offers a combination that's unique among the river towns of the Upper Mississippi: outstanding **historic architecture** and **natural areas**, *plus* urban conveniences, good food, and **cultural events** sponsored by St. Mary's College and Winona State University.

You can actually do without a car here, for a relaxing, exercise-oriented vacation. Everything is easily reachable by foot, bike, or canoe. Easy side trips by car or bike explore interesting small towns, Mississippi locks, the Trempealeau National Wildlife Refuge, and blufftop parks with spectacular views across the winding river channels and valleys.

A car-free holiday by bike and train

Winona is two hours from the Twin Cities and 5 hours from Chicago, virtually all by interstate. It is almost unique in being easy to get to by train, and you can bring your bike along. The reservations-only **Amtrak Empire Builder** leaves Chicago's Union Station at 3:15 p.m. and Milwaukee at 4:51, arriving in Winona at 9:18 p.m. The east bound trainaves the Twin Cities at 7:10, arriving in Winona at 9:27. Both feature a full-service dining car, observation lounge with floor-to-ceiling windows, and on-train movies. A boon to bicyclists: a baggage car. You can take your bike for $5 extra each way. Bikes and cars can also be rented in Winona and on nearby bike trails.

Winona motels are favorites with bicyclists; two extensive bike trails on former railroad beds are

Distance from Winona
327 miles to Chicago
123 miles to Minneapolis
182 miles to Madison
259 miles to Milwaukee
151 miles to Dubuque
29 miles to La Crosse
16 miles to Trempealeau
17 miles to Galesville, WI

For a visitor packet or questions
call the Winona Area Visitors' Bureau, (507) 452-2272, or write Box 870, Winona, MN 55987.

not far away. The delightful 22-mile **Great River Trail** begins in nearby Trempealeau, Wisconsin, 16 miles from Winona by car or an easy bike ride with moderate traffic. The scenic 35-mile **Root River Trail** through Lanesboro, Minnesota is 45 minutes away by car. You can bike there in a day of moderately challenging bicycling and reserve a room in one of several area bed and breakfasts.

Bird-watching around here is outstanding. Finding good spots is made easy with an excellent color brochure and map outlining eight tours, six within easy biking (or hiking) range of town. A YMCA and a YWCA offer daily passes to fine co-ed indoor **sports facilities**. They're handy to an attractively restored downtown hotel with terrific, moderately priced food. **Movies** are a block away. An Olympic-size pool and 208-foot **water slide** is a mile ride away, and eminently affordable. A bed and breakfast by Winona State University provides bikes at no extra charge.

Winona's architecture is mainly from the decades around 1900, and much of it is splendid. Many fortunes were made here in wheat, lumber, banking, Watkins extracts, and other products. Local wealth is reflected in elaborate municipal, commercial, and religious buildings of the late 19th and early 20th centuries. Architecture fans would want to visit Winona for three remarkable Prairie School buildings alone — two banks and the Watkins Company headquarters. A more modest charm is revealed in walks through the eastside neighborhood settled by Kashubian Poles, who came to work in booming lumber and flour mills of the 1880s. Delightful tableaus of yard art and stops at a corner bakery and antique shop enliven an expedition to this area.

Beautiful **Lake Winona** (once the main channel of the Mississippi) separates the city from the traffic of U.S. 61, which hugs

Two indoor sports centers right downtown
The **YMCA**, 207 Winona Street, has an **Olympic pool, youth center** with video games & ping-pong, weekday child care, running track, fitness center, gym. $3/day adults, kids less. Racquetball extra. (507) 454-1520. The **YWCA**, 223 Center, has a warmer pool, women's gym, and indoor tennis ($32/hour). $5/day guest pass. (507) 454-4345.

The Wisconsin bank of the Mississippi offers close-up looks at two locks and dams; two state parks; small pretty towns; a regionally popular restaurant; a live music venue that brings back the counterculture of the 1960s-1970s, and ▼ an interpretive drive through a national wildlife refuge. See Trempealeau chapter, pp. 184-205.

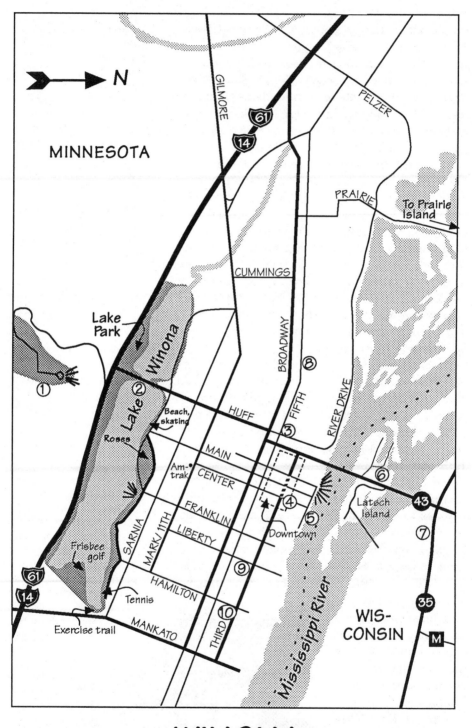

• WINONA •

Winona Map Notes

① **Garvin Heights Park.** Fabulous view looks down across Lake Winona & the city's steeples & big grain elevators to the Mississippi's twisting backwaters and the Wisconsin bluffs beyond.

② **Lake Park and Info Center.** Retirees staff this delightful & helpful visitor center (p. 151). Nifty displays show off local products: Winona and St. Croix sweaters, Peerless chains, Watkins spices, stained glass, sheet music, canoes. Park paths around both lakes (6 miles in all) have beautiful views of Sugar Loaf (illuminated at night). Frisbee golf, rose gardens, beach at park. P. 172.

③ **A walk through Victorian Winona.** Winona families with fortunes from steamboating, land, lumber, and wheat competed in the 1800s with these unusually ornate homes. Start at Huff House with Moorish lattice porch.

④ **Downtown and Merchants National Bank.** Spectacular 1912 bank highlights a stroll along architecturally rich Third St. The bank is a subtle masterpiece, with big stained-glass windows, Arts & Crafts murals.

KEY

. . - - Main channel, Mississippi R.

A fine view

0   1/2 mile   1

⑤ **Jollie Ollie river cruises.** Harbor cruise offers a rare chance to observe up-close the workings of a commercial harbor, where barges are loaded and unloaded. Evening cruises to Ed Sullivan's restaurant in Trempealeau combine good food, sunset views of river and Trempealeau Mountain.

⑥ **Houseboat community.** Last permanent boat colony remaining on the Upper Mississippi has a funky, improvised aura. Jacques Cousteau considered it Winona's most interesting sight. Some boats are crude floating shacks, others charming, with upper stories, deck gardens.

⑦ **Still more on the Wisconsin side.** Herb farm (p. 195), river wildlife refuge with interior trail & drives (p. 192), 22-mile bike trail with great bird-watching (p. 197), Perrot State Park with canoe trail and beautiful blufftop hiking trails through uncommon goat prairies (p.189), good food and good music at the Mill Road Cafe (mostly folk; p. 204) and Trempealeau Hotel (more rock and blues, p. 205).

⑧ **Winona Aquatic Center.** Unlimited use of 208-foot water slide for $1.25 a kid. Wading pool with mushroom waterfall a hit with kids. Lap lanes in Olympic pool for serious swimmers.

⑨ **Watkins Administration Building.** Grand 1911 headquarters of nationally famous door-to-door peddling firm. Inside: old Watkins peddler's wagon, Tiffany art glass dome and romantic landscapes. Buy current Watkins products at outlet prices.

⑩ **Church of St. Stanislaus.** Saints perch atop all the many towers of this splendid Polish church. It looks like a cathedral, glimpsed from all over the east side. Open weekdays for a peek inside.

500-foot limestone bluffs. The bluffs, with Sugar Loaf Mountain their focal point, form a dramatic background for lake and town. Having such clear-cut edges at the river and bluffs is part of what makes Winona so pretty and serene, compared with the traffic-clogged sprawl of cities like La Crosse to the south 5.25-mile jogging and bike path and pretty **city park** surrounds the lake, with picnic facilities, a rose garden, exercise trail, Frisbee golf course, and bandstand. A delightful visitor **information center** and concession stand is on the dike crossing Lake Winona into town. It is a logical first stop for visitors. The retirees who staff it make it a wonderful place to come for suggestions on where to go, and for explanations of how things came to be.

▲ **Sugar Loaf Mountain is Winona's signature landmark, illuminated at night. It is actually a man-made formation — what remained of a natural limestone dome after quarrymen in 1887 were prevailed upon to stop their destruction of a beloved natural feature.**

Wealth from wheat, lumber, and transportation

The river town that is so settled and shady today began as an unusually large Mississippi River sandbar on a treeless plain. Minnesota was still a wilderness in 1851, when a steamboat captain founded Winona, intending that its settlers would supply his fuel. Steamboats consumed immense quantities of cordwood. Though the townsite had no trees, it was a good landing for steamboats, and logs could be floated down the river to it.

In the 1850s Winona was the southernmost port in the rapidly developing Minnesota Territory. Soon it became the jumping-off place for new settlers arriving by the boatload. Winona was the last place they could buy supplies before striking inland. Grocers and outfitters prospered.

Wheat was always the first cash crop on the westward-advancing frontier. Winona shipped Minnesota grain to downriver markets, and soon milled it, too. The second railroad constructed in Minnesota struck west from Winona. Winona became the "Gate City of the Northern Plains." Here raw materials were shipped from the hinterland

Amtrak's
Empire Builder
leaves Chicago's Union Station at 3:15 p.m. and arrives in Winona at 9:18 p.m. The views of the Wisconsin Dells are memorable. Summer round-trip rates $87-$116, depending on how early you reserve space. Children 2-15 get half fare. (Call (800) USA-RAIL to confirm current schedule and fares.)

Take your bike
on the train
It's a simple matter to check bikes in a bike box ($5 extra; advance arrangements required). Turn the handlebars with an Allen wrench to fit the box; check in at least 40 minutes early.

and manufactured goods were distributed to the frontier. Logs cut in the pineries of the Chippewa and St. Croix valleys were floated down to Winona to be milled. Sawdust from lumber fueled the flour mills. Lumber was shipped west to build houses on the treeless plains.

By 1856 1,300 steamboats a year docked at the still-raw frontier town. Here, as everywhere in the Middle West, the Civil War stimulated transportation, agriculture, and industrial development. Between 1870 and 1900, Winona was a major U.S. lumber producer. When grain shipments peaked in 1875, Winona was the fourth-largest U.S. grain market. As one industry faltered, wealth was invested in others: dairying, meat-packing, sauerkraut, hay and clover seed, straw insulation, heavy farm wagons, gloves, pails, and all the usual products of diversified turn-of-the-century cities before industries consolidated into large national corporations. Winona made carriages, cigars, sashes and doors, beer, harnesses, and much more.

Winona liked to boast that it had more millionaires than any other city of its size at the turn of the century. Bankers, grocers, land developers, lumbermen, and other entrepreneurs — usually of New England or German stock — competed in

The heyday of lumbering on the Upper Mississippi was at the turn of the century. Steamboats like this pushed vast floating log rafts, cut in northwoods pineries, to be milled into lumber, doors, and sashes at Winona and Dubuque. Many of those cities' churches, elaborate homes, and public buildings were built with lumber money. ▼

building their residences and businesses stylishly.

Two homegrown institutions from Winona's glory days retain an important presence today. **Winona State University** was the first teachers' college west of the Mississippi, founded in 1858. The fabulously successful **Watkins Products** direct-sales firm was launched by a liniment cooked up on J. R. Watkins' kitchen stove and sold from a peddler's wagon. He moved from the country to town in 1885. Watkins soon became as well known as Avon is today. By 1912 the Watkins offices and plants assumed palatial proportions.

A diversified economy in graceful equilibrium

Since its boom times in the late 19th century, Winona has enjoyed far more stability than most American cities. It declined as a trade center after the steamboat and railroad eras, but the slack was taken up by growth of its colleges and by a manufacturing base that has remained unusually diversified. Ten manufacturing firms employing from 200

By standards of today's metropolises, places like Winona with populations of 15,000 to 25,000 are seen as small towns. In fact, Winona was quite an urban place by 1906, as the streetcars and four-story buildings in this photo show. ▼

to 450 have plants and often headquarters here.

Hemmed in by encircling bluffs, Winona is a mile wide and five miles long, with no room for growth. By 1900, in the last prosperous years of the lumber era, Winona had nearly 20,000 residents. Today it has only 5,000 more. (Its only suburb, Goodview, has another 2,800.)

At a time when the American clothing industry is vanishing, Winona has *two* sweater factories, medium-priced Winona Knitting Mills (385 employees) and Knitcraft (215), manufacturers of upscale St. Croix sweaters, starting at over $100. Other local specialties include plastics composites, printing all the sheet music for Hal Leonard, the leading publisher of school sheet music, and manufacturing stained glass. Hauser Art Glass, the biggest U.S. manufacturer of stained glass, is headquartered here. Its former employees are responsible for starting six other studios in town.

It takes a delicate balance of economic forces to create livable cities, without wrenching booms or busts. Winona has managed to come out on the bright side. There's not so much money or land here to propel massive suburban reorientation, but enough money and economic growth to maintain what's here and build a little, too.

Winona's ethnic and economic mix has helped create an easygoing atmosphere where people seem able to respect differences. It's the only town on the Upper Mississippi that still tolerates a permanent, year-round **houseboat colony** — over 100 floating shacks and cottages. Jacques Cousteau found these boat people the most fascinating aspect of Winona when the *Calypso* visited town. Here on the banks of the Mississippi a colorful collection of independent types — carpenters, fishermen, day laborers, and various river rats — live on the shady backwaters of Latsch Island across the main channel from town. (See p. 163.) They have organized a tight little informal, self-governed community to take care of trash, sewage, and other potential problems that might make local government decide to get rid of them.

A nice ethnic mix
Because most river towns haven't grown much in the 20th century, they can become ossified and insular. Winona is proud of its mellow diversity. Its lumber mills advertised in New York and abroad for immigrant labor.

By 1880, 29% of the population was first- or second-generation German, 11% Polish (both dominated the east end), 9% Irish (largely railroad workers living on the west end), 4% Norwegian, and 4% Bohemian.

WHEN TO VISIT

Winter: excellent cross-country skiing at St. Mary's, state parks in Minn. & Wisc. Skating at Lake Park. College-sponsored plays & music. Cold, mostly sunny continental climate, usually good snow cover. Active snowmobile clubs have created many miles of interlinked trails.

Spring: Bird migrations begin in March. Eagles, swans, waterfowl mid-March thru mid-April, warblers from late April thru May. Spring bulbs come up in later April, gardens pop in May. Woodland wildflowers on state park trails. Most historic sites, Jollie Ollie cruises open May 1. Nice for bicycling. canoeing.

Summer: ideal for canoeing, swimming, river activities. August often muggy. Wed. band concerts, rose garden in Lake Park. Herb farm. Water slide at Aquatic Center. Upland prairies bloom. Outdoor rock, blues at Trempealeau Hotel. Bird-watching highlights: orioles, woodpeckers, bluebirds, herons, egrets, other wading birds.

Fall: wonderful color on forested bluffs, not so crowded as Galena and vicinity. College events in full swing. Fall bird migration begins in mid-Sept., ends with eagles, swans in early to mid-Nov.

ANNUAL EVENTS

Winter Carnival: 3 days of races, ice sculpture, softball, golf, etc. in late Jan. or early Feb. **Steamboat Days:** Week before July 4. Parades, contests, carnival, fireworks at Lake Park. **Windom Park Jazz Festival:** last weekend of July at Windom Park. Outdoor jazz, food. **Victorian Fair:** sometime in late Sept. or early Oct. Old-time crafts & music, food & festivities. **Victorian Christmas:** 1st Sun. in Dec. Homes tour, holiday activities. *For more info,* call (507) 454-1724.

ENTERTAINMENT

Movies in downtown Winona at the Excellence Cine-Four, 70 W. 2nd. $5 adults, $3 kids and seniors, $3 weekend afternoon matinees. (507) 452-4172. **Summer band concerts:** Wed. evenings at Lake Park Band Shell, mid-June-mid-August. **THEATER: Winona Community Theater.** (507) 454-1202. **Commonweal Theatre Co.** in Lanesboro MN. Professional nonprofit summer theater. Each 3-play season includes a musical, Shakespeare, and a contemporary playwright. (507) 467-2525. **THEATER, DANCE, MUSIC. St. Mary's College.** Full season of touring classical music, dance, opera, children's theater, musicals and drama. Jazz & other concerts by music department. (507) 457-1715. **Winona State University.** (507) 457-5235. **T. B. Sheldon Auditorium** in Red Wing MN, a beautiful hour's drive up the Mississippi. (612) 388-8877. **Pumphouse Regional Arts Center,** half an hour's drive south in La Crosse. (The Minnesota side is the prettier route.) (608) 785-1434.

LIVE WEEKEND MUSIC: Leading regional & national folk acts at **Mill Road Cafe,** Galesville, WI. Sometimes in midweek, too. (608) 582-4438. Blues, rock, jazz by well-known performers at **Trempealeau Hotel,** Trempealeau, WI (608) 534-6898. Check at Bluff Country Co-op for music schedule of **Alive & Well Music Coffeehouse** in Lanesboro, MN (closed for winter, no phone). Folk, bluegrass, blues, jazz.

POINTS OF INTEREST

Downtown Winona

Third Street is the main commercial street, Second is more oriented to services and warehouses. Major public buildings are clustered between Third and Fifth, from Winona to Center. Handiest parking: lots off Center near Third, reachable by taking Second or Fourth to Center. Most stores open Mon-Sat 10-5, Sun 12-4.

A leisurely walk on Third, east from the courthouse to Center and back on Fourth, offers lots of visual delights if you look up at upper windows and rooflines. Elaborate pressed-metal cornices, pressed brick and stone detailing, bay windows, towers, and turrets abound.

◆ **The Winona County Courthouse**, *Third and Washington. Open business hours Mon-Fri.* (1888) A massive stone castle in the Romanesque Revival style of H. H. Richardson. Built during Winona's flushest days as a lumber mill town and shipping center, it stands out in its vivid use of contrasting colors and patterns of stone. Though the interior has been remodeled, the original woodwork and stained glass inside are still well worth a look.

◆ **Country Comfort Antiques**, *79 W. Third at Main. Mon-Sat 10-5, Sun 12-4.* *(507) 452-7044.*

Winona County's Romanesque Revival courthouse from 1888 shows the level of elaborate architectural detail that went into local public buildings.

Country Comfort has built a regional reputation with choice items, mostly 18th- and 19th-century but with some 20th-century objects, and old and rare books. Now, joined by a few fairly select dealers, it has expanded into a 6,000-square-foot space in an attractive old building. Furniture comprises 80% of its stock, especially strong in country primitives and elaborate Victorian furniture acquired from estates of old Winona families.

◆ **Statue and fountain of Princess Wenonah.** *On Plaza Square, Third at Center.* Romantic 1901 statue of Winona's namesake, the stereotypical Indian maiden who jumped off a cliff when her father, a chief, forbade her marriage to her true love. At least that's the oft-repeated legend, concocted for the benefit of sentimental Victorians.

◆ **The Levee Plaza pedestrian mall,** *along Third from Lafayette to Main.* Along with the small **Plaza Square** mall, on Third between Main and Center, and the four-screen movie theater, turning the main business blocks into a pedestrians-only mall was part of a 1977 effort to revitalize downtown. Urban renewal appealed even to cities as placid as Winona, untroubled by waves of 20th-century industrial booms and busts.

In retrospect, the low, modern buildings here already look dated. They're out of character with the impressive, richly detailed downtown streetscape of three- and four-story buildings from the 1880s and 1890s. But the mall's tables and benches are a nice place to sit, eat, and take in the wonderful old architecture — at least until 1993, when the mall is taken out and opened to vehicular traffic. **The Bun Barn** (inside Plaza Square) has takeout sandwiches, salad fixings, and baked goods. Also worth checking out in Plaza Square are attractive shops for women's and men's clothing.

◆ **Heart's Desire**, *Second at Center. Mon-Sat 10-5, Sun 12-4.* In this unusually well preserved Gothic Revival bank building from the 1860s, two large floors are filled with gift and decor items, mostly either very feminine (loads of lace, pot-

▲ Princess Wenonah, Winona's namesake, was commemorated in this romantic 1901 statue, now on the Third Avenue pedestrian plaza.

The legend of Princess Wenonah is the kind of romantic legend Indians cooked up for the sentimental white man of the 19th century. The Indian princess Wenonah, prevented by her father from marrying her true love, flings herself from a blufftop in a lover's leap. Stories like this pop up throughout the western lands taken over by white Americans.

pourri, dried flower arrangements, porcelain dolls,
etc.) or distinctively masculine (duck prints and
plaids). Big selection of cards and kitchen items.
Well done for its kind.

◆ **Bluff Country Co-op**, *114 E. Second a little east
of Lafayette. Mon-Fri 9-6, Sat 9-4. (507) 452-1815.*
Pleasant little natural foods grocery with organic
fruits and vegetables, cheese, the usual trail mix
and granola, and a small deli section with
sandwiches and spreads. Two excellent wholegrain
breads, Mill City sourdough from St. Paul and Wild
Flower Bakery from Richland Center, Wisconsin,
make this a good picnic stop. Interesting bulletin
board includes some entertainment events.

◆ **Choate Building**, *51 E. Third at Center.* Unusual
five-story Romanesque department store (1888)
with elaborate arched windows, terra cotta details,
recessed balconies, and corner tower. Off the
Center St. side is the attractive **Rivertown
Gallery**, known as the largest gallery of limited-
edition prints in the region. Subjects include
wildlife, southwestern and western, marine, military, and more. Bronzes, animal carvings, and
woodburnings are other specialties. A new section
features paintings and prints of **area artists** from
Red Wing to La Crosse. *Mon-Fri 9-6, Sat 10-5. (507)
452-8922.*

◆ **Merchants National Bank.** *102 E. Third at
Lafayette. Lobby open Mon-Thurs 9-3, Fri 9-6.* This
extraordinary Prairie Style building is well worth a
peek inside, even if you're not an architecture buff.
It looks like one of Louis Sullivan's famous rural
banks, with the same strong, simple, flat-roofed
shape. Played off against that monumental simplicity are wonderfully delicate decorative effects:
Sullivan's characteristic twining terra cotta ornament and a huge stained glass window.

This is actually an early (1911-12) work of the
illustrious firm of Purcell and Elmslie. They are
direct descendants of Sullivan's inspired approach
to architecture and decoration — a fresh,

*Prairie Style
explained by the master*
Wrote Frank Lloyd Wright,
"We of the Middle West are
living on the prairie. The
prairie has a beauty of its
own and we should recog-
nize and accentuate this
natural beauty, its quiet
level. Hence, gently sloping
roofs, low proportions,
quiet sky lines, suppressed
heavy-set chimneys and
sheltering overhangs, low
terraces and out-reaching
walls sequestering private
gardens."

American approach that lost out to Daniel Burnham's Beaux Arts classicism beginning with the Chicago World's Fair of 1893.

George Elmslie had been Sullivan's assistant for 21 years. Architectural historian and connoisseur Wayne Andrews wrote in his fascinating and profoundly wise book, *Architecture, Ambition, and Americans,* "Elmslie came closer than anyone to understanding Sullivan, and the firm was loyal, as was none other, to his principles. . . . Since it was Elmslie who suggested the great arches of Sullivan's Owatonna [Minnesota] bank, the new firm could hardly avoid specializing in banking houses for country towns. The finest of these, the Merchants National Bank of Winona, Minnesota, . . . was an achievement with which Sullivan himself

▲ A bold, self-confident architectural statement, Merchants National Bank by Purcell & Elmslie is considered a masterpiece of the Prairie Style.

could have found no fault."

If at all possible, plan a visit when the bank is open, and ask for a souvenir postcard. Thanks to a sensitive restoration, the interior in every detail remains true to the calm, powerful original spirit of the place. The two huge expanses of stained-glass curtain walls, seen from within, have a wonderfully subtle effect. The mural of the farms and hills of Winona County's West Burns Valley, just behind Sugar Loaf, is closely related to Arts & Crafts and Mission styles

◆ **A longer, optional walk down Third** to the huge Watkins Administration Building (on Liberty between Third and Fourth, p. 167) takes you past some holdovers from earlier eras that have disappeared in many towns: a trim 1950s pharmacy, neighborhood taverns, the Odd Fellows Hall, a pawn shop, a onetime harness shop, and some tiny workmen's cottages, still immaculately maintained, on 25-foot-wide half lots. If you've been around many Great Lakes industrial cities, you can tell that this part of town was settled by Poles. Few other peoples have such flair in lending such homey charm to the most modest urban environments.

◆ **Exchange Building**, *51 E. Fourth at Center.* Impressive, four-story Beaux Arts office building (1900) built for Winona's Grain and Lumber Exchange. Each floor has ceiling-to-floor picture windows, an unusual feature for that era.

◆ **Winona National and Savings Bank**, *204 Main at Fourth. Lobby open Mon-Thurs 8:30-4:30, Fri to 6.* An odd blend of Prairie Style and Egyptian Revival, built in 1916. Architect George Maher had recently produced the monumental Watkins Building. The bank president and his wife, a Watkins daughter, were enthusiastic big-game hunters in Africa. African decorative motifs (a repeated lion's head, the Egyptian temple facade, and lotus ornamentation) are the result. This bank uses swankier materials than Purcell and Elmslie's masterpiece a few blocks away: perfectly matched

A readable, informative souvenir guide to Winona's history and architecture is **River Town Winona**, full of historic and contemporary photos and a map. Find it at the Armory Museum for $5. The 1938 **state guide to Minnesota** is among the better ones in the landmark WPA series; reprints are at the museum.

A steamboat captain founded Winona on an unusually large sandbar as a fueling stop for steamboats, which burned huge quantities of cordwood. An outstanding collection of steamboat photos is at the **Winona Historical Society's Armory Museum and Archive.**

granite, subtly shaded imported marble in the interior, and a beautiful huge window from the Tiffany studio in delicate shades of blue, peach, and beige. Go up either stairway flanking the doorway, and on the second- and third-floor mezzanines you'll come upon some startling souvenirs of the Kings' African safari.

Winona Armory Museum

Mon-Fri 10-5, Sat & Sun noon-4. $3/adults, $1 ages 7-17, 6 & under free.

160 Johnson, between Third and Fourth, downtown. (Johnson is 2 blocks west of Center and 2 blocks east of Winona). (507) 454-2723.

At this large historical museum of the Winona County Historical Society, the collection of things isn't in any way amazing. The recreated Main Street (dry goods emporium, blacksmith shop, Victorian parlor, fire equipment) may be fun for some kids. The diorama of Winona lumber history is interesting, and some unusual old vehicles are on display. A contemporary stained-glass window by one of Winona's big studios incorporates local scenes and symbols.

What does stand out is an excellent archive, interesting **changing exhibits,** and the unusually intelligent writing in the upstairs **timeline display**, from geology and prehistory to the present.

Most local history museums never get around to making coherent sense of their own social and economic history, telling it honestly, or setting it in a larger context. This does. The writing is good and refreshingly honest, and the photos and small artifacts are interesting. (How many historical societies would think to promote their fall Victorian Fair by pointing out how "the Victorian era was a study in contradictions. . . telegraphs and tepees, opera and illiteracy, absolute affluence and abject poverty"?) The timeline segment on Native Americans and the government's Indian removal policy is enlightening.

The **archive** excels in regional genealogy. History-minded visitors may enjoy looking at photographic souvenir books circa 1900 and the outstanding collection of old photos of the Mississippi levee and steamboats in their heyday.

The well-done **museum shop** has an outstanding selection of regional books, plus area products, traditional handcrafts, penny candy, and inexpensive historical reprints of colorful Victorian books and cutouts.

Levee Park

Take Johnson or Walnut from downtown across the levee to the Mississippi. Parking along river or off Johnson or Center. From Wisconsin, take U.S.54 to Fourth, left to Johnson, left to Front and the park.

Good in-town spot for watching the river. Picnic tables. Murals with river scenes have been painted along the dike.

Jollie Ollie Cruises

In operation from May until sometime in October, depending on weather. Docked at Levee Park. Get tickets at neighboring Wilkie Steamboat Center (below). (507) 454-6027. Visa, MC. Reservations required for Sullivan Shuttle and dinner cruises.

▲ An unusual chance to see the workings of a commercial harbor, where barges are loaded, is offered on the Jollie Ollie's sightseeing cruise.

A small new paddle-wheeler has a first-deck restaurant with big windows, upper-deck tables and chairs under canvas. The two-hour **sightseeing cruise** passes the entire Winona waterfront, up to Lock 5A at the tip of Prairie Island. It offers a rare chance to observe up-close the workings of a commercial harbor, where barges are loaded and unloaded. The Jollie Ollie is owned and operated by the Winona Fleeting Company, whose tugboats shuttle individual barges out onto big barge tows, so the guides know what they're talking about. The tour costs $10 for adults, $5 for kids 10 and under; it leaves at 2 p.m. every day but Monday.

Also recommended is the evening **Sullivan Shuttle** (also $10 and $5) to Ed Sullivan's highly regarded restaurant in Trempealeau. This longer trip passes most of Winona's riverfront and also an especially scenic stretch of river, including Trempealeau Mountain. Around sunset, the changing light makes the river especially dramatic and primeval-looking. The dinner shuttle usually leaves at 6:40, returning about 10:30. Exceptions: on Sundays it's 4:15, in May and after Labor Day it's 6 p.m. On-board meals are served at the 2-hour *Sunday brunch cruise* ($18; leaves at 11:30), the *Friday buffet* ($25, includes entertainment, leaves at 6), and Saturday *prime rib cruise* ($23, leaves at 7, 6:30 in May and fall).

Winona's waterfront in 1868: bustling and bawdy

"Warehouses lined the levees; paddle-wheeled steamboats, barges, flatboats backed into the landing. . . . For the competing railroads the scorn of the rivermen was boundless, and for years they expressed it by spitting a vociferous curse on every track they came upon. Day and night hip-booted rivermen challenged swaggering lumberjacks to contests of drinking, cruising, singing, or fighting. Farmers from the back country packed up wives, children, shotguns, and milk cows, came with wheat-laden oxcarts to the city, and purchased their winter's supplies.
— Minnesota WPA Guide, 1938

Julius C. Wilkie Steamboat Center

Open Memorial Day-October. Call (507) 454-6027 for details. On Levee Park.

A nonprofit museum built this authentically detailed, full-size steamboat. So much money was lost on its restaurant that it closed to regroup. Now it's re-opened in conjunction with the Jollie Ollie cruise boat.

The beautiful big boatis permanently anchored atop a riverside dike.

The **river museum** on the first deck has old photos and prints of steamboats, letters from steamboat inventor Robert Fulton, and many miniature models of actual steamboats, made by steamboat personnel in their spare time. Interpretation is minimal. The second-deck **grand salon** has all the wine-red drapery, gold and white gingerbread, and brass chandeliers and sconces that you'd expect Victorian steamboats to have. From the open-air **top deck** and **pilot house**, it's easy to think you are actually on the Mississippi. Fine views survey river and island, city and bluffs.

Latsch Island and Beach

No posted hours. No charge.

Opposite downtown across the Main Channel of the Mississippi. Take Route 54 east as if you were going to Wisconsin, but turn off onto the island. Beach is opposite town.

A big frame bathhouse and commercial beach stood here from 1906 through the 1960s. You can still swim here today, though the park is not very well maintained. One plus: a good view of the city and any barges that go by. Most Winonans prefer to swim at the Aquatic Center with its popular waterslide, or from river sandbars reached by boat.

The north part of the island is ringed by the modest **year-round houseboats** that so fascinated Jacques Cousteau on his visit to Winona. Some boat-houses are on the crude side, like floating shacks, while others have been improved and expanded to be quite charming in a rustic way, with decks and potted plants, second stories and bay windows. The boat-house neighborhood is an interesting place to walk or canoe by. The houses face the waterfront, so you see more from a canoe. There are big woodpiles, improvised sheds, and an odd menagerie of old cars, operating and abandoned. Residents, concerned lest they be booted out from their rent-free spots, have organized to

Get a Winona area canoe and bike guide with suggested trips and overview maps of town, two-state vicinity, and the river (all marked with bike and canoe routes) by calling the Visitors' Bureau, 800-657-4972.

undertake sanitation improvements like sewage disposal and recycling bins.

For a really weird little adventure to the backwaters along the Wisconsin shore, take the abandoned **dike road** that angles off northeast from Latsch Beach. Its concrete surface is so pocked and crumbling, and the vegetation so rank, you feel like you are in a Pompeii of 20th-century civilization. This eerie sidetrack allows naturalists to explore the backwaters on foot. (The Trempealeau National Wildlife Refuge, p. 192, has constructed a 6-mile roadway/nature trail for this purpose.)

Winona Aquatic Center

Open daily, Mem. Day-Labor Day, noon-8. $2.25 adult, $1.25 under 18.

780 W. Fourth at the just west of John, about a mile west of downtown. (507) 457-8210.

Fantastic for kids, who can use the Olympic-size pool and 208-foot water slide as much as they want for $1.25. Two playgrounds, a very gradual wading area, and a mushroom waterfall and spray fountain make this ideal for little kids, too. Several pool lanes are reserved for lap swimming. Volleyball court, concession stand, grass lawns.

Prairie Island

Mississippi River island 2 miles northwest of downtown. Most easily reached by taking Huff north to the river, then west on River View Dr. to Prairie Island Rd.; or, north along Pelzer from the junction of U.S. 14 and 61.

This is more of a boater's and fishermen's park than an especially scenic spot. An exception is the area along the new one-mile **nature trail**. It passes through a restored prairie and hardwood forest, and a boardwalk crossed the marshes along the river bottom. Look for the trailhead by the deer park, and pick up a brochure for a **self-guided tour**. Benches are in a pine plantation, along river backwaters, and by the prairie. They make this a nice place to sit and take in the

Swimming
is varied here. **Lake Winona** *offers a most pleasant view but has a grassy bottom. At the* **Aquatic Center** *(p. 164) the Olympic pool, zero-depth wading area, and big water slide are a hit with kids. People with kids consider the* **Mississippi** *risky, with its current. But for many, swimming off a* **sandbar** *reached by boat is a tremendous treat. At* **Latsch Beach** *(p. 163) on Latsch Island across from town, you can swim and watch river traffic on the main channel.*

Rookeries
of great blue herons
and great egrets can be seen by canoe northeast of Prairie Island and elsewhere.

wildlife around you.

Mourning doves, vireos, and owls live in the pines and hardwoods, and warblers are seen in spring. Bluebird boxes attract that beautiful little bird. Taking the dike road west leads to more terrific **bird-watching** for great blue herons, double-crested cormorants, great egrets, and spectacular diving osprey looking for fish in the water.

70 shady **campsites** with hookups are near the river. Pit toilets, no showers, no privacy landscaping. Campgrounds are open April to November. Often fills up on summer weekends; call (507) 452-4501 for reservations. $6.50/night; $7.50 with electricity.

A walk through the showiest neighborhood in Victorian Winona

Park along Fourth or Fifth by the Huff House facing Huff (Route 52).

Winona's most prominent and memorable Victorian fantasy, the massive **Huff House**, sits on a huge lot at 211 Huff, the main street into town from Lake Winona and U.S. 61. In 1857, when Winona was just a raw frontier port, land developer Charles Huff built this huge, showy Italianate Villa with much stone trim and a chunky big tower with mansard roof. Most aspiring architecture on the frontier was decades behind Eastern styles, but Huff made his mark being right in step with the latest fashions, and on a very grand scale. The house, now known as the Lamberton Residence, today consists of very nice retirement apartments. It is not open to the public, but it's worth walking along Fourth Street for a good look at the Moorish arches and lattice of the elaborate side porch.

Over the next six decades, Winona's wealthy new entrepreneurs also built in this neighborhood, next to the business district along West Fifth, Broadway, and Wabasha. They made sure "their grand style and ornate detail could be admired by passers-by," as *River Town Winona*, an interesting history and architecture guide available at the historical mu-

For a fine bird-watching pamphlet
with clear directions for 8 expeditions, 6 within easy biking from Winona, phone the Visitors' Bureau, 1-800-657-4972. The **canoe and biking guide** *and* **bird checklist** *are also helpful.*

Local history from an auto tape tour
A one-hour narrated drive fills visitors in on history, hits high spots & more. $3 at the Armory Museum (p. 160). Not for impatient people.

seum (p. 160), points out. "There was a some-times not-so-subtle competition among these families for the most imposing home."

♦ **Books Unlimited**, a large and inexpensive used book store at the rear of the Red Cross building, a handsome Italianate house. *276 W. Fifth at Huff. Open Mon-Fri, 1-4:30.* From here go west (away from downtown) on Fifth to Harriet, turn left to reach 275 Harriet.

♦ **Hodgins House**, *275 Harriet at Broadway.* 1890 Queen Anne lumber baron's house, loaded with projections and a tower, porches and nooks. Continue down Broadway, away from Huff, until you reach 451 Broadway.

♦ **Gallagher House**, *451 W. Broadway west of Grand.* 1913. Simple, stucco Prairie School house with horizontal bands of windows. Designed for a dentist by Purcell and Elmslie, masters of the Prairie Style. (See p. 157.) Backtrack to Grand, go right to Wabasha, then left on Wabasha to 402.

♦ **Meginiss House**, *402 W. Wabasha west of Wilson.* Circa 1894. Eclectic version of the Shingle Style with New England colonial touches. Built for a manager of Latsch & Son grocers. Go 4 blocks east on Wabasha past Huff to 203 E. Wabasha.

♦ **Nevius House**, *203 W. Wabasha.* Circa 1895. Earnings from a livery stable built this gracious Queen Anne/Classic Revival house with a curved, wrap-around porch. Go 4 more blocks east on Wabasha to Lafayette and the Octagon House.

♦ **Octagon House**, *317 Lafayette at Wabasha.* 1887. One of the few octagons west of the Mississippi. A very late result of the 1850s octagon craze, promoted by Orson Fowler for greater economy (an octagon's walls enclose more space than a rectangle or square) and heating and step-saving efficiency. Early concrete walls (recommended by Fowler) now stucco-covered. Wrap-around veranda is gone. Continue half a block east on Wabasha and you'll be at the Watkins House entrance.

♦ **Watkins Home**, *175 E. Wabasha at Walnut.* See separate entry. Here you may want to return to your car by going a block north to Broadway, then west to Huff.

▲ **Striking 19th-century architecture is the legacy of fortunes made in land, lumber, wheat, industry, and retail businesses geared to Minnesota home-steaders, for whom Winona was a jumping-off point. This unusual tower is on the Central Methodist Church, on Broadway. It and other beautiful old churches are on this walk.**

◆ **Schmitz House,** *226 E. Wabasha at Franklin. 1895. (This makes the walk four blocks longer.)* Especially lively Queen Anne concoction built by the second-generation owners of a harness and saddle factory. Lots of dormers, bays, patterned shingles, and a tower topped by a bell-shaped cupola.

◆ **Sinclair House,** *73 W. Broadway.* 1881. Newspaper publisher's impressive Italianate house with ornate brackets on big front porch and eaves. Go north on Franklin to Broadway, then left on Broadway. At Huff, go right and return to your car. *Return along Broadway, and you'll see some wonderful old churches.*

Watkins Home

Drop-in visitors are welcome to look in Great Hall. one-hour tour by appointment; call a day ahead. $2/person.

175 E. Wabasha at Walnut, midway between the river and lake. (507) 454-4670.

This 39-room Tudor mansion was built in 1924-27 for the nephew of the man who founded Watkins Products. It's more on the scale of a college dorm or administration building than a home; the Great Hall, a huge, vertical space with massive Old English beams and braces, could house a good-sized church. Today the house forms the basis for a retirement center and nursing home owned by the Methodist Church. Visitors can see major public rooms and the grand central stairway, and hear a brief concert on the mammoth **Aeolian organ** and Steinway concert grand piano in the Great Hall. 4,000 of its 6,000 pipes are housed in a 30-foot-long chamber that's 40 feet high. Player rolls play both organ and piano, separately or together.

Watkins Administration Building

Mon-Fri 7:30-4:30. No charge.
150 Liberty between Third and Fourth, six blocks west of Center and the heart of downtown. (507) 457-3300.

Watkins liniment, "good for man and beast," was

the product that launched this immensely successful direct-sales firm. By 1911, Watkins Products
had grown large and rich selling patent medicines,
cosmetics, seasonings, and home products through
a nationwide network of independent distributors.
It erected this monumental headquarters in front
of a new 10-story plant. The exterior, impressive
to the point of intimidation, resembles an art
museum or hall of justice. Architect George Maher
blended the block-like, dramatic massing of the
Prairie Style with neoclassical detailing.

The lavishly decorated interior — two barrel-
vaulted business halls flanking a Tiffany glass dome
— is quite interesting and well worth a visit. Much
beautiful leaded art glass shows romantic landscape versions of local scenes. Displays show a
century's worth of Watkins products (the evolving
packaging styles are worth a look), along with an
old Watkins peddler's wagon that made neighborhood rounds selling to busy housewives.

After a decline in recent decades, Watkins is
coming back, thanks to a new owner and a new
influx of energy and cash. The **lobby store** sells
Watkins products, including its famous vanilla ex-
tract. A low-cost factory outlet is open occasionally,
usually the first full weekend of a month. Call first.
Sometime in 1992 a full-fledged museum/store is
due to open on the premises.

Polish Cultural Institute and Museum

*Open May-Oct. Mon-Fri 10-3, Sun 1-3. Donation
requested.*

*102 Liberty at Second, 1 block north of Watkins
Administration Building (above). (507) 452-2141.
Call for information on occasional presentations of
folk dance, classical music, etc.* **Polish Heritage
Days** *(May): banquet of ethnic foods, traditional
hymns.* **Apple Fest** *(Oct.): Polish music, apple foods
and crafts.*

Poles, mainly from the Kashubian region of
Pomerania around the city of Gdansk, were second
to Germans among Winona's ethnic groups. Men

worked in lumber and flour mills, on railroads and
in construction; women served as domestics. In
this east end neighborhood, Polish immigrants
built little houses, one room wide with back additions, over one side of 50-foot-wide lots, leaving
the other 25 feet for a relative to build on. Backyard gardens were the rule, usually with chickens,
ducks, and geese. Many Polish farmers lived in
nearby Arcadia, Pine Creek, and Independence
townships. *Wiarus*, a Polish-language newspaper
published in Winona, was widely circulated in
North and South America. It championed the
workers' causes in labor disputes.

▲ **Religious art of the
19th and early 20th
centuries that fell vic-
tim to church remodel-
ing after Vatican II,
lives on in all its sen-
timental glory at Wino-
na's Polish museum.**

Intermarriage and dispersal have shrunk the
Polish community to an estimated 5% of the population. The cultural center is the inspiration of
Father Paul Breza, a native Winonan who serves a
parish in Hokah, Minnesota (across from La
Crosse). He raised funds to purchase this large,
two-story brick building, built in 1894 as the office
of Laird-Norton, one of Winona's big lumber mills.
It has been renovated with a great deal of volunteer
work.

The museum is a real community attic. Miscella-
neous contributions are presented without much
interpretation or perspective. A guided tour lets
visitors ask questions, which helps. To enjoy this
place, it requires patience to put up with boring
collections of local sports team photos and the
like.

Highlights include:

◆ **religious paraphernalia** of numerous Catholic
churches that were closed or fell victim to the
simplification of remodeling inspired by Vatican II.
If you grew up in the Catholic Church before
Vatican II in the 1960s today and you miss all that
wonderfully sugary ornament, pink and blue and
gold, from churches of the late 19th and early
20th centuries, you'll love seeing all this great old
stuff in the large second-story space: pulpits and
baptistries, statues and sick call sets, a recreated
19th-century chapel, rows up to the ceiling of religious pictures showing the Black Madonna of

Czechostawa, passionate saints, and noble priests.

◆ a **folk art board ceiling**. Each board is colorfully painted in a different folk art motif, for a delightful vivid, random effect. Castle ceilings were finished in this manner, which could be easily adopted in modern homes.

◆ changing **family displays**. One is about a local priest, from boyhood to old age. It included many photos and flowery certificates, along with the crown presented at his first Mass, and the accompanying presentation pillow handpainted by his favorite teacher, an artistic nun. Rounding out the exhibit was a funeral photograph of the nun in her coffin.

Winona Glove factory outlet

Mon-Sat 9-5, Sun 11-5.

412 E. Second between Chestnut and Laird, a few blocks northwest of Watkins. (507) 452-6973.

For a hundred years this firm (it used to be the Winona Whip Company) has been wholesaling gloves. Some gloves used to be made right here, too, but now the dies and patterns are at a Missouri factory that makes them on contract. Gloves sell here for 30% to 50% under suggested retail prices. One-size Magic Gloves that sell for $3.49 at Wal-Mart are $2 here. What really makes this place special is that it offers good values on a huge selection, including specialties like:

◆ better leather work gloves in elk and deerskin

◆ small sizes in a full line of Wells-Lamont work gloves (most stores only stock medium and large)

◆ heavy-duty split leather gloves for masons

◆ good women's work gloves and gardening gloves

◆ cashmere- or silk-lined dress gloves, to size 13

◆ traditional functional wear like wool boot socks from Seneca Mills

Savings can really add up if you can think of all the things required for different seasons and pur-poses. Winona Gloves also sells caps, socks, and hats, along with accessories like wallets, umbrel-

las, and more. If you're looking for a good value on
Ragg mittens, rabbit-fur trooper hats, work socks,
dress gloves, golf gloves, rain hats, ski gloves,
check this store out.

Church of St. Stanislaus

Open weekdays until 5.
    625 E. Fourth. Faces Carimona. (507) 452-5430.

St. Stan's is one of those splendid Polish
churches that stand out like great cathedrals of old
in neighborhoods of modest workers' homes. Built
in 1894 to seat 1,800, it's a one-of-a-kind blend of
Baroque and Romanesque. The high, silvery dome
is a landmark visible throughout the east side.
Saintly statues perch atop smaller towers on each
façade of the squarish church, for a delightfully
lively silhouette against the sky. The inner dome
makes for an impressive space inside.

Devotion to church and a fanatical pride in the
family home are Polish-American traits that stabil-
ize and enliven many cities of the industrial
Midwest. Families of very limited means cheerfully
tithed to support a grand church like this, a focus
of community pride.

Mary Twyce Antiques

*Open by chance or by appointment. Closed week-
days for lunch. Open most Saturdays 10-4:30.
Closed Sundays.*
    601 E. Fifth at Carimona. (507) 454-4412.

Winona's largest antique shop is strong on the
stuff of average American families from the past
hundred years: a lot of Red Wing pottery, furniture,
glassware and china, old post cards and printed
ephemera, jewelry, silver, campaign buttons,
framed and unframed pictures — all very well
organized and reasonably priced. The used and
rare book shop has a good regional selection, and
old magazines, too. A most pleasant place to
browse.

Bloedow's Bakery

Mon-Fri 7:30-5:30, Sat to 5.
451 E. Broadway at Laird. (507) 452-3682.

Unaffectedly old-fashioned corner bakery. Bloedow's (pronounced BLAY-doe's) seems like it hasn't changed much since it started in 1924, incorporating ornate old fixtures from an even earlier era. It's a fantastically popular local institution, especially for glazed donuts, long johns (the ones with maple frosting stand out), and Danish — rich and loaded with sugar. Not an upscale trend in sight. Prices are terrific. Also known for rye breads. Many kinds of cookies and buns make this a good stop for assembling a picnic basket.

Lake Park

Around Lake Winona, just north of U.S. 61, forming the southern edge of town. See map for details.

It would be hard to come up with a prettier place for a park, surrounding a two-mile-long lake.

Rentals for cross-country skis, bikes & roller blades (ideal for Lake Park) are at Adventure Cycle & Ski, 4th at Center. (507) 452-4228. Opens at 9:30, to 6 most nights, to 9 Mon & Thurs, to 5 Sat. Sun closed. Sample rates: skis $15/ day, $20 Sat & Sun. Bikes: $10/day, $25 tandem.

Lake Park, with its rose garden, beach, and view of Sugar Loaf, has been a favorite picnic spot for generations. A 7-mile bike-jogging path and a Frisbee golf course are ▼ recent attractions.

High bluffs form the backdrop, with Sugar Loaf as the focal point. Many of Winona's most impressive homes, from the 1920s and 1930s into the 1960s, line Lake Park Drive on the park's north end.

The park itself features a nice range of activities and interest centers. A **bike path** surrounds the lake, which is divided by the Huff Street dike, the main road into town. The East Lake bike path is 3.7 miles, the West Lake path 1.8 miles. The lake's grassy bottom impairs the **swimming beach** but makes for great **fishing**. Lake Winona is said to have more panfish per acre than any other lake in Minnesota.

In winter the bath house and **concession stand** becomes a warming house with hot drinks for the natural ice skating rink kept clear here. **Band concerts** are held in the band shell on Wednesdays at 8, June through August. East of it is a **rose garden** with 3,000 plants (250 varieties), in bloom from June through September. **Picnic tables**, grills, and shelters are at several locations. **Tennis courts** are at two places. An **exercise trail** and 18-hole **Frisbee golf course** are near the hospital on the lake's east end. At Huff and Lake streets are another nine holes of Frisbee golf. The marshy west end is good for **bird-watching**: warblers in spring, orchard orioles, rails in the marsh, and loons, terns, and diving ducks in open water.

Winona Knits

Mon-Sat 8-8, Sun 9-6. Shorter hours Jan.-March. U.S. 61 at Sugar Loaf, across from the east end of Lake Winona. (507) 454-1724.

This Winona-based specialty sweater retailer now has some 30 stores in seven states, usually in vacation areas. At a time when the Far East dominates ready-to-wear clothing, it seems like a miracle to find these stores full of reasonably priced sweaters ($25-$100) made in the United States, some right here in Winona. That's in line with owner Pat Woodworth's convictions that Americans should support American products. This is

Best picnic spots
◆ *Levee Park (p. 161) for river views.*
◆ *Lake Winona (p. 172) for views of bluff and lake.*
◆ *Levee Plaza downtown (p. 156) for its beautiful turn-of-the-century commercial buildings.*

Where to find good takeout food
◆ *Bun Barn (p. 182) for soups, salads, sandwiches by the pound.*
◆ *Bluff Country Co-op (p. 157) for wholegrain breads, organic produce, cheese.*
◆ *Beno's Cheese & Del, 72 Center, for huge deli sandwiches & muffins, salads, soups. Picnic baskets.*

not a factory outlet; broadly appealing sweaters for men, women, and children are all first-quality, made for Winona Knits. A few accessories are on hand, such as blouses, skirts, and nifty reversible $6 adult mittens of heavy wool yarn, made by retarded people in town.

Winona Knits got its start in 1943, when Walker Woodworth moved from Pennsylvania to open his third sweater factory, a wholesale business geared to the likes of L. L. Bean and Pendleton. One grandson, Pat, started a retail outlet that grew into the present Midwestern chain. His brother, Pete, owns Winona Knitting Mills, which employs 385 in Winona.

A German who discovered Winona when he sold knitting machines to Winona Knitting Mills liked the area so much that he stayed to start his own firm, Knitcraft. Its survival secret: a local work ethic that's "second to none," in the words of a company manager. High Minnesota taxes are off-set, he feels, by a motivated, educated work force and outstanding quality of life.

Garvin Heights Park

Up Garvin Heights Road, which intersects with U.S, 61 just east of the south end of Huff.

From this blufftop park 500 feet above the city, you can look past Lake Winona and the city's steeples and towering grain elevators, to the Mississippi's twisting backwaters and the Wisconsin hills beyond. It's an "America the Beautiful" view, especially when the light is right and a train and barge are moving through the river valley far below. Picnic tables dot the parks at the foot of the bluffs. Trails lead up and go along the blufftop.

Hiking, jogging, and cross-country skiing at St. Mary's College

Daylight hours. Typical ski season: early Dec. to mid-March. No charge; $2 donation suggested.

On Gilmore Valley Rd. At the southwest edge of town. From U.S. 61 west of Lake Winona, take Hwy.

14 1/2 mi. south to college. (507) 452-4430. Park behind the theater.

This four-year liberal arts Catholic college is run by the Christian Brothers. It has strong ties to the Chicago area for alumni and its student body of 1,200. A men's college until 20 years ago, it now has women as half the student body.

St. Mary's local reputation is one of sparing no expense for developing a beautiful campus. It nestles into the bluffs above a trout stream and overlooks the Mississippi River valley. Behind the buildings, these **scenic, bluffside trails** run through birch, pine, oak, and walnut woods. They make for an exceptionally beautiful and challenging cross-country track and ski course, recommended as the best around. (For beginning skiers, there's a 1K loop around Frontenac Field across from the College Center.)

A 5K main loop is supplemented by loops totaling 15K. Intermediate and advanced trails are clearly marked. *Park behind the theater* and ski from there. The map and sign for the trails are by in the right field of the main baseball diamond.

Bunnell House

Open in summer Wed-Sat 10-5, Sun 1-5. Thru early October, weekends only. Or by appt. $3/adult, $1/ ages 7-17, 6 & under free.

5 miles south of Winona on U.S. 61 near Homer. Watch for sign. (507) 452-7575.

This Gothic Revival house overlooking the Mississippi is most unusual. It was built by the very first European-American resident of what became Winona County. It's never been painted, and the weathered wood and ornate sawn trim looks a little like country

The Bunnell House overlooking the Mississippi south of Winona has its roots in fur-trading times when it was part of Dakota Territory. ▼

houses in Russia. Willard Bunnell built this house in 1859, 10 years after he first came to the area to trade for furs. Many original furnishings, a good gift shop, and an interesting tour set this apart from ordinary house museums.

O. L. Kipp State Park

Open year-round. Park hours 8 a.m.-10 p.m. Minnesota state park vehicle sticker required; $18/year, $4/2 days. Visa, MC accepted.

About 17 miles southeast of Winona and 18 miles northwest of La Crosse on Mississippi River bluffs. From La Crosse, take I-90 w. About 4 mi. west of where I-90 turns away from the river, look for signs to park entrance off Rte. 3. From Winona, take U.S. 61 12 mi. e. to Rte. 3, then 4 1/2 mi. to entrance. (507) 643-6849.

These 3,000 acres of rolling blufftops and steep valley walls overlook the Mississippi across from Trempealeau. Like other blufftop parks, this is mainly a native hardwood forest (dominated by oaks and hickories) and it offers spectacular views across the river valley. At this point the bluffs overlook a wide marsh just downstream from Trempealeau.

Two unusual natural features are a blufftop stand of northern **white cedar**, twisted and misshapen like bonsai, and some 30 **goat prairies**. The uncommon Henslow's Sparrow prefers these elevated prairies.

In Minnesota, unusual biological communities may be deemed "Scientific and Natural Areas," with restricted access. Queen's and King's Bluff here have that designation. The 1 1/4-mile **King's Bluff Nature Trail** (2 1/2 miles round trip) passes a huge goat prairie on its way to a scenic overlook that lets you see up the river to Trempealeau Mountain, a steep-sided island hill in the Mississippi. Interpretive signs point out area history and typical and unusual aspects of the geology and plant life.

Twenty **picnic spots**, each with fire ring and

8 cross-country ski trails near Winona from 1 to 8.8 miles are described in a guide from the Visitors' Bureau, 1-800-657-4972. Many are atop Mississippi River bluffs for great views. Some are beginners' trails along nature paths on bottomland. Most have options for all skill levels. For the prettiest and most challenging, see additional info for St. Mary's College (p. 174).

table, enjoy considerable privacy from landscape buffering. From the north picnic area, it's a short 40-yard walk to an overlook with a sweeping Mississippi River view. From the south picnic area the trail to the river view is about 1/4 mile.

The 6.5-mile system of **hiking trails** has color for all seasons: loads of spring and summer wild-flowers, sumac and hardwood foliage in fall, and the green of pines in winter. **Blackberries** are abundant and ripe for picking in August. This land was acquired as state forestry land, and old fields were planted in pine, ash, and walnut in the early 1960s. Those trees are now medium-size. Public demand for park land along the Mississippi later led to this becoming a park.

Cross-country ski trails, 9.2 miles in all, are groomed in winter. Most are easy to intermediate. Their variety of habitat makes them popular: hard-woods, pine plantations, old fields and sidehill prairies, and spectacular views of the river valley.

The single-loop **campground** with 31 campsites ($9/night) has showers, flush toilets, but no elec-tricity (60' trailer limit). Trees are relatively young, but there's unusual privacy between camp-sites because of wider spacing and lots of black-berry and sumac screening. This campground hasn't been as busy as many, but with the new showers, reservations are increasingly advisable (1-800-765-CAMP).

Nearby at the Dresbach Visitor Center are Mississippi River **boat launches** and picnic tables and an observation deck at Lock and Dam No. 7.

Minnesota Travel Information Center/ Lock and Dam No. 7

*Off I-90 just north of the Mississippi River bridge from La Crosse. **Travel Info Center** open daily 9-5; from Mem. to Labor Day 8-6. (507) 895-2005.*

Here the state of Minnesota and the Army Corps of Engineers have designed a joint wayside that incorporates a large terrace/**picnic area** overlook-ing the Mississippi, **boat launches** above and be-

State forest campgrounds are less crowded and more rustic than state parks. The very large Whitewater Wildlife Management Area west of Weaver and not far from Winona is great for nature observation, hunting, and trout fishing.

For printed info on Minnesota state parks, forests, and bike trails, call (612) 269-4776 (week-days 8 a.m.-4:30 p.m. Central Time). Or write DNR Info Center, 500 Lafa-yette Rd., St. Paul, MN 5515. Naturally is a very helpful booklet guide to the state parks system. Ask for state forest info by area.

low the dam, and an **observation deck** at the locks. Upstream from La Crosse, the dam forms Lake Onalaska, some eight miles long and up to five miles wide. It's one of the widest points across the Mississippi. The travel information center is loaded with brochures, maps, booklets, and such.

John Latsch State Wayside

State park vehicle sticker required; $4/2 days, $18/year. Parking area open 8 a.m.-10 p.m. On U.S. 61, 12 mi. northeast of Winona.

This beautiful, unstaffed 400-acre park consists of a **picnic area** and small primitive campground off busy U.S. 61. It's tucked beneath Faith, Hope, and Charity, three rocky bluffs used as landmarks by steamboat captains. Once a logging camp here cut timber for Winona's sawmills; now the railroad and backwater pool of Lock and Dam No. 5 have covered all remains of that ghost town. A fairly rough **trail** leads up a steep ravine to the peak of Charity, with a good view of the valley. For a beautiful all-day adventure, you could hike through back country (no trails at all) to the other two bluffs.

This isn't a quiet, get-away-from-it-all kind of place, what with the highway and the train. But it is convenient to Winona, seldom used, and good for watching the slow-moving drama as downriver barges pull up in the main channel right by this bank, waiting to go through Lock 5 just a couple miles south of the campground.

A 12-site **primitive campground** (with pit toilets and a water pump) has the virtues of being pretty, private, and little-used. Walk-in sites are a short

▲ **Tundra swans in unparalleled numbers (3,000 and up) pause near Winona as they fly from arctic nesting grounds to winter in the Carolinas. At Weaver Bottoms, 12 miles north off U.S. 61, they feed on wild celery & other aquatic plants. An annual Swan Watch is held a weekend around Nov. 1.**

ways from the parking area; tents only, no reservations.

Lock and Dam Number 5

Just off U.S. 61 13 mi. northwest of Winona.

The Corps of Engineers has provided a pleasant visitor wayside and viewing stand to watch the slow-paced action as barge trains are broken apart and locked through in two sections. A fine place for a picnic if there's some traffic. Ask for a free pamphlet about lock and dam operation and the history of developing the 9-foot channel in the 1930s.

Arches Museum of Pioneer Life

Open May-Oct., Wed-Sat 10-5, Sun 2-5 or by appt. $3/adult, $1 ages 7-17, 6 & under free.
11 miles west of Winona on U.S. 14. (507) 523-2111.

Before interstate highways whooshed motorists past the quaint byways of America, private roadside museums like this were common. Founder Walter Rahn was "motivated by a love of children and a genuine appreciation of pioneer ingenuity," according to the Winona County Historical Society, which runs his place today. He "collected everything imaginable to illustrate the past, and what he couldn't collect, he created." His hand-made models of pioneer machines, vehicles, and processes are charming. A furnished **log home and barn** from the 1860s and a **one-room school** are across a brook from a shady, pleasant **picnic spot**.

Whitewater State Park

Open all year, 8 a.m.-10 p.m. daily. State park vehicle sticker required: $4/2 days, $18/year.
3 miles south of Elba and 22 miles west of Winona. Take U.S. 14 west to 74, then north. (507) 932-3007.

One of Minnesota's oldest and better-known parks consists of a stretch of the Whitewater River

▲ **Picturesque limestone bluffs like these are found along river valleys throughout the Driftless Region—that corner of southeast Minnesota, northeast Iowa, and all of southwest Wisconsin untouched by the bulldozing effects of glaciers. Scenery like this can be seen in Whitewater State Park, along the Root River Trail, and in Iowa around Decorah and on the Heritage Trail west of Dubuque.**

The Whitewater River is a fast trout stream as it flows through 3,000-acre Whitewater State Park and the much larger adjoining wildlife area. ▼

Valley and the beautiful back country around it, studded with vistas and rugged limestone outcrops and chimneys. The river itself, spring-fed, rocky, and full of riffles, is a fast-moving trout stream. **Fishing** is excellent (the season is from mid-April through September), but the river has too many shallow spots to be good for canoeing or tubing.

The picturesque **visitor center**, built by the Civilian Conservation Corps in the 1930s, is a good place to get an overview of southeastern Minnesota's unusual natural history. Here in the northwestern corner of the Driftless Region (p. 16), many plant and soil communities coexist: fertile but vulnerable loess soils (formed by wind-blown dust gathered from glacial till), clay, sand, and limestone. Here plants and wildflowers of the Eastern woodlands, at their western range, meet prairie grasses. Spring wildflowers in these deep-cut valleys are spectacular; some flood plains are covered with bluebells. Fall colors are especially dramatic where hardwood forest meets rocky outcrops. Ten miles of **hiking trails** include the 2-mile **Chimney Rock Nature Trail**, which has interesting interpretive signs. A warming house is kept open for 5 miles of **cross-country ski trails**.

106 drive-in **campsites** have good landscape buffering and tree canopy. Showers and toilets are handicapped-accessible. The campground fills up on summer weekends with good weather; reserve them 3-120 days in advance by calling 1-800-765-CAMP. $5 non-refundable fee.

The **Whitewater Wildlife Management Area**, a much larger area of public land, extends between here and the Mississippi, adding to the a ppeal for outdoorsmen. For information about its State Forest **campgrounds** (more rustic and far less crowded), call (612) 296-4776.

Lanesboro

45 minutes southwest of Winona. Take Hwy. 43 to Rushford, then Hwy. 16 west to Lanesboro. For a visitor packet on the entire area, write Historic Bluff Country, Box 609, Harmony, MN 55939. For local phone info, call Brewster's Outfitters, (507) 467-3400.

A delightful pre-industrial town, Lanesboro isn't too cute or slick. It's on a beautiful stretch of the Root River with such rugged limestone bluffs, it looks like a greener, gentler Wild West. The beautiful **Root River bike trail,** 35 miles of a former railroad bed, goes along the valley through Lanesboro. It makes terrific family bicycling. In summer Lanesboro is lively with antique shops, B&Bs, Commonweal (an innovative summer stock

▲ An affectionate, useful introduction to Lanesboro, where "down-home character and elegance go hand in hand," can be had for $2.50 from Ode Design, 2706 Glenwood Dr., Des Moines, IA 50321. Native son Carson Ode describes the highlights of his revived home town; his crisply detailed drawings enliven the dense, interesting 8-page booklet.

theater), and now a folk music coffeehouse, Alive and Well, open Friday through Sunday. Canoes, tubes, bikes, and cross-country skis can be rented at **Brewster's Outfitters** (507-467-3400). Two large caves and Amish farms are in the vicinity. Lanesboro is very busy on good-weather weekends; advance reservations are advised for the area's many inns and B&Bs.

RESTAURANTS & LODGINGS

Minnesota sales tax is 6 1/2%; Winona room tax is an additional 4%.

Bun Barn. *3rd between Main and Center, downtown Winona. Parking lots on Center at 2nd and 4th. (507) 452-5700. Mon-Fri 8:30-3:30, Sat 9-3. No credit cards or alcohol.*

Popular little self-serve spot for coffee, good house-baked muffins (80¢), house-made soups (95¢ cup/$1.40/ bowl), build-your-own sandwiches and salads (34¢/oz.). Takeout to eat on 3rd street mall, interior mall, or eat in at 6 tables. Pies are $1.25/slice, rhubarb is a special favorite.

Finn & Sawyer's. *At the foot of Walnut on the Mississippi, over the levee from downtown Winona. Parking adjoining. (507) 452-3104. Mon-Thurs 11:30-9, Fri & Sat to 10, Sun 10-1:30 (brunch), 1:30-9 (dinner). Visa, MC. Full bar. Children's menu.*

Winona's most ambitious menu. Outstanding river view from all tables. Chef Anthony Pepe combines classical training with his own Italian background to produce the likes of seafood ravioli w/ homemade pasta ($14 at dinner), char-broiled roast pork marinated in fresh citrus & bourbon ($12 at dinner). Known for fresh seafood. Dinners (mostly $11-$15) include potato or fresh pasta, fresh vegetable, salad bar, and good housemade French bread. For lunch, Reubens ($5), French bread pizza ($4), specials like ginger shrimp over rice ($5) for kabob week. Cocktails served on riverfront deck. Weekend jazz or light classical music.

Hot Fish Shop. *965 Mankato Ave. (Hwy. 43) at the east end of Lake Winona. From U. S, 14/61, turn north onto Mankato at Holiday Inn, look for sign. (507) 452-5002. Tues-Sat 6 a.m.-10 p.m., Sun to 8 p.m. Visa, MC, Diners, CB. Full bar, separate lounge. Children's menu. Reservations in winter.*

Considered *the* place to go in Winona, for occasional visitors and businessmen's lunches alike. Since 1931 it has evolved from a simple fish shop on the Polish east end to a sprawl-ing, rather plush place that focuses on basic food, well prepared. Decor is fish, either mounted or alive in three nifty aquariums by the cash register. (In the larger tank of tropical fish, the orange and white-striped clownfish nestling inside the anemone is something to see.) Broiled fish is available in season, and many kinds of seafood are available, but walleye fried in a secret batter is the thing here, in a hot sandwich ($5.75), in a small lunch portion ($8), regular lunch portion ($11.50), or at dinner ($13.25). You can also get walleye, or any other fish, broiled or pan fried. Lunches include beets, slaw, and potato; dinners come with soup and salad, too. Beverages come with all meals. Breakfasts include the usual (for instance, a full order of pancakes is $2.25, including drink) and more: eggs benedict ($4.50), a Spanish omelet big enough for 2 ($4.50), steak tenderloin and eggs. Separate lounge. Dance floor, **dance combo** (mostly Big Band era or 50s-70s) nightly exc.

Sun at 7:30; no cover. **Fish store** in separate building.

McVey's Ice Cream Parlor. *451 Huff across from 2 4-story dorms of Winona State U. From U.S. 14/61, turn north onto the Huff St. dike across Lake Winona, go about 5 blocks north. (507) 452-7173. Mon-Fri 10-10, Sat & Sun 8 a.m.-10 p.m. Closes at 9 Nov.-April. No credit cards or alcohol; out-of-town checks OK.*

Updated soda shoppe goes back to 1929. Cozy & bright. Popular lunch spot for college faculty during school year. 1/3 lb. burger, from leading local butcher, is $3.25 w/ fries, fixings; soups $1.25/$1.75. Full sandwich menu, pies. Weekend breakfasts include cinnamon rolls, Belgian waffles ($2.75), omelets. Known for homemade ice cream (especially Palmer House flavor: vanilla w/ maraschino cherries, almonds), turtle sundaes (caramel, hot fudge, pecans over 3 scoops vanilla; $2.75).

Zach's on the Tracks. *On Front at Center, across the levee from downtown. (507) 454-6939. Mon, Wed-Fri 11:30-2:30 and 5-9:30 (to 10 Fri). Sat 5-10, Sun 10:30-2, also 5-9 May-Oct. Visa, MC, AmEx, Diners. Full bar, separate lounge.*

Historic railroad freight house with 3 dining rooms. Well regarded. Soup/ salad bar w/ pasta, marinated and fresh vegetables, fruit: $4.50 at lunch, $6.50 at dinner. All-day sandwich menu runs $6 w/ fries, slaw. Lunch highlights: crab salad w/ muffin ($6.50), stuffed shrimp ($8.50), ham croissant ($4.75). Dinners include soup, potato, salad bar: pork parmesan in marinara sauce $11, filet mignon $13.50.

Best Western Riverport Inn and Suites. *(507) 452-0606. Across from the Hot Fish Shop.* The best location of any motel in town, with a nice view and miles of park walkways across the street. Opening as we go to press. Call for details.
Indoor pool, across from Lake Park & Hot Fish Shop

Carriage House Bed and Breakfast. *(507) 452-8256. 420 Main Street.* 2 rooms with private bath, $70 and $85. 2 rooms share a bath, $60.Business weekday rate $40. Air-conditioned. In pleasant residential neighborhood across from Winona State University. The upper floors of a very large 1870 carriage house behind the innkeeper-owners' big house have been turned into guest rooms. Decor is country with dark colors; table and chairs, pedestal sink in all rooms. Attached 4-season porch. Big continental breakfast. Refrigerator stocked with soft drinks and mineral water. Guests can borrow tandem bikes or other bikes, fishing gear from sociable hosts. Walking distance to areas of historic homes, downtown, Lake Park.
Winona's only B&B, in good central location, with loaner bikes

Days Inn. *(507) 454-6930. On U.S. 14 just west of U.S. 61.* 58 rooms on 2 floors. $48. Cable TV, HBO. Continental breakfast. Next to several restaurants on commercial strip/retail area 2 or 3 miles from downtown.
Well-regarded chain, moderate prices

See also: **Trempealeau** and **Galesville**, p. 204.

Trempealeau

*Where life slows down to the river's pace,
and people have time for music, fishing,
and just taking in an amazing natural world.*

"**E**VERYBODY'S HAPPY down by the river,"
says a transplant from southeastern
Wisconsin who feels he's been reborn
since he quit his high-pressure job to run a motel
in Trempealeau. "Fishermen *expect* to wait. It
doesn't help to hurry to get fish to bite. The barges
move so slowly, it's pointless for the bargemen to
get uptight. Sunrise, sunset, the seasons, the
weather — down by the river, everything happens
in its own time. That makes people relax."

Life slows down — *way* down — when the river
becomes your focus. That's the way it is at the village of Trempealeau. A few old Victorian storefronts are what's left of a once-lively port and rail
station after the demise of steamboats, an 1888
fire, and the railroads' later decline. The tone is
now set by retirees in neat ranch houses. A big
event here is an early-morning game of dice at the
Country Corners convenience store/cafe, or the
coffee klatsch at the Eatery on Main, or watching a
barge tow being split up and moved through the
locks right by the village.

What's riveting about this place is the constant
backdrop of the river. It makes a tight bend here,
creating especially interesting and complex views.

At the **Trempealeau Hotel,** a plain frame vestige
of river port days, you can sit in a light-filled back
room of the restaurant or on the deck and watch
the sun set behind the bluffs. Often there's a barge
waiting to go through the locks on the south side
of the village. On weekends the hotel offers live
music — bluegrass, folk and vintage rock. On an
outdoor stage in summer, touring national acts

**Distances from
Trempealeau**
*139 mi. to Minneapolis
309 mi to Chicago
239 mi. to Milwaukee
162 mi. to Madison
145 mi. to Dubuque
24 mi. to I-90, LaCrosse
16 mi. to Winona*

To find out more
◆ *Trempealeau Chamber
of Commerce, c/o Pleasant
Knoll, Box 426,
Trempealeau, WI 54661.
(608) 534-6615.*
◆ *Galesville Business Assn.
C/o Ardelle Williamson,
819 W. Gale, Galesville, WI
54630.*

perform. The surprisingly tasty vegetarian walnut burger is the specialty of the house. A freshly painted, clean room with an iron bedstead and chenille spread rents for $22 a night, with bath down the hall. There's likely a weekend crowd around the big-screen TV in the bar, or by the volleyball court in summer.

But during the week and off-season, the main attractions are things like:

◆ fishing and canoeing.

◆ bicycling on the remarkably scenic Great River State Trail almost to La Crosse — and beyond.

◆ hiking or cross-country skiing in Perrot State Park just north of town.

◆ a good meal at Ed Sullivan's celebrated riverside restaurant.

◆ bird-watching in the marshes of the nearby Van Loon Wildlife Area and the ponds of Trempealeau National Wildlife Refuge.

◆ visiting apple orchards around nearby Galesville.

◆ swimming in the Olympic-size city pool at the south end of Fourth Street.

▲ **The blufftop trails at Perrot State Park offer both magnificent Mississippi vistas and natural prairies that have never been plowed.**

Acoustic music — folk, bluegrass, and occasionally jazz musicians from the Midwest and beyond — is also booked at the Mill Road Cafe, 6 miles north in the picturesque town of Galesville.

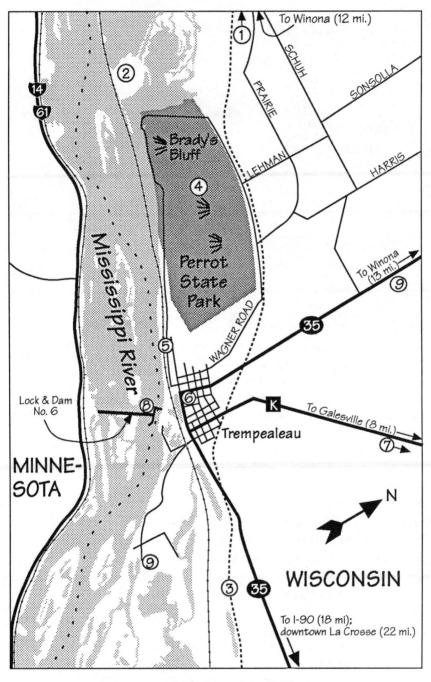

To Winona (12 mi.)

SCHUH

PRAIRIE

SONSOLLA

14

61

②

Brady's Bluff

LEHMAN

HARRIS

④

Perrot State Park

To Winona (13 mi.)

⑨

WAGNER ROAD

35

Mississippi River

⑤

Lock & Dam No. 6

⑧

⑥

K

To Galesville (8 mi.)

⑦

Trempealeau

MINNE-SOTA

N

⑨

WISCONSIN

③ 35

To I-90 (18 mi.);
downtown La Crosse (22 mi.)

• TREMPEALEAU •

Trempealeau Map Notes

① Trempealeau National Wildlife Refuge. Explore by foot, canoe, bike, or car this huge wetlands teeming with wildlife. See herons, egrets, swans & ducks, which come here to eat aquatic plants. 4-mile self-guiding wildlife drive. Canoe rentals at nearby state park.

② Trempealeau Mountain. Striking island mountain, formed when ancient river changed course, turning bluff into island. Early French gave this landmark its name, which means "the mountain with its foot in the water."

③ Great River State Trail. Bicyclists enjoy terrific views of Mississippi R. on this easy 22.5-mile trail. Also splendid birdwatching. Joins La Crosse River and Elroy-Sparta trails for 76 miles of beautiful bicycling. Bike rentals in Trempealeau.

④ Perrot State Park. Showcase park offers both access to backwater channels and blufftop nature trails with grand views, rare goat prairies. Canoes for rent. Marked canoe trail.

⑤ Ed Sullivan's. Good food and splendid views overlooking the Mississippi River at this restaurant. Fish, ribs, special touches like Irish brown bread muffins, crusty round potatoes.

⑥ Trempealeau Hotel. Spare, simple frame hotel from 1890s. Watch river traffic from deck while eating a tasty walnut burger. 60s-flavored rock, folk, and blues music on weekends. $21 rooms have chenille spreads, bath down the hall.

⑦ Mill Road Cafe. Good deli sandwiches, vegetarian dishes. Top regional and some national folk musicians on weekends. Next to pretty bluffside park in the picturesque small town of Galesville. Winter ice skating on pond; curling.

⑧ Lock & Dam No. 6. See the slow-moving drama of big barge tows going through locks. Wait for them while hanging out at the nearby park or the Trempealeau Hotel's pleasant deck. Viewing stand, picnic tables.

⑨ Long Lake Canoe Trail. This marked water trail lets you glide through a maze of sloughs & marshes without getting lost. You may see blue herons, egrets, ducks, eagles, hawks. Canoe rentals at Larry's Landing on Lake Rd.

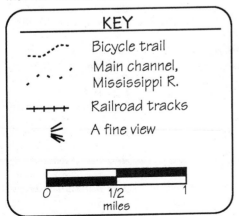

KEY

- ·--·--· Bicycle trail
- · · · · Main channel, Mississippi R.
- +++++ Railroad tracks
- ⇐ A fine view

0   1/2   1
miles

WHEN TO VISIT, ENTERTAINMENT

See Winona, p. 154.

ANNUAL EVENTS

Winter Festival. Last weekend of Jan. Candlelight skiing, snow sculpture, ski & bike races, skating, ice fishing contest. Trempealeau.

Catfish Days. Weekend after July 4. Crafts & flea market, carnival, car show, live music, catfish burgers. Sun. afternoon parade, 10 p.m. fireworks. Trempealeau.

Apple Affair Festival. First weekend of October, Galesville. Bike tour. Crafts, apple events. (608) 582-4460.

POINTS OF INTEREST

Perrot State Park

Open all year. Wisc. state park vehicle sticker required. $24/year non-residents, $15 residents; day pass $6/$4.

*Entrances are **1.** on the Mississippi, about 1/2 mile west of village of Trempealeau, and **2.** off the Great River Road (routes 35 and 54) about 3 miles northwest of Trempealeau. (608) 534-6409. Pick up a copy of the excellent park guide/newspaper, or request a copy ahead of time by calling or writing Perrot State Park, Route #1 Box 407, Trempealeau, WI 54661.*

The don't-miss sight of this big (1,400 acre) riverside park is the panoramic Mississippi River view from 520-foot **Brady's Bluff.** An Indian mound and a rest shelter are near the top of Brady's Bluff. Downstream you see almost to La Crosse; upstream, you're directly across from **Trempealeau Mountain**, a 384-foot peak completely surrounded by water. This dramatic oddity fascinated Indians and 19th-century travelers.

Trempealeau Mountain was formed when the Mississippi changed its course quite recently, some 10,000 to 15,000 years ago, as the last glacier receded. The river had turned sharply east at the present-day site of Winona to a point near Galesville, before turning south again. As the river swelled and flooded with glacial meltwaters, it cut a new channel *behind* Trempealeau Mountain and

The legacy of Winona conservationist John Latsch

By the 1920s, hunters and fishermen across the Midwest were organizing to protect and enlarge vanishing wildlife habitat. Winona grocer John Latsch helped found the Izaak Walton League that established the Upper Mississippi Wildlife Refuge. He gave 2,200 acres on **Prairie Island** *and* **Latsch Island** *to Winona and donated three state parks (***Latsch*** in Minnesota and* **Perrot** *and* **Merrick** *in Wisconsin) and the core of the* **Trempealeau National Wildlife Refuge.**

Brady's Bluff. These bluffs *had* been on the
Minnesota side of the river. The present channel
south of Trempealeau Mountain is quite new in
geological time. It's one mile wide, the narrowest
point on the Mississippi. But it's also the widest —
six miles wide — if measured from the north side
of the island mountain. The old, abandoned river
bed, covered by sandy outwash from the glacial
meltwaters, is the flat, sandy farmland north and
east of Perrot State Park.

Brady's Bluff is reachable by two trails off the
main road. **Brady's Bluff West Trail** is .5 mile,
doable in half an hour both ways if you move right
along. The .7-mile **Brady's Bluff South Trail** is
under an hour, up and back. It passes a rare **goat
prairie** (see p. 12) full of prairie wildflowers unusual for these parts. In spring, these include pale-
blue pasque flowers on grassy stems, bird's-foot
violets, and more. More spectacular is the prairie's
riot of color in late summer and fall, with purple
coneflowers and tall, multi-flowered blazing star.

Exceptional opportunities for **bicycling** and

▲   Trempealeau is a
nickname French fur
traders applied to Trem-
pealeau Mountain, the
landmark island moun-
tain north of Perrot
State Park. The name is
a shortened version of
"la montaigne qui
trempe l'eau," or, "the
mountain with its foot
in the water." It's pro-
nounced TREM-puh-low.

backwater canoeing are available here. Many kinds of birds and other wildlife can be seen by canoe in the adjacent estuary of the Trempealeau River, or by canoe, foot, car, or bike in the 5,900-acre **Trempealeau National Wildlife Refuge** immediately west of the park. The **Great River State Bicycle Trail** passes the campground and links the park with the wildlife refuge and, to the south, miles of marsh along the former railroad tracks.

Other park highlights include:

◆ A **marked canoe trail** starting at the **nature center**. It goes through backwater channels of the Trempealeau River; canoeing across the narrow Mississippi main channel here is discouraged. **Canoes** can be rented at the park office ($8/2 hours, $10/4 hours) from early April into November.

◆ The two-mile **Riverview Trail,** roughly paralleling the main road by the water's edge. You can often see brown water snakes and many kinds of turtles here, along with beavers, muskrats, and mink.

◆ The 1/2-mile **Black Walnut Nature Trail** with interpretive signs is before you get to the campgrounds. An unstaffed **nature center** nearby is open daily from early May through September.

◆ The park naturalist leads frequent summer **walks and talks**. (Times vary with the current naturalist's expertise; call for details.)

◆ Several **Indian mounds** are within the park, including Nichols Mound, the largest Hopewell mound in Wisconsin, on the Great River State Trail.

Seen from the main entry road, Perrot State Park is deceptively tidy and suburban-looking, with mown grass and trees that have obviously been planted as part of a landscape plan. Actually, there's a wilder wetland and cottonwood trees back along the Trempealeau, and rugged, woodsy terrain up on the bluff away from the road. **Trails** of the 8-mile trail system branch off from the entry road and climb to rewarding lookout points. Oak-

A car-free vacation
It's possible to visit Perrot State Park and the Trempealeau area without using a car at all. The park is quite close to Trempealeau and right on the Great River Road bike path originating in Onalaska. You could leave your car there, or farther east at West Salem or Sparta. Or you could take your bike on the train to Winona (p. 150).

Several miles of a traffic-clogged commercial strip make it unpleasant to bike from the La Crosse train station.

Excellent river maps of every pool and dam within the 284-mile Upper Mississippi Wildlife and Fish Refuge are available from its headquarters, 51 E. 4th, Winona, MN 55987. (507) 452-4232. Ask for each dam and pool you want to canoe by number.

hickory forests are along the **Perrot Ridge hiking trail.** As the main road curves back away from the Mississippi along the Trempealeau River, it borders wetlands and cottonwoods.

CAMPING. 97 sites ($7/$9), 36 with electricity, 1 handicapped. Flush toilets, showers. Grassy, multi-loop campground with some landscape buffering between sites. Medium-size trees, no canopy. Fills up 6-7 times/summer, inc. holiday weekends. Call for reservations.

SPRING WILDFLOWERS. Hepatica, jack-in-the-pulpit, ferns, wood geraniums. Some prairie flowers on bluffs.

FISHING: Bluegills, crappies, large and smallmouth bass, northern pike, walleye, catfish, striped bass.

SUMMER WILDFLOWERS. Unusual goat's prairie with colorful summer blooms.

FALL COLOR is best enjoyed from Brady's Bluff Trail.

WINTER ACTIVITIES. Early winter, before snowfall, is best for viewing landforms and Indian mounds. 8.3 miles of groomed cross-country **ski trails** varying in difficulty levels. The long loops atop Perrot Ridge offer excellent views across the valley, without difficult hills once you get up onto the plateau. A flat ski trail goes by the Trempealeau River. Ice fishing is for bluegill, bass, crappies, and northerns.

Lock & Dam No. 6

From Third St./U.S. 35 at the east side of Trempealeau, turn south on Fremont St./Lake.

After crossing tracks, turn right again to enter lock area. No admission charge.

Seeing a quarter-mile-long tow of barges moved through a Mississippi River lock is a slow-moving, impressive drama. The vast scale of everything makes it a spectacle. You may be watching grain from the Red River Valley of the North going down

▲ A riverfront beach and picnic area and an exceptionally beautiful campground characterize Merrick State Park (above) 22 miles north of Trempealeau. Its focus is the Mississippi's floodplain, backwaters, and boat landings, while most Mississippi River parks are centered on the bluffs. For more info, call (608) 687-4936 or write Box 182, Fountain City, WI 54629.

to New Orleans, or oil heading up to Minneapolis.

This lock and dam has an ideal location for convenient viewing. It's easy to spot a downbound barge train from Perrot State Park or from the pleasant, sunny dining room or deck of the Trempealeau Hotel, and then bike or drive the short distance down to the locks.

The tow of 15 barges (five barges long and three abreast) has to be broken in two to fit into the 600-foot-long locks. "Towboaters" (as the crew is called) untie the cables that join the first three rows of barges to the last two. (The cables are attached to huge cleats on each barge.) The tug moves around to push the first section (nine barges in all) into the lock, where it is cabled to the side walls to keep it in place. A valve is then opened to raise or lower the water level within the lock. Then the gate opens, and a wench on the lock pulls the tow through the open gate. The operation is repeated again to lock through the last two rows of barges and the giant tugboat. The entire process takes about an hour.

The Corps of Engineers spares no expense in courting public favor; their visitor facilities are first-rate, immaculately landscaped and sodded. **Picnic tables** let you sit down and eat while watching. An **elevated, covered observation stand** beside the lock lets you view the locks in bad weather. Mists make the bluffs look even more romantic and Rhine-like than on sunny days.

Trempealeau National Wildlife Refuge

Open daylight hours, year-round. No charge. Office hours: Mon-Fri 7:30-4. (608) 539-2311; or write Box 1602, Route 1, Trempealeau, WI 54661. A **map** *is available at the entrance.*

On the Wisconsin side of the Mississippi, about 10 miles east of Winona, Minn. and just west of Perrot State Park. From Trempealeau, take South Prairie Rd. west past Perrot State Park. From bridge to Minnesota, take Route 54 6 miles east to West Prairie Rd., turn right and follow signs.

The 50th anniversary of the 9-foot channel was commemorated by the U.S. Army Corps of Engineers with an interesting publication on its history and design. Ask for a copy of "Old Man River," a 50th anniversary publication, from the Corps of Engineers Public Affairs, 180 E. Kellogg, St. Paul, MN 55101.

Usually wetland refuges like this are inaccessible to all but canoeists, who can only see the water's edge. But here an extensive system of service roads and a four-mile drive allow hikers, bicyclists, and motorists to explore many kinds of habitats. In summer **herons** and **egrets** can often be seen from the observation platform by the hiking trail and parking area, feeding on fish among the aquatic plants. Nesting summer residents include **bitterns**, black **terns**, double-crested **cormorants**, and many ducks. **Wood ducks** that nest in bottom-land hardwood tree cavities.

Many kinds of migrating waterfowl stop to rest and feed in the marshes in April, late October, and early November. **Tundra swans, Canada geese**, and wigeons, scaup, mergansers, and other **ducks** are common. Large numbers of the colorful wood ducks have been seen in fall feeding on acorns

Bird-watching near
Winona & Trempealeau
is outstanding for several
reasons:

◆ *The Mississippi*
Flyway is used by migrat-
ing birds as a map and
place to find water & rest.

◆ *The entire area of the*
Upper Mississippi Wildlife
*Refuge (p. 7) includes **many***
***habitats:** open water*
year-round, remote bluffs,
marshes, forest.

◆ *Many **nature trails***
***and publications** of area*
naturalists make access
easy. Call (507) 452-2272
and ask for an area bird-
watching guide.

around the shores of a wooded island here. In January and February, wintering **eagles** can be seen in water kept open by artesian wells.

The four-mile **self-guiding wildlife drive** shows visitors three distinctive plant communities here: the **sand prairie** formed by the ancient riverbed. now being restored with native prairie grasses; **backwater marshes**; and **bottomland hardwood forests** made of shallow-rooted trees like silver maple and river birch that can survive spring flooding and wet soils. Of course, the drive can also be biked or hiked; the **Great River Road bicycle trail** ends at the refuge. (Hikers can also use service roads closed to visitors' vehicles.) Pick up the accompanying **leaflet** at the information center at the refuge entrance; it's full of valuable hints for observing wildlife. An **observation deck** and half-mile **trail** take visitors up to wetlands where diving and wading birds and beaver can be seen.

The refuge can also be explored by **canoe**. Canoes can be **rented** at adjacent Perrot State Park.

The long, straight dike of the Burlington Northern Railroad separates the refuge's vulnerable open water and wetlands from the Mississippi's main channel. The dike keeps the river's huge load of sediment away from the vulnerable wetlands, extending their life by centuries.

The U.S. Fish and Wildlife Service first established the refuge in 1936 to provide habitat for migratory birds. With the acquisition of the former Delta Fish and Fur Farm, it extends some five miles along the river. Of the refuge's 5,600 acres, 70% are open water or wetlands that are flooded, seasonally or permanently. The rest is bottomland, upland forest, and some prairie grasslands now being restored after blight killed the trees that invaded them.

Canoeing
is the way to get in touch with the Upper Mississippi's hidden world of maze-like streams and backwater pools. The quiet canoe lets you get close to birds and wildlife and takes you to shallow fishing spots unreachable by larger craft.

Valley Herb Gardens

In Wisconsin not far from Winona, Minn. or the Trempealeau National Wildlife Refuge, at 148 Piepers Valley Rd. From Route 35/54 about 4 1/2 miles east of Route 54 bridge to Minnesota, take County Rd. P less than 1 mile northeast, turn left (west) onto Piepers Valley Rd. Stop at ranch house at 148.Owners are usually home. Stop by or call ahead (608) 687-8566.

What started 25 years ago as a summer hobby growing herbs for cooking has evolved into rather a large place in a beautiful valley that attracts quite a few garden tours. Display gardens include some 300 kinds of herbs — medicinal, ornamental, and culinary. Hops grow on a trellis; a thyme garden spreads over rocks. The plants aren't for sale, but dried arrangements, more informal country than High Victorian, are for sale in the barn, at prices that are very reasonable compared to city prices. So are stained glass and paintings by the owners, who are retired educators.

Galesville

19 miles east of Winona via Hwy. 54/35; 6 miles northeast of Trempealeau on Country Road K.

The pretty town of Galesville (population 1,200) is a popular side-trip from Trempealeau, six miles away to the southwest. Galesville enjoys a beautiful setting between the limestone bluffs and spring-fed creek of High Cliff Park on its south side and Lake Marinuka (actually a mill pond) on its north. The flat, sandy prairie of the old Mississippi River bottom extends west and south toward Winona. Two **antique stores** are on U.S. 53 west toward Centerville, and several **apple orchards** are in the vicinity.

A bandstand has long accented Galesville's quaint **town square**. Two blocks north, horseshoe pits and an information gazebo draw visitors to **Triangle Park**, between Ridge Avenue and the lake. It's just across from the **Lake Marinuka dam**, a favorite fishing spot for bass, sunfish, and

crappies. Some of Galesville's finest old houses
line the lakeshore. Each winter a **natural-ice rink**,
lighted at night, is maintained, approximately from
December through February. A warming house
makes it even nicer. *(To get to the rink and adjoining boat landing, go west on Ridge, and turn north to
the lake at the bottom of the hill.)*

Galesville was founded in 1850 — quite early for
the west part of Wisconsin — by George Gale, a
surveyor, lawyer, and later a judge. He had come
west from Connecticut to found a college. After his
efforts were rebuffed by La Crosse, he started his
own town here. He platted the lots, built a dam for
flour and sawmills, and induced a Chicago &
Northwestern spur to come here. The plain,
three-story Victorian home of his coeducational
Gale University sits on a high, peninsula-like
plateau at the southwest edge of town, overlooking
fields and the valley of Beaver Creek. The quaint
college building, surrounded by stately old ever-
greens and orchards, is now the ecumenical
Marynook Conference and Retreat Center (608-
582-2789), available for many kinds of confer-
ences. Visitors are welcome to see the grounds.

Cance Memorial Park has tennis courts, picnic
tables, and a playground. It's in a lovely neighborhood of Queen Anne houses along Ridge Avenue, on
the so-called "upper table" or plateau west of
downtown.

The popular **Mill Road Cafe** is in one side of an
old warehouse at 219 East Mill, at the south
entrance to town, shared by the **Common Market**
natural foods grocery. The cafe hosts an attractive
lineup of folk, blues, and other acoustic musicians
on Fridays and Saturdays year-round. Its rear windows look out onto Beaver Creek and the **swinging
bridge** to **High Cliff Park**. A **waterfall** drops some
25 feet down the side of sandstone outcrops. A
trail winds along the base of the cliffs; the clifftop
trail can be reached from the cemetery off the
upper the road. **Picnic tables** make the park a fine
spot for a takeout sandwich from the cafe or lunch

from the Common Market

The real showplace of Victorian Galesville was, and is again, A. A. Arnold's **East Side Farm**, once a grand 256-acre estate. The 15-room Italianate house has asymmetrical tower and a big barn. It's now being restored. Visitors can climb the spiral staircase up into the tower for a fine view. *The house is open Sundays from 2 to 4, June through the first week of October, or by appointment (find phone number on door).*

A series of religious revivals left mid-19th-century Americans imbued with the sense that their land was uniquely blessed by God for some higher purpose. So it didn't seem too far-fetched for a Galesville minister to argue that, based on the topographic description of the Garden of Eden in the Bible, the Garden had probably been right here in the vicinity of Galesville.

▲ **East Side Farm, a fancy stock farm in the 1870s, is again a Galesville showplace, open Sunday afternoons in summer and fall.**

The Great River State Bike Trail

22.5 mi. from Onalaska (north of La Crosse) to Perrot State Park & Trempealeau National Wildlife Refuge.

Pass required for ages 18 and up: $2 daily, $6 annual; at bike shops, Mac's Bait, Perrot State Park. **Trailside parking**: *in Onalaska, by Mac's Bait, U.S. 53 at Main by light; in Midway at QT and ZN; in Trempealeau, 1 block south of Route 93 on east side of village; and at Trempealeau Wildlife Refuge at Route 35 and Prairie Rd. Open year-round except in deer-hunting season.*

This superb trail on an abandoned Chicago and Northwestern railroad bed gives even infrequent

Bike rentals in Trempealeau

◆ *Tremplo Bike Shop, Third (U.S. 53) at entrance to trail, east side of town. (608) 534-6217.*

◆ *Trempealeau Hotel Trading Post (150 Main in rear, facing First). (608) 534-6898.*

bike riders a delightful, 11-mile look at the dramatic lowlands next to the Mississippi. The trail, 24 miles in all, lets you quietly pass through some outstanding bird-watching habitats (prairies, marshes, creeks, backwaters) and take in some beautiful views of Trempealeau Mountain and the Mississippi River valley. The trail includes **18 bridges** crossing the marshy mouth of the **Black River** and several creeks.

▲ **18 bridges are a highlight of the Great River State Trail.**

The trail's western section is along the northern edge of **Perrot State Park** and the **Trempealeau National Wildlife Refuge**, whose **five-mile wildlife drive** is ideal for bicyclists; be sure to pick up the accompanying interpretive pamphlet at the entrance. Signs are clear for turnoffs to the wildlife drive, to a one-mile hiking trail, and to the state park campground.

Trempealeau has all the services a bicyclist would want: two places with **bike rentals**, a **repair shop**, a **grocery/fast food mart**, and two good **restaurants with river views**, Ed Sullivan's Supper Club, and the quaint Trempealeau Hotel.

The isolated 10.8-mile stretch between Trempealeau and Midway has a remote aura, removed from the sound and sight of traffic and for long stretches even from farms. A passing freight on the Burlington Northern is all that interrupts the quiet. It's a striking ride. The long railroad bridge across the Black River is especially memorable. The great horizontal sweeps of marsh, sky, and distant bluffs make the ride especially rewarding to those who stop to look up at the sky — and down into the waters at the bridges. In the distance north of the Black River bridge you see the oaks, elms, and cottonwoods of the hardwood swamp within the **Van Loon Wildlife Area** (p. 199). This is such a lonely stretch that finally coming upon farms and homes is a welcome sight.

Most of the trail is completely flat, and the surface of fine-crushed lime makes for easy cycling. That and the distinctive, remote scenery make it ideal for the most casual cyclists, and for families with young children. It's surprising how far an

Good overnight stops for bicyclists
◆ *along and near the Great River StateTrail: anything in Trempealeau, Perrot State Park, most lodgings in Winona, a riverview motel in Onalaska (p. 204).*
◆ *on the adjoining La Crosse River Trail: the county campgrounds at beautiful Neshonoc Lake ; or a dairy farm bed and breakfast near Bangor. Call Wolfway Farm, (608) 486-2686.*

inexperienced bicyclist can go on such an unde-
manding route, where it's easy to make 15 miles
an hour.

The Great River State Trail connects with the
23-mile **La Crosse River Trail** and the 32-mile
Elroy-Sparta Trail via a 1 1/2-mile link along a
moderately busy road through Onalaska. Signs from
the trailhead by Mac's Bait make this clear. On the
La Crosse River Trail, the distant hills flanking the
wide La Crosse River valley make for an attractive
backdrop. West Salem, about 10 miles east of
Onalaska, is an interesting town to ride through.
Progressive Era author **Hamlin Garland's home**
there is well worth a visit for lovers of American
regionalism and Mission furniture.

SPRING: Many kinds of migrating ducks, geese seen in April.
SUMMER: Bring mosquito repellent. Watch egrets, heron,
osprey hunting for fish. Prairie grasses at west end of trail
bloom in August and September.
FALL: Wetlands add a special dimension to fall color. Trail
closed in deer firearms season (Nov. 15-30).
WINTER: From Midway west (19.1 mi.) is for **snowmobiles**;
from Midway east (3.2 mi.) is for **cross-country skiing**.

Long Lake Canoe Trail

*Two-hour marked trip along backwaters south of
Trempealeau. Starts at the Long Lake boat landing.*

*From U.S. 35 in Trempealeau, go south on
Fremont St./Lake Rd. (it's the way to the lock and
dam), continue past tracks 1.4 miles.*

Canoe trail signs mark a route that lets you quietly glide through a maze of sloughs, marshes, and
islands without getting lost. You're likely to see
blue herons, common egrets, ducks, eagles, and
hawks. Rent a canoe and get a trail map from
Larry's Landing, on Lake Road 1/2 mile below Dam
6. Maps are also available at Perrot State Park.

Van Loon Wildlife Area

*Midway between Trempealeau, Galesville, and
Holmen. Four **access sites** to trails: **1.** Off U.S.
53/Route 93, 3 miles south of Galesville. Park just*

*To find out about the
La Crosse River and
Elroy-Sparta bike trails,
contact Wildcat Mountain
State Park, Box 98,
Ontario, WI 54651. (608)
337-4775.*

Rent a canoe at
◆ *Trempealeau Hotel
Trading Post, faces First
behind the hotel on Main.
(608) 534-6898. Above
Dam #6.*
◆ *Perrot State Park.
For use on Trempealeau
Bay only.*
◆ *Larry's Landing. 1/2
mi. below Dam #6 on Lake
Rd. (608) 534-7771.*

south of Black River bridge. Short trail starts just west of bridge. **2.** *From Amsterdam Prairie Rd. (joins Route 35 and Route 93). Look for sign for Van Loon Wildlife Area/McGilvray Rd. McGilvray Rd. (foot access only) leads to main trails.* **3.** *Off Route 35, 5 miles east of Trempealeau at West Channel of Black River. 4-mile riverside trail starts east of channel, on north side of road.* **4.** *Off Route 35 just west of previous access site. 1-mile trail starts west of channel on south side of road. No charge.*

For a map and McGilvray Rd. history, contact Wisconsin DNR, La Crosse office: (608) 785-9000. 3550 Mormon Coulee Rd., La Crosse, WI 54601.

A store, blacksmith shop, school, and roadhouse once were here along the bottomland of the Black River; now it's a vanished ghost town reached by an abandoned road over five striking historic bridges. McGilvray's Ferry developed around the ferry across the Black River here that joined La Crosse and Trempealeau counties by road, back before there were bridges. During the logging era, log jams on the Black River and adjoining McGilvray Bottoms often isolated the hamlet for months. A series of bridges were built to bring McGilvray Road across the bottoms to the town — hence, the surviving nickname, "Seven Bridges Road." Five bowstring-arch bridges survive, all designed in La Crosse and built by the La Crosse Bridge and Steel Company between 1905 and 1908. They were designed to use specially designed hook-clips to eliminate rivets and bolts.

Seven Bridges Road, repeatedly flooded, was abandoned, along with the town after farming here failed. Today the road makes for an interesting walk from the Black River's East Channel near Amsterdam Prairie Road, across several small streams, to the West Channel less than two miles away. Near the West Channel, the road connects with **trails** extending two miles north and two miles south along the river. Friends of the McGilvray Road are working to preserve the his-

▲ **Saving the backwaters**
is a very emotional issue along the river. Insidious sedimentation is caused by runoff from agriculture, construction sites, road edges, etc. Sediment makes open water turn into marsh, marsh turn into dry land. Once-deep backwaters become too shallow to even canoe through.
State and federal agencies are working on education, management, and enforcement programs, but conditions aren't improving.

The Black River lumber boom
provided the capital that launched La Crosse as an important industrial city. The Black River begins well northeast of Eau Claire and drains much of northwestern Wisconsin.

toric bridges.

The public wildlife area consists of 3,800 acres of bottomland hardwoods (mostly oaks, cottonwoods, elm, and ash) extending for five miles along the Black River between its east and west channels. It's flooded in spring, permanently in places where beavers have created dams. Used mostly by deer hunters and duck hunters, the area is also used by hikers, canoeists, bird-watchers, naturalists, and old bridge buffs.

A **canoe launch** is at the south side of Hunter's Bridge over Highway 53/93. A **rustic campsite** is on 2/3 mile downstream on the south bank. Mosquitoes can be fierce! A **boat landing** is on the south side of Route 35 on the east bank of the West Channel.

Onalaska

Immediately north of La Crosse on the north bank of the La Crosse River. U.S. 35 parallels the river; the old downtown is on Main, the cross-street near the crest of the hill. Chamber of Commerce: (608) 781-7210.

Today this town with the poetic Aleutian name is a long, rivertown suburb of La Crosse, strung out along an old highway commercial strip with a new regional shopping center at its east edge. This exploding suburb hardly looks like a 19th-century lumber boom town. But some six billion board feet of white pine have floated down the Black River to the sawmills and shingle mills from here to La Crosse. Four railroads served the the town's lumber industry here in its heyday in the 1890s; 4,400 people worked here.

At Onalaska, the Mississippi River is so wide as it bends south that it's referred to as **Lake Onalaska**, five miles wide and eight miles long. It looks so wide, it hardly seems like a river at all. U.S. 35, as it passes through Onalaska, offers some stunning views, especially toward twilight. Several **waysides** let you stop and take it all in.

Panfishing, always good here, became even better after the dam. Responding to the promotional

Onalaska was called a "boom town,"
wrote Hamlin Garland, "for the reason that 'booms' or yards for holding pine logs laced the quiet bayou and supplied several large mills with timber. Busy saws clamored from the islands and great rafts of planks and lath and shingles were made up and floated down into the Mississippi and on to southern markets."

The view from Green's Coulee, just outside Onalaska, as depicted in a 1927 edition of Hamlin Garland's *A Son of the Middle Border.*

obligation of every small town to celebrate something, Onalaska has styled itself "Sunfish Capital of the World."

Lock and Dam Number 7 has made the Mississippi even wider than it was naturally. The lock and its operations can be observed close-up at the **Minnesota Travel Information Center** in nearby Dresbach (p. 177), across the river from La Crosse.

Modern roads move us so fast by car and even by bicycle that our sense of space has shrunk, and in many ways, our powers of detailed observation have dwindled with it. It's startling to read about Onalaska in the 1860s, in Pulitzer Prize-winning author Hamlin Garland's evocative autobiography, *A Son of the Middle Border.* His family were pioneers living in a cabin in Green's Coulee, a scant two miles from Onalaska. Occasionally they came to town to visit his father's parents and sister. La Crosse, six miles to the south, was a world away.

Onalaska, Garland wrote, "was a rude, rough little camp filled with raftsmen, loggers, mill-hands and boomsmen. Saloons abounded and deeds of violence were common, but to me it was a poem. From its position on a high plateau it commanded a lovely southern expanse of shimmering water bounded by purple bluffs. The spires of La Crosse rose from the smoky distance, and steamships hoarsely giving voice suggested illimitable reaches of travel. Some day I hoped my father would take me to that shining market-place whereto he carried all our grain."

Hamlin Garland's summer home
after he became a successful writer can be seen in West Salem, not far from the La Crosse River State Trail. It's a rare restoration of a middle-class home of the Progressive Era just after the turn of the century. Its mix of Navajo rugs, Mission furniture, and family heirlooms gives the sense of simplicity and higher purpose that characterized the Progressive spirit. The home is at 357 W. Garland, northwest of downtown.

A good shop has many out-of-print Garland books. Open Memorial Day thru Labor Day 1-5 and by appointment other times. (608) 786-1399.

Onalaska's interesting early history
is on display at the Onalaska Historical Museum in the big new library building at 603 S. 3rd at Oak, east of the first stop north of La Crosse on U.S. 35. Hours: Wed-Fri 12-4, Sat 10-2. (608) 783-1586. Parking for the La Crosse River Bike Trail is here, too.

RESTAURANTS & LODGINGS

GALESVILLE (population 1,300)

Mill Road Cafe. *219 East Mill, at the southwest entrance to town. (608) 582-4438. Mon-Thurs 9 a.m.-4 p.m. Fri & Sat to 11 p.m., Sun 9-2. No credit cards. Beer.*

Cafe and natural foods grocery share space in an old warehouse that looks out in back onto Beaver Creek, High Cliff Park with rock outcrops, waterfall, swinging bridge, and picnic tables. Sandwich, soup, and salad menu with reliably good food — homemade soups at $2 a bowl, soup and salad bowl $3.50. Sandwich favorites: grilled chicken fajitas with avocado, tomato, cheese, sprouts in pita ($6), veggie sandwich with melted Swiss ($4.75), taco pita with refried beans ($5.25). Ten-inch whole wheat veggie pizza entire ($12.50 to $15.50) or by the slice. Cashew chicken curry stir fry ($6.75) is also popular. Espresso, rich homemade desserts ($2-$2.50). Breakfast ($3.50-$4.75) served to 11 a.m., Sun to 2 p.m. Weekend **acoustic music concerts** feature well-known regional and national performers on the folk coffeehouse circuit. Audience drawn from as far as Madison and the Twin Cities. Saturday evenings, special dinners before concert. Most shows 8:30, sometimes 2 shows at 7 & 9 or 8 & 10.

Sonic Motel. *(608) 582-2281. On Hwy. 93/54, 1 mile west of Galesville.* 24 rooms on 1 floor. $32, 4-poster bed $36. Cable TV, HBO, coffee in room and in lobby. J. J. Stephens Supper Club next door. Quiet rural location surrounded by cornfields, apple orchards, within sight of Minnesota bluffs. A favorite with musicians appearing at Mill Road Cafe.

Nice, inexpensive motel in country setting

ONALASKA (population 11,300)

Shadow Run Lodge. *(608) 783-0020. 710 2nd Ave. (Hwy. 53) at the north end of Onalaska.* 20 rooms on 2 floors. May-Oct: $38-$45 (depends on weekend). Nov.-April: $29-$38. Cable TV. Coffee in office. Picnic tables in back. Half of rooms overlook Lake Onalaska (actually a wide pool on the Upper Mississippi). Great River Road Trail and a park going down to the lake are across the street. Next door is the Chicken, Steak and Chocolate Cake restaurant. Both are north of downtown Onalaska and the hectic commercial strip between Onalaska and I-90.

Good river view, quiet location next to restaurant, bike trail

TREMPEALEAU (population 1,050)

The Eatery on Main. *220 Main in center of Trempealeau. (608) 534-6866. Mon 6 a.m.-2 p.m., Tues 6-6, Wed & Thurs 6-7, Fri 6 a.m.-9, Sat 6 a.m.-7 p.m., Sun 6 a.m-7. May stay open later in summer. No credit cards. Out-of-town checks OK. Beer & wine coolers.*

Well regarded small-town cafe under new owners. Basic breakfasts include 3 pancakes ($1.75), 2 eggs and hash browns ($2.10). Homemade soups, chili, sandwiches, pies ($1.30/slice). Specials may be roast beef dinner with real mashed potatoes ($4), Friday night all-you-can-eat fish fry ($5.25). Broiled fish also available.

Ed Sullivan's. *On the Mississippi between village of Trempealeau and Perrot State Park. (608) 534-7775. Mon-Tues, Thurs-Sat 5-10, Sun 11:30-4. Closed Jan. 1-10. Visa, MC. Full bar.*

Visitors keep coming back because of uniformly good food and service, great view from all tables of river, barges & bluffs. Reasonable prices. Fun Irish theme. Special touches like Irish brown bread muffins, crusty round potatoes. Menu is big on fish (steamed or batter fried), scalloped seafood, combos like battered tenderloin tips and shrimp ($10). BBQ pork ribs a specialty, too. Wide variety of smaller portions, lighter food like chicken dinner ($6.75). Children's menu; lunch portions at dinner; 500 Club (500 cal. balanced menu, designed by hospital). All meals include soup, salad bar, bread basket, beverage. Harp lager beer. Emerald Isle **gift shop** w/ Aran sweaters, Duiske glassware, claddaugh rings (circle w/ hands, heart). **Boat dock** in season. Scenic evening **boat cruise** from Winona, dinner here — see p. 182.

Trempealeau Hotel. *At the foot of Main overlooking the Mississippi in Trempealeau. (608) 534-6898. Summer hours (Mem.-Labor Day): 7 a.m.-9 p.m. daily. Otherwise: Mon-Fri 1102, 5-9, Sat 7 a.m.-9 p.m., Sun 7-7. Bar open to 2 a.m. May close Jan-March. Visa, MC. Full bar.*

A pure and simple restoration of a plain frame hotel from the 1890s. Back dining room has big southwest windows overlooking river. Long outside deck has same view. Great barge-watching. Menu designed for vegetarians (including both owners) and meat-eating traditionalists alike, with sandwiches like tenderloin steak ($6.25), chicken fajita ($5.25), good meal-size salads (around $5), homemade soups ($2.75/bowl with good whole wheat bread), homemade desserts like Swedish apple pie, poppyseed cake ($2.50). Signature walnut burgers ($4.50) are surprisingly good and filling. Spinach lasagna ($7 with interesting house salad, French bread) is another favorite. Wide-ranging **weekend entertainment** may be blues, jazz, reggae, classic rock. Ten **outdoor concerts** (2 a month from May through September) include for '92 Arlo Guthrie, Steppenwolf, Rare Earth. **Sand volleyball** has league nights, pickup games, 6 or 8 tournaments a year. Bike, canoe rentals.

See also **Winona**, p. 146.

Pleasant Knoll Motel. *(608) 534-6615. 361 Main in Trempealeau.* 10 rooms on 1 floor. Regular rooms with 2 beds $35 in season, $32 from Nov-April. 4 kitchenettes are $39. Cable TV, HBO. Coming by fall, 1992: sunroom with whirlpool overlooking river, with coffee, donuts; 3 new rooms with river views. Sits back from road. Picnic tables, lawn chairs.
Well-maintained older motel; lawn has river view

River View Motel. *(608) 534-7784. First and Main in Trempealeau, on road to Perrot Park but in town.* 8 rooms on two floors. May-Nov. $38. Dec-April: $30. All rooms have river view, 2 beds, cable TV; most have refrigerators. Basketball hoop.
Pleasant, inexpensive rooms with river views

Trempealeau Hotel. *(608) 534-6898. At the foot of Main overlooking the Mississippi in Trempealeau.* 8 rooms share 1 bath. $21. Very clean and freshly painted, with period furniture just refinished. 7 rooms have river views. Spartan accommodations, the way most Victorian hotels really were. Most rooms have chenille spreads. It's definitely something different, not for everyone. But to many people (including some seniors) it's fun, and you can't beat the prices. Be sure you're prepared to wait to use the bathroom. Music downstairs (blues, classic rock, reggae) plays on weekends until 1 a.m. or so. Nearby **riverview cottage** with 2 bedrooms, living room rents for $65/night.
1891 hotel restored by preservation purists